The Immortal "I"

A Unified Theory of
Psychology, Neurology,
and the Perennial Philosophy

Eugene B. Shea

Copyright © 2005 by
The Shelton Group
24W500 Maple Avenue - Suite 209
Naperville, Illinois 60540
TheSheltonGroup@cs.com

Shea, Eugene B.
The Immortal "I": A Unified Theory
of Psychology, Neurology, and the
Perennial Philosophy / Eugene B. Shea

Includes bibliographical references and indexes.
1. Psychology   2 Neurology
3. Mystical Theology   4. Soul
5. Mind   6. Love   7. Belief and Doubt
8. Psychotherapy   9. Kingdom of God

ISBN 0-615-12924-2

Acknowledgements

Excerpts from Toward a Psychology of Being by Abraham H. Maslow reprinted with permission of Van Nostrand Reinhold.

Excerpts from Christian Mysticism by William McNamara, O.C.D. reprinted with permission of Franciscan Herald Press.

Excerpt from The Perennial Philosophy by Aldous Huxley. Copyright © 1970 by Aldous Huxley reprinted with permission of Harper & Row, Publishers, Inc. and Chatto & Windus, Ltd., London

Excerpt from The Choice is Always Ours edited by Dorothy Berkley Phillips. Copy-right 1948 © 1960 by Dorothy Berkley Phillips. Copyright renewed 1988 by Dorothy Berkley Phillips reprinted with permission of Harper & Row.

Excerpts from Maslow comments at the Second Interdisciplinary Conference on the Voluntary Control of Internal States - Council Grove, KS. 1970 reprinted with permission of The Journal of Transpersonal Psychology. Copyright © Transpersonal Institute.

Rendering from The Brain - Mystery of Matter and Mind Copyright © Marshall Editions Ltd., London, reprinted with permission.

Excerpts from Human Behavior: The Role of the Brain by Ronald H. Bailey and the editors Time-Life Books reprinted with permission © 1975 Time-Life Books.

Excerpts from Mysticism East and West by Rudolph Otto. Copyright © 1932 The Macmillan Company; copyright renewed © 1960 The Macmillan Company. Reprinted with permission of Macmillan Publishing Company.

Excerpts from On Human Nature by Edward O. Wilson reprinted with permission of the publishers: Harvard University Press Copyright © 1975 by the President and Fellows of Harvard College.

Excerpts from The Brain - A User's Manual by the Diagram Group reprinted with permission of The Putnam Publishing Group, and The Diagram Group.

Excerpts from Creative Evolution by Henri Bergson reprinted with permission of The Macmillan Press.

Excerpt from The Stairway of Perfection by Walter Hilton translated by M. L. Del Mastro Copyright © 1979 reprinted with permission of Doubleday & Co., Inc.

Excerpt from Beyond Ego reprinted with permission of Jeremy. P. Tarcher, Inc. Copyright © 1981 by Walsh and Vaughan

Excerpts from Your Four-Year Old by Louise Bates Ames, Ph.D. & Frances L. Ilg, M.D. Copyright © 1976 by the Gesell Institute of Child Development reprinted with permission of Dell Books.

Excerpt by John Hick from Mystics and Scholars edited by Harold Coward and Terence Penelhum reprinted with permission of the Canadian Corporation for Studies in Religion, 1977, Waterloo Canada.

Excerpt from The Machinery of the Brain by Dean Wooldridge. Copyright © 1963 reprinted with permission of the publisher, McGraw-Hill, Inc.

Excerpt from Finding the Real Self. Copyright © The American Journal of Psychoanalysis published by The Association for the Advancement of Psychoanalysis of the Karen Horney Psycho-analytic Institute and Center.

Excerpts from Motivation and Personality by Abraham H. Maslow. Copyright © 1954 by Harper & Row, Publishers, Inc., Copyright © 1970 by Abraham H. Maslow. Reprinted by permission of HarperCollins Publishers, Inc.

Excerpt from Practical Mysticism by Evelyn Underhill reprinted with permission of Tessa Sayle Agency, London

To my Lord, Jesus Christ,

and an incredible family:
a loving and patient wife, Terry,
now in Heaven,
Pat, Pam, Peter, Paul,
George, Rod, Linda, Kathy,
eight loveable grandchildren,
a great grandchild,
Mom, Dad, and Vince

Also, to some for their suggestions,
to a few for their endorsements,
but to all for their uncommon kindness
and encouragement, I am deeply indebted to

Robert T. Sears, S.J., Ph.D.
Carolin Keutzer, Ph.D.
Philip G. Zimbardo, Ph.D.
Gerald F. Kreyche, Ph.D.
Michael Washburn, Ph.D.
Frank Haronian, Ph.D.
Sebastian P. Grossman, Ph.D.
William McNamara, O.C.D.
Dennis T. Jaffe, Ph.D.
J. Harold Ellens, Ph.D.
Piero Ferrucci, Ph.D.
Roger D. Snyder, Ph.D.
Stanislav Grof, M.D., Ph.D.
Stanley Krippner, Ph.D.
Charles E. Bennett, Ph.D.
James E. Liebig
M. Scott Peck, M.D.
Dorothy Gundling, Ph.D.
Ken Wilber
Huston Smith, Ph.D.
James Fadiman, Ph.D.
Bernard Tyrrell, S.J., Ph.D.
Rollo May, Ph.D.
Gary Emery, Ph.D.
Roger N. Walsh, M.D., Ph.D.
Michael J. Mahoney, Ph.D.
Albert Ellis, Ph.D.
and my dear friend, Tom Powers

Table of Contents

What is man? An angel, an animal, a void, a world, a nothing surrounded by God, indigent of God, capable of God, filled with God, if it so wills.

—CARDINAL DE BÉRULLE
(1575-1629)

Now that cognitive psychology has taken the head once lopped off by radical behaviorism and returned it to the body of psychology, we might in the next 10 years consider implanting a heart or a little soul in the same body. When that takes place, it may be easier to know what psychologists can offer to people and how they can do so, because then they will be us.

—PHILIP G. ZIMBARDO
Professor of Psychology
Stanford University - 1982

Preface

In his 1935 masterwork, *Man the Unknown,* Nobel laureate surgeon and biologist, Dr. Alexis Carrel, says that the observations of Jan of Ruysbroeck, a brilliant 14th century Christian mystic, were every bit as valid and realistic as those of our contemporary physiologists, each of them simply describing different aspects of the same mystery—the human being. He also wrote:

> *In learning the secret of the constitution and of the properties of matter, we have gained the mastery of almost everything which exists on the surface of the earth, excepting ourselves. The science of living beings in general, and especially of the human individual, has not made such great progress. . . Man is an indivisible whole of extreme complexity. No simple representation of him can be obtained. . . Man should be the measure of all. On the contrary, he is a stranger in the world that he has created. . . We must realize clearly that the science of man is the most difficult of all sciences. . . [and it] has become the most necessary of all sciences.* [Ch. I]

In 1971, after some early career success, but now deeply in debt and having exhausted all my resources, I was, in the words of Abraham Lincoln, "forced to my knees in the certain conviction that I had absolutely nowhere else to go." I returned to pray at the church I had left 32 years earlier, and began to intensify my avid lifelong avocational study of human behavior and the human potential. During the years that followed, I haunted the church, the library, the bookstores, and redoubled my volunteer work at Pace Institute, a life-transforming school in the Cook County Jail—a school created as a veritable miracle by the saintly chaplain, Reverend John Erwin.

Praying and reading voraciously, I added more than 200 books to my studies, literally steeping my brain in the classics by Evelyn Underhill, Aldous Huxley, William Law, Huston Smith, Augustine, Aquinas, Richard Bucke, Suzuki, Fénelon, Watts, Eckhart, de Caussade, à Kempis, Ruysbroeck, Idries Shah, Ernest Becker, Merton, Walter Hilton; the apologetics of every major religion and their exemplars: Hebrew prophets, Christian saints, Islamic Sufi adepts, Buddhist bodhisattvas, Zen masters, Hindu gurus, Taoist enlightened ones; all the major schools of psychology and psychiatry from Watson, James, Freud, and Jung, to Horney, Assagioli, Maslow, Glasser, and Perls; the philosophers from Socrates to Heidegger; Nag Hammadi Library, Upanishads, Dionysius, The Cloud of Unknowing, Theologia Germanica, Bhagavad Gita; scores of other major and minor works; and of course, the Bible—though I had already been through several readings of more or less the whole Bible, and enough study of the Gospels to memorize most of Christ's admonitions.

Obviously, this was a very perplexing study since the authors all seemed to be speaking different languages, often using ill-defined or undefined terms. Psychologists spoke of the ego, id, superego, repression, subconscious, parent/child/adult, complexes, tapes, transference, denial, isolation, rationalization, psychosis, neurosis, character disorders, basic needs, metaneeds, values, belief-system, self-image, archetypes, shoulds, constructs, ideas, mind, psyche, self-actualization, transactional analysis, etc., whereas theologians and philosophers spoke of the heart, the soul, repentance, purgation, contemplation, liberation, enlightenment, samsara, nirvana, the Kingdom of God; and others spoke of the power of visual imagery, positive thinking, a positive mental attitude, etc. Though all seemed valid observations, the idea of integrating them into a coherent framework seemed like an impossible dream.

Therefore it came as a thrilling revelation when, during a sleepless night in March, 1978, after seven years of intensive, agonizing and tortuous, study, thought, and prayer, the apple hit me on the head for about the tenth time, and the two keystones in the yawning arch between most major schools of psychology and the *perennial philosophy* [1] began to slip neatly into place. Suddenly I realized that these authors, each from their own perspective, like the blind men describing an elephant, had finally provided enough pieces of the puzzle to see how they could be merged into a coherent outline of the whole person. Suddenly, I saw the elephant—saw with startling clarity the essential components and their functions of the heretofore undefined *psyche*, the governing system of humans—components and functions which yielded a complete explanation of human motivation and behavior.

---

[1]   **Perennial Philosophy:** . . . often used as a synonym for Sanatana Dharma (Sanskrit for "Eternal or Perennial Truth"). It was used by Leibniz to designate the common, eternal philosophy that underlies all religious movements, in particular the mystical streams within religions. The term was popularized by Aldous Huxley in his 1945 book *The Perennial Philosophy* . . .(From Wikipedia, the free encyclopedia). For a fuller discussion, related to Christianity, see www.religioperennis.org/Document/Pdf/Christ_Perennial.pdf

In just a few days, these scores of viewpoints and millions of observations all came cascading, coalescing together into a new, relatively simple paradigm of the human being, a paradigm which reconciled all their findings, made comprehensible human motivation, behavior, the development of character and personality, and explained the mental processes of all human functions. In a single stroke, it reconciled the teachings of Christ and the exemplars of several major religions and philosophies, with all the observations—though not, of course, all the theories—of most major schools of psychology and psychiatry—and later, neurology, physiology, and cybernetics as well.

In answer to Cardinal de Bérulle's question, "What is man?". . .

The paradigm reveals that the human,
created in the image and likeness of a Triune God,
can only be defined as a *trinity* of soul, mind, and body.

This may sound like old news to some. But this paradigm, by providing a cogent delineation of the heretofore undefined "mind," and the apparent needs and faculties of the heretofore undefined "soul," enables us to understand our mental and spiritual components and their functions. It yields a "working model" of the human, a model which illustrates and explains motivation, behavior, and spiritual enlightenment. It gives us that "simple representation" of the person, which 43 years earlier Dr. Carrel said could not be obtained.

The paradigm fulfills Zimbardo's suggestion (fsp.) by providing impeccable inductive proof of the existence of both the spiritual soul and a neurologic "heart." It makes manifest the needs and faculties of the soul—faculties which invest it with the power of "Governor" of the person, *affirming our essentially spiritual nature*—and the constitution and functions of the heart.

It explains how *all of us,* in childhood, by the placid assumption
that our little milieu was representative of the world, and our avid
adoption of the beliefs, values, and mores of some random set of
significant but unenlightened others, have been *brain-wire blinded*
to the real world, and divested of most of our autonomy. As we
shall see, the naive soul has blithely overseen the creation of a
neurologic "Hal" heart, with a life and a will of its own.
But the paradigm also clarifies the process by which the soul
may recover its majesty and restore us to wholeness.

We are all living in a post-hypnotic trance,
induced in early infancy.
R. D. LAING

I was graced with a second thrilling insight in 1986—eight years after I had deduced a spiritual soul and mental heart, and, in my enthusiasm, feverishly completed the first six or seven rewrites of this book—when I learned that physiologists had identified the mind's heart more than 40 years ago, but not realizing what they had found, named it the *reticular formation* (RF). The RF is an uncharted—because unchartable—amorphous mass of millions of neurons located inside the brain stem, about the size and shape of one's little finger. In 1958, physiologist H. W. Magoun described some of its functions in *The Waking Brain.* Together with its millions of communication pathways to and from the brain and the body, it was named the *Reticular Activating System* (RAS), because stimulation of the RF caused sleeping subjects to awaken, while damage to the RF resulted in coma. (See page 192)

But now, even after fifty-plus years, neurologists have identified only a few of its purposes. It is so complex that research on it has practically come to a halt. Although its centralized location and countless connections would seem to enable it to perform myriad functions, it is impossible, using current research methods, to identify more than a few of them.

As we shall see, the known functions of the reticular formation, its commanding centralized location, and its vast two-way communications network linking it with all of the senses, muscles, and practically every part of the brain, make it the perfect candidate for the human "heart," which theologians and philosophers have spoken of for thousands of years, and which I had inferred from theologic and psychologic evidence, must exist in the human brain. I felt sure they would find the mind's heart someday—I didn't know they already had. But neither did they at the time, nor do they now.

This new paradigm, demonstrating the equivalence of the theologic heart and the neurologic RAS, lends compelling credibility to Dr. Carrel's assertion that saints and physiologists—and by extension psychologists and neurologists—are simply describing different but real aspects of the same mystery: the human being.

This book then, is about people; but not about "them"—any minority. It is a book about *us,* the great majority of the human race who live typical "lives of quiet desperation;" we so-called "normal" people who live out our days obeying most of the rules, but never knowing who or what we are, and who die in ignorance of why we were here. It is a book about our mental and spiritual constitution; our needs, our capabilities, our potential; about how we perceive, how we interpret, and how we respond to the world's stimuli. It is a book about our potential for enlightenment, liberation, self-actualization, realization of the Kingdom of God; about our ability to live purposeful, meaningful, fulfilling lives, simply through the (difficult) development of some significant and rational Loves and Beliefs. It is a book about what we are, and what we can be.

I have risked boring the reader with the preceding list of my major sources in order to indicate the universality of the derivations of my thesis, and to credit the hundreds of geniuses and saintly people—many of whom were also geniuses—who provided all the grist for my mill. Every important fact and idea in this book was derived from the work of someone else. My only contribution, if I have made one, is to integrate their most significant discoveries and credible insights into a coherent framework, somewhat as Mendeleef organized the atoms into a "Periodic Table of the Elements." If, as I firmly believe, this theory provides a cogent synthesis of some of the best thoughts of practically all these writers, representing several different disciplines and schools of thought, the credit lies with my 31 years with Christ, and to my studies at the feet of scores of His "MVP's" and many of the world's foremost authorities on these subjects.

The single most important question facing the human race is Cardinal de Bérulle's, "What is man?"—followed closely by the perennial puzzle, "What are the determinants of human behavior?" Based on the works of these great People, this book presents some new answers to those age-old questions. It is, therefore, "our" response to Alexis Carrel's inspired and inspiring call for a "Science of Man," to Roberto Assagioli's insightful advocacy of a "Science of the Self," and to Abraham Maslow's clairvoyant vision of a "still higher, Fourth Psychology."

1
Introduction

Dr. Maxwell Maltz, in his landmark work, *Psycho-Cybernetics,* states, "The most important psychologic discovery of this [20th] century has been the discovery of the 'self-image'." He explains that from our experiences and reflections (both kinds) we all gradually build up a mental picture of a self, a person, whose characteristics are represented by our beliefs about ourselves: our worth, our intelligence, personality, character, physical prowess, appearance, etc.; and that once a belief about ourselves goes into this picture, whether or not it is true, it becomes true as far as we personally are concerned, and tends to be realized in our lives. The beliefs which make up the self-image become what we have now labeled (but not heretofore explained), "self-fulfilling prophecies." He then proves beyond any reasonable doubt that not only do we always tend to act in a manner consistent with this self-image, it is extremely difficult for us to act otherwise.

Conversely, he proves that a change in our self-images, our beliefs about ourselves, automatically results in a change in our personality, our character, our behavior; it can actually change our capabilities.

Along with Freud's "ego," "id," "libido," "superego," "subconscious," and "repressed desires," Jung's "complexes," "personal unconscious," "persona," and "shadow," Horney's "neurotic trends" and "tyranny of the 'should'," Ellis' "irrational ideas," Maslow's "basic needs," and "metaneeds," Kelly's "personal constructs," Assagioli's "higher self" and dominance of entities of self-identification, Becker's "denial of death," and dozens of other important psychologic discoveries, Maltz' explication of the self-image opened up a whole new world to our understanding of human behavior. But none of these people suggested that their concepts could explain all human behavior.

To do that, we must consolidate these ideas and incorporate them into two new concepts in psychology and theology, concepts which represent the two keystones in the arch between most major schools of Psychology and the Perennial Philosophy.

The first concept is that all of these psychologic phenomena, as well as many others, are subsumed in one specific, extremely complex neurologic "system" in the brain, a system best described as:

The Love/Belief System

The Love/Belief System is a marvelous neurological computer/servo-mechanism in the brain of the human, between the senses and the Center of Consciousness—a system of which the superego, the personal unconscious, the persona, the shadow, the neurotic trends, the personal constructs, the complexes, the self-image, the shoulds, the irrational ideas, many of the basic needs, the denial of death, etc., are only a few of its most important "programs." All of these wellsprings of human motivation and behavior will be seen to represent "clusters," or individual elements, of the thousands of conscious and subconscious Loves, Beliefs, Values, Needs, Desires, and Fears which constitute the preponderant programs of the Love/Belief System. And it is this System, operating on these programs, that determines most of our actions and all of our emotions. It generates most of our motivations, and exercises a commanding influence over all of our mental, physical, verbal, and emotional responses to the circumstances of life.

Neurologists have been studying the Love/Belief System for over forty years, only they call it the Reticular Activating System (see illustration, page 192). The "RAS" is an extremely elaborate and complex neural communication and control network emanating from a finger-shaped "reticular formation" (RF) inside the brain stem. The RF is uniquely located and connected to monitor, interpret, and initiate responses to all communications between all parts of the brain, and between brain and body. Many of its functions have been identified with complete scientific rigor, and, as we shall see, are identical to those I will define as functions of the Love/Belief System.

The "programs" of this computer/servo-like Love/Belief System, or RAS, are the needs we share with all social animals (which I shall refer to as the SA-Needs), plus all of our *self-adopted conscious and subconscious Loves, Beliefs, Values, and Needs.* Now both the SA-Needs and our self-adopted Loves, Beliefs, Values, and Needs, give rise to Desires and Fears. I will designate all of these Loves, Beliefs, Values, Needs, Desires, and Fears as "Elements," which, together with the SA-Needs, constitute the programs of the Love/Belief System.[1] Since Loves, Beliefs, Values, and Needs form such an important part of the Love/Belief System, and since references to these four Elements will occur so often in this book, I will in the future refer to them

---

[1] I'll explain how our Loves, Beliefs, Values, and Needs become wired in our Love/Belief Systems in Chapter 4, page 58.

simply as "Loves and Beliefs." Please note that "Loves and Beliefs" represent our self-adopted, conscious and subconscious, Loves, Beliefs, Values, and Needs.

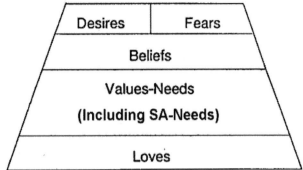

Figure 1 - The Love/Belief System or Reticular Activating System Programs

As we shall see, it is the Love/Belief System, or RAS, operating from 10 to 1,000 times faster than the best (1998) computer, which determines what we perceive in the world, then interprets those percepts—tells us what to think of them—and then tries to implement its illations by generating corresponding "Response Impulses" to our brains and bodies, all *before* those percepts fully penetrate our consciousness; and that this is why, as saints and psychologists alike keep telling us, we are *not* the masters of our own lives.

What Christ and all enlightened people are saying is that fully 99.99% of us are not experiencing the real world at all, the world they inhabit. For example, when you look through the bottom of a wine bottle, everything appears distorted and murky. Well, these enlightened people have bad news for us. They tell us that we are all wearing *permanent* lenses over our eyes so dark and distorted they make the wine bottle look like plate glass. They say that all of us "normal" people see the world and our neighbor only very super-ficially and deficiently, because we can only see and hear them through these uncompromising filters, through our diffracting and obscuring Love/Belief Systems, or what they call our "hearts." [2]

As Jerome Bruner has stated, "the human mind has an 'inhibitory system' which routinely and automatically removes from *perception,* reason,

---

[2]   The "lenses" analogy is deficient since it is not just our visual percepts that are distorted, but also the *selection* and *interpretation* of all our sensory percepts. The "filter" is between the world and our *understanding,* our objective appreciation, our ability to be fully and sensitively *aware.*

and judgment, over 99% of available fact." ! ! We now know that it is the RAS which performs this very necessary function. Our senses are forwarding 100 million signals to the brain every second. It is obviously impossible for us to be conscious of any but a small portion of these impressions—some screening is essential to our sanity and our safety. But, as we all know, over and above our sanity and our safety, each of us tends to perceive a different one percent of the total impressions available to us; each individual always tends to see the same one percent; and each of us interprets, and therefore reacts, differently, even to the same stimulus.

But not only does the RAS select, evaluate, and determine "appropriate" responses to our percepts, it is also, since it is a servomechanism, the "implementer" or "executor" of all of our actions. Not only its own responses, but also all of our acts of will are implemented by the RAS which translates the pictures we create into neural signals to the motor neurons which will effect the actualization of those visions. But of course our acts of will are enacted by the RAS only after they have been "processed." Try pricking your finger to get a drop of blood and watch the RAS spring into action!

This book presents, for the first time to my knowledge, a delineation and description of the constitution and functions of this "mental inhibitory system," this RAS, with which we are all endowed, and shows that it is best described as a Love/Belief System, a computer/servo-like system whose programs are made up of the SA-Needs we share with all social animals, and all of our self-adopted, conscious and subconscious Loves and Beliefs, and their resultant Desires and Fears.

The simple explanation of all human behavior is that the Love/Belief System is always determining: 1) our psychological "set:" what we look for in the world, and therefore what we see—which of the less than one percent of the world's stimuli are even perceived; 2) how those few impressions are interpreted, cognized; 3) what our responses "should" be; and 4) initiates the implementation of those responses, all before the percepts fully penetrate our consciousness. As we shall see, only then are these *Response Impulses* subject to review. Therefore, to our great misfortune, the great majority of our actions and emotions are simply conditioned Love/Belief System responses to stimuli which *it* has selected as being important!

Because of the incredible speed of the brain,

**No percept enters our consciousness
until it has first been "processed" by the RAS.**

**Every act of will is implemented by the RAS,
only after it has *processed* those commands.**

**We are all blinded to the *real* world, and disenabled
by the machinations of our Love/Belief Systems.**

The only way we can significantly and permanently improve our lives then, from a psychological or spiritual standpoint, is by changing some of our basic Loves and Beliefs. By changing Elements of our Love/Belief Systems, we immediately change *what* we perceive, *how* we perceive (re-cognize), and therefore, change our autonomic Response Impulses—how we involuntarily tend to act and feel in response to all the circumstances of our lives. Unlike efforts to change our behavior, these become perception/cognitive-shaping changes—basic, permanent changes in the person, changes which make us new people (and if towards Love of God and our neighbor, born-again people).

Now the idea of improving our lives by changing some of our basic Loves and Beliefs is not new, having been definitively explicated about 2,000 years ago in Galilee. But I will propose that Christ's "Kingdom of God" also represents the highest possible form of what psychologists call mental health and self-actualization—which, as we shall see, is "Soul-actualization."

As for the mystics/saints/sages of most religions—who keep telling us that in order to share their beatitude and "peace that passes understanding," nothing need change but our *hearts*—they are generally thought of as wild-eyed visionaries whose experiences bear little significance or relevance to what most of us think of as the "real" world. On the contrary, I will contend that many of these enlightened people are the most intellectually gifted and most rational of all people. As the brilliant Sigrid Undset, recipient of the Pulitzer prize for literature, concluded, "The only *sane* people are the saints." Many of them are the best balanced, most self-actualized of all people, because they sought, not self-actualization, but the Kingdom of God and His righteousness, or some form thereof, and as a result, have been graced with a Knowledge of God's Love and their own immortality. They have ascended into the peace of "The Freedom of the Will of God." They prove the axiom, "The most evident token and apparent sign of true wisdom is constant and unconstrained rejoicing." If the human race is to have a future, they are indeed its precursors, the harbingers of the millennium.

On a scale of mental health and self-actualization, Christ and most saints and sages must be seen to be on the highest end of the continuum, psychotics and neurotics on the lowest, with the great mass of humanity in between, neither mentally disturbed, nor self-actualized, enlightened, or liberated. Psychotics and neurotics only suffer from more deleterious root Loves and Beliefs than those of us "normal" people. But the saints say we are *all* suffering spiritual blindness, as well as innumerable psychopathologies, from the irrational and haphazardly adopted Loves and Beliefs and their resultant Desires and Fears, which, together with the Needs we share with all social animals, constitute the programs of our Love/Belief Systems, or hearts.

> *Fully developed mystics state unequivocally that our usual state of consciousness is not only suboptimal, it is dreamlike and illusory. They assert that whether we know it or not, we, as untrained individuals, are prisoners of our own minds, totally and unwittingly trapped by a continuous inner fantasy-dialogue that creates an all-consuming illusory distortion of perception of reality. However, this condition goes unrecognized until we begin to subject our perceptual-cognitive processes to rigorous scrutiny as in meditation.*
>
> *Thus, the "normal" person is seen as "asleep" or "dreaming." When the "dream" is especially painful or disruptive it becomes a nightmare and is recognized as psychopathology, but since the vast majority of the population "dreams," the true state of affairs goes unrecognized. When the individual disidentifies from or eradicates this dream he or she is said to have awakened and can now recognize the true nature of both his or her former state and that of the population. This awakening or enlightenment is the aim of the consciousness disciplines.[3]*
>
> *To some extent this is an extension rather than a denial of the perspective of Western psychology and psychiatry which have long recognized that careful experimental observation reveals a broad range of perceptual distortions unrecognized by naive subjects. The consciousness disciplines merely go further in asserting that we are all subject to distortions, that they affect all aspects of our perception, that without specific remedial mental training all remain unaware of them, and that the consensual reality we share is thus illusory. This has also been suggested by a number Western investigators. . . .*
>
> *The implications of this are awesome. Within the Western model, we*

---

[3]   But, as we shall see, it is the fruit only of the *spiritual* disciplines.

recognize and define psychosis as a suboptimal state of consciousness that views reality in a distorted way and does not recognize that distortion. It is significant to note that from the mystical perspective, our usual state fits all the criteria of psychosis in that it is suboptimal, has a distorted view of reality, and does not recognize that distortion.

To hold this as an interesting objective concept is one thing. To consider it as something directly applicable to our own experience is . . . considerably more difficult.

'We have studied some aspects of samsara (illusion, maya) in far more detail than the Eastern traditions that originated the concept of samsara. Yet almost no psychologists apply this idea to themselves. They assume . . . that their own states of consciousness are basically logical and clear. Western psychology now has a challenge to recognize this detailed evidence that our 'normal' state is a state of samsara.'
C. Tart

Of course, this is very difficult, if not impossible, to recognize the limitations of the usual state of consciousness if that is all one has ever known. However, mystics repeatedly claim that anyone who is willing to undertake the strenuous but necessary training to extricate their awareness from the conditioned tyranny of the mind will be able to look back and see the formerly unrecognized limitations within which they lived. A common present-day analogy is that of people who live in a chronically smog-ridden environment but only see the full extent of the pollution once they get out of it. [BE:37]
—WALSH & VAUGHAN

Or, in a profound earlier observation:

What does he of England know, who only England knows? [4]
—RUDYARD KIPLING

---

[4] The profundity of this question is easy to overlook. What does she of femininity know, who only femininity knows? What does he of living as a member of the majority race know, who only living as a member of the majority knows? What does he of Christianity know who only Christianity knows? etc., etc., etc.

What the mystics/saints/sages are trying to tell us is that all of us "normal" people are suffering this "conditioned tyranny of the mind," and getting a distorted view of reality, because each of us is looking at the world through our own peculiar Love/Belief System, and all our responses are determined by how that System selects and interprets the world's stimuli to us. It is only when we have learned to look at the world "through the eyes of Love," i.e., with attentive and selfless (Frommian) care and concern, responsiveness, respect, and knowledge, that we can possibly begin to see it as it really is; see it as it was designed to be seen, and as we were ordained to see it; see it as Christ and all the saints have seen it: infinite; "see" God in the world. Truly, "the world is full of beauty when the heart is full of Love."

To illustrate, picture a young couple in a nursery of unmarked babies, trying to figure out which one is theirs. Then imagine the nurse coming in and pointing out their baby. How differently they will look at it now that they know it is theirs! This is looking with the eyes of Love, albeit in this instance a possessive Love. And Christ and His saints say we can all *learn* to see the world and our neighbor this way—but unpossessively; can learn to see the miraculous, and therefore the Loveable, not only in all babies, but in everything, even down to the "flower in the crannied wall."

Late in life, after his heart attack, Abraham Maslow, at best an agnostic, discovered what he called "plateau experiences," this new way of perceiving and re-cognizing the world:

> *I can define this unitive consciousness . . . as the simultaneous perception of the sacred and the ordinary, or the miraculous and the ordinary, . . . I now perceive under the aspect of eternity and become mythic, poetic, and symbolic about ordinary things. . . I think you can teach plateau experiences; you could hold classes in miraculousness. . . it is possible to sit and look at something miraculous for an hour and enjoy every minute of it.*

> *The important point that emerges from these plateau experiences is that they're essentially cognitive. . almost by definition, they represent a witnessing of the world. The plateau experience is a witnessing of reality. It involves seeing the symbolic, the mythic, the poetic, the transcendent, the miraculous, the unbelievable, all of which I think are part of the real world instead of existing only in the eyes of the beholder.*

[I can] walk on the prairie and see the buffalo and the Indians and the pioneers. . . the surf is more beautiful to me now . . . It can be very, very touching. This whole business of witnessing eternity means you are mortal and your mortality produces a fear of the witnessing. It is happy and also sad. It's a mixture, and very beautiful.

Maslow had begun to see the world through the eyes of Love. With Blake, he began . .

To see a World in a grain of sand, and a Heaven in a wild flower, hold Infinity in the palm of your hand, and Eternity in an hour.

Or, as Traherne said it should be seen:

Your enjoyment of the world is never right till every morning you awake in Heaven; see yourself in your Father's palace; and look upon the skies, the earth and the air as celestial joys; having such a reverend esteem of all, as if you were among the Angels. The bride of a monarch, in her husband's chamber, hath no such causes of delight as you.

You never enjoy the world aright till the sea itself floweth in your veins, till you are clothed with the heavens and crowned with the stars; and perceive yourself to be the sole heir of the whole world, and more, because men are in it who are every one sole heirs as well as you. Till you can sing and rejoice and delight in God, as misers do in gold, and kings in sceptres, you can never enjoy the world.

. . . till you love men so as to desire their happiness with a thirst equal to the zeal of your own; till you delight in God for being good to all; you never enjoy the world. . . .

The world is a mirror of Infinite Beauty, yet no man sees it.[5] *It is a Temple of Majesty, yet no man regards it. It is a region of Light and Peace, did not men disquiet it. . . . [It] is none other than the House of God and the Gate of Heaven.*

---

[5]   Because the world is only a *mirror* of our Love/Belief Systems. See pps. 118-120. This is the way we all saw the world when we were four, but at five, we began to undergo the "hypnosis of social conditioning." (pps. 46-47)

"But," some say, "that's a simplistic and artificial way of looking at the world—that's just putting on rose-colored glasses, and ignoring all the suffering in the world." But the saints and sages, all of whom have seen the world both ways, say this is not putting on rose-colored glasses—it's taking off our dung-colored ones; not being hypnotized, but *de*-hypnotized; that while it is a simplistic way of looking at the world, it is anything but simple to do, requiring great personal courage, integrity, and faith; and, rather than ignoring suffering in the world, they say,

> *None can usurp this height*
> *But those to whom the miseries of the world*
> *Are misery, and will not let them rest.*

And because it is only when we look through the eyes of Love that we receive a clear and honest view of the world and our neighbor, it is only then that we can begin to lead whole, fulfilling, self-actualizing, and *rational* lives.

This was Christ's message: "Blessed are the pure in heart, for they shall see God." In order to see the world as it is, infinite—to see God in the world—we must see it through the eyes of Love; through our own efforts and the grace of God, we must learn to Love God with all our heart, soul, mind, and strength, and our neighbor as ourselves.

> *Our whole business in this world is to restore to health*
> *the eye of the heart whereby God may be seen.*
> —ST. AUGUSTINE

Now not only do we fail to see the world as it really is, but much more importantly, Christ and all these enlightened people tell us, we do not see ourselves the way they saw their "selves." This is because we have all been callously indoctrinated to believe, "I am my mind and body." You see, you are not your mind/body. Instead you are spirit, the spirit of Free Being, Loving, and Knowing, associated with the mind/body of a very proficient social animal. But you are not that animal. What you call "I" is pure spirit; you don't *have* a soul—you *are* a soul. But you haven't realized this since you were a child, when you lost the awareness of your True Self, the glorious nature of your "I", primarily because, as a child, one of the first beliefs to enter your Love/Belief System was, "I am my mind/body." This is one of your most basic beliefs, and has dominated and diminished your life in ways you may not believe possible. Later we'll see how thousands of enlightened people throughout the ages have eliminated this erroneous belief, recovered the joy of existence as a Loving, Knowing soul, and in so doing, found a piece of pure heaven, here on earth, while they lived.

Therefore, to explain all human behavior, we must reintroduce and now define, a second element in the human:

The Immortal "I"

The immortal "I" is the soul, the Governor of the person, and the "programmer" and "overseer" of the Love/Belief System. Again, for the first time to my knowledge, I will define in psychological terms, the Needs and Faculties of this mysterious element in people, the one element which makes us human, and differentiates us from the animals. As I will describe it, the immortal "I" will be seen to represent the theologian's "soul," both Horney's "real self" and Assagioli's "higher self" (but adds their Needs and Faculties), Freud's "I" (reconstituted), Jung's "self," or "God within us" (radically reconstituted), Buber's "I" and "Thou," Deikman's nebulous "Observing Self," Damasio's nebulous "proto self," the naive creator of LeDoux's "synaptic self," and the source of some of Maslow's "basic needs," and all of his "metaneeds."

Enlightened people tell us that there can be no higher form of self-actualization than that which begins with *Self-realization,* recognition of the True Self, or "I"—what they call the "opening of the eye of the soul."

> *Having realized the Self, nothing remains to be known,*
> *because it is perfect Bliss, it is the All.*
> —RAMANA MAHARSHI

The path to attainment of this Self-realization can be derived not only from the words and example of Christ, and from the saints of several of the world's major religions, but also from the works of some purely secular philosophers, and several leading psychologists. It is now becoming increasingly apparent that these great writers and thinkers, theist and non-theist alike, are all working towards and approaching, one definition, or description, or identification, of the highest possible form of human self-actualization: the fulfillment of the promise that we have the power to become, while we live, sons and daughters of God; to actualize, to realize, and to live that relationship.

Christ and the saints tell us how we can realize and live that relationship. It's not an easy way, so precious few pursue it. But those who persist eventually find a peace and fulfillment which exceeds all other gratifications.

Therefore, the theological foundations of this book are not the ordinary garden-variety of "observe the Sabbath and pray when you're in trouble" kind of religion, the religion of those whom Huxley describes as "ordinary, nice, unregenerate people," and Huston Smith depicts as the "exoteric," as opposed to the "esoteric," practitioners of their religions. Rather, these principles have been derived from the Perennial Philosophy (as expounded by Huxley), from the words and example of Christ and many great Christians, as well as the exemplars of several major religions—people who had learned to live their whole lives religiously. Our subject, then, from a spiritual standpoint, is not about changing some surface aspect of our lives, but about being literally reborn, spiritually and psychologically, into an entirely new person; not about an altered state of consciousness, but an altered state of being; about realizing, not as a mental concept, but actually experiencing, one's own immortal, spiritual Self, or "I", and one's kinship with God—not in days or weeks or even months, but, if you are importunate, certainly much sooner than anyone could possibly deserve such a great gift.

Although I hope this book will help to explain the process, there seem to be no fast, easy ways to realize the "I", since it is known only to the "pure in heart," those who have undergone the arduous restoration of their childhood innocence and humility. As Evelyn Underhill says, "It is reasonable, even reassuring, that hard work and discipline should be needed for this: that it should demand of you, if not the renunciation of the cloister, at least the virtues of the golf course." Godsmanship is at least as difficult as golfsmanship. I'll explain "miraculous" instantaneous conversions later, and show that they are neither instantaneous nor miraculous. Saul, for example, was a very religious person.

Unfortunately however, their reports have caused a great movement in the world today of people seeking enlightenment by use of drugs, encounter groups, meditation, consciousness disciplines, prayer, psychoanalysis and psychotherapy, revival meetings, "est," and many other means, without any effort to change their lives outside of those practices. But surely for those who believe there is a God, and that He is a living Being Who is best thought of as our heavenly Father—One who has numbered the hairs of our heads—then the highest form of true enlightenment must be the one the saints of most religions keep telling us about: the attainment, with God's grace, of the state in which one becomes aware of, experiences, becomes absolutely assured of, Knows, while he lives, his kinship with God; comes to Know God, as Ken Wilber puts it, "directly, non-conceptually, and immediately;" or, as St. John of the Cross describes this "awakening:"

> *And here lies the remarkable delight of this awakening: the soul knows the creatures through God, and not God through the creatures. . . . That which a person knows and experiences of God in this awakening is entirely beyond words. Since this awakening is the communication of God's excellence to the substance of the soul, which is its heart, . . . an immense, powerful voice sounds in it, the voice of a multitude of excellences, of thousands of virtues in God, infinite in number. The soul is established in them, terribly and solidly set in array in them like an army, and made gentle and charming with all the gentleness and charm of the creatures.* [CW:645]

But this "awakening" cannot be the result of any single act, or even many acts, out of context with the rest of our lives, e.g., going to church, saying some words, taking a drug, going into a trance—what Evelyn Underhill calls "the psychologists' error of looking for the soul in 'psychic states'"—but must be the result of what we *are*. As our evidence shall show, we are what we Love, Believe, Value, and Need. Therefore it is to our Loves and Beliefs that we must turn if we are to Know God's Love and His Peace in our lives.

For the first time in the history of the human race, we are now able to intelligently participate in our own evolution, in the discovery (recovery?) and development of our *essentially spiritual natures.*[6] For 20,000 years or more, we identified ourselves with our bodies, and believed that all our powers were in our muscles. In the last several thousand years we have learned to identify ourselves with what we call our "minds," and our accomplishments have multiplied exponentially. But now a new age for humanity is dawning. The Spirit of God is sweeping the world, and we must learn to identify ourselves with our spirits, our true selves, our immortal "I"'s—learn to appreciate fully this highest aspect of the trinity of our being. The millennium will come when we learn that all our real satisfactions, and all our real power—our power as creators, made in the image and likeness of God—derive not from our minds or bodies, but from our spirits, our immortal "I"'s, from the exercise of our uniquely human capabilities to Love, to Believe, and to Envision—and to freely choose the objects of our Loves, Beliefs, and Visions.

---

[6]   Both St. Augustine (p. 42) and Lao Tse (p. 133) use the word "restore."

It can never be too strongly emphasized that the crisis which Western man is undergoing today is a metaphysical one; there is probably no more dangerous illusion than that of imagining that some readjustment of social or institutional conditions could suffice of itself to appease a contemporary sense of disquiet which rises, in fact, from the very depth of man's being.

—GABRIEL MARCEL

The "sense of disquiet" to which Marcel refers arises primarily from the fact that we don't know what we *are*, and therefore, we don't know what to *do* with our lives. We are unique in the universe, and can find no standards or guidelines for our lives. We find it impossible to achieve the "integrated outlook and attitude," which John Dewey says, is "the basic cause of the despair [representing] the chief intellectual characteristic of the present age;" impossible to find a "knowledge of the right direction—of orientation," which William Sheldon says is "the most universal craving in the human makeup."

As Maltz has proved, our lives are shaped largely by our self-images, our beliefs about ourselves. (Over and above our SA-Needs, human nature can perhaps only be described as a compulsion to always act in a manner consistent with one's self-image!) But the self-image consists not only of our beliefs about what kind of a person we are, but also of our more basic, implicit beliefs about what a person *is*. Obviously then, the single most effective way in which we can significantly and permanently improve our human nature— and with it, the world—is to enhance our understanding of what it is to be human, our implicit, thoughtless, but inexorably self-constricting answers to Cardinal de Bérulle's question, "What is man?"

**To the extent that we can control our own destiny,
the fate of the entire human race depends
primarily on how we explicitly or implicitly
answer that question—how we define "person."**

Therefore, even without "religious" considerations,

**The single most important objective for the human race,
individually and collectively, is the realization and
appreciation of our *essentially spiritual nature*,
our immortal "I"'s.**

Drawing on scores of the most authoritative sources from the disciplines of psychiatry, psychology, theology, philosophy, neurology, hagiography, physiology, and cybernetics, I will submit new delineations of the constitution and functions of the necessary and sufficient components—the mind, heart, and soul—for a new paradigm of the human, which, with a few theorems, can illustrate and elucidate all our faculties, capabilities, motivation, behavior, and the mechanics and interrelations of our animal and spiritual natures. The paradigm also yields a new hierarchy of needs, modifying and completing that of Maslow, and a promising new psychotherapy, Open-Heart Therapy.

I will suggest that the immortal "I", though ultimately unknowable, is a realizable, experiencable entity, and that realization of the "I" brings instantaneous awareness, Knowledge, of our kinship with Ultimate Being; that the "I" is spirit, inherently the Governor of our lives, but a Governor which delegates most of its powers to its Love/Belief System.

I will show how the Love/Belief System develops, and comes to dominate our lives; identify some of our most significant Loves and Beliefs; show how they can be changed, using the creative powers of the "I" itself; and indicate the direction in which the mystics/saints/sages of all ages (and lately some few psychologists) tell us we must change those Loves and Beliefs for our own benefit, for our greatest self-fulfillment and satisfaction here on earth, to actualize, to realize, and thereby enable us to live and die in peace in our true stature, as sons and daughters of God.

Since these paradigms were induced from the research and experiences of others, I must quote these People rather copiously to show their derivation and validity. But of course this book cannot be an exhaustive treatment of how these theories apply in all of their ramifications to all of the schools and disciplines mentioned. The reader is referred to the standard works on the major schools of psychology/psychiatry, and the bibliography—especially the Gospels and the works of Huxley, Maslow, Maltz, Underhill, Freud, Becker, and Assagioli— for a more comprehensive substantiation of these theories.

Three qualifications: First, this book is not offered as a scientific work, presenting theories which can be proved or disproved, nor conclusions which can be replicated by skeptics. Rather it is a work of philosophical anthropology derived from the best thoughts of many the world's greatest thinkers, and representing a multidisciplinary systems analysis of brain/mind/behavior. Although its conclusions derive from well-established scientific facts in the fields listed above, and the thoughts of the most highly regarded philosophers and theologians of many faiths, the validity of this theory will not satisfy "Scientismists" (those who believe that someday all our problems will be solved, all our questions answered, in the laboratory, by the figment they revere as "Science"), since they were derived inductively—the same way Newton's laws of motion, the Copernican system, and many other scientific discoveries were derived (often by considering multiple similar anecdotes as *data*). They can be proved the way these theories were initially "proved"— by showing that they explain all the facts. No single example will prove my thesis, any more than the falling apple alone convinced Newton's contemporaries of the validity of his laws of motion. It is only the great accumulation of well-documented scientific and cumulative anecdotal evidence from many different sources that give credence to this thesis.

Also, while Newton's laws of motion "explained," in terms of gravity and inertia, the motions of physical bodies from a falling apple to the trajectory of a cannon-ball to the orbits of the planets, we still don't know what gravity or inertia *are*, nor how they generate their forces. Newton didn't know *how* the earth and apple attracted each other, and neither do we. As my beloved physics professor, Dr. Valasek, said, "You think you know why a rubber band stretches and contracts;" then, after a pregnant pause, concluded indulgently, emphatically, "but you don't." In the same manner, this hypothesis, by identifying and delineating the necessary and sufficient components and their functions of the heretofore undefined "psyche," yields an explanation of all human capabilities, motivation, and behavior. But we don't know now, and may never know, *how* these components accomplish their functions.[7]

Second: Rather than the cumbersome he/she, hers/his, etc., I have used masculine and feminine pronouns in alternate chapters; but I have not felt licensed to change the sexist language used by my sources. Knowing them as I do however, I feel sure that most of them, if they were living today, would be at the forefront of the crusade for equality; many of them felt that women were better endowed for the enlightened life. Too, it is my hope this book will help prove that gender is one of the least important characteristics of people; the really important part, the "I", is certainly genderless. One day men and women will realize their essential oneness.

---

[7]   A personal anecdote: When I heard Richard Feynman, one of the world's leading theoretical physicists, say that he once asked his father why the ball kept rolling to the back of his wagon when he pulled it, I smugly recalled Newton's laws of motion. But my attitude was instantly transformed into pride's inseparable counterpart, the gall of envy, when Feynman related his father's *correct* answer, "Son, nobody knows. They call it *inertia*." Now, 70+ years later, the answer is still the same.

Third: Since I am personally committed to Christ (indentured might be a better word—He owns me), and since I believe that Christ's words represent the definitive exposition of the Perennial Philosophy, I must ask the indulgence of readers who are atheists, agnostics, or adherents of other faiths, as well as those millions of Christians who do not share my interpretation of the four Gospels (which, like my approach to psychology, is an existential one), and/or my friendly attitude toward other faiths. I request of them the charity to ignore our religious differences and consider the overwhelming multidisciplinary evidence for the theses presented here. To those who cannot accept Christ's divinity, perhaps they will consider another aspect of his many-faceted being: the incredible profundity of his knowledge of human nature— the sheer genius which made him the first, and still the foremost proponent and exemplar of the psychology of—not self-actualization—but *Soul*-actualization.

If you find the book difficult, I plead the task of integrating ideas from hundreds of books and a half-dozen different disciplines, to introduce a central idea, a unifying principle, which was derived inductively; therefore a principle which can render comprehensible—explain—hundreds of facts about human nature, but which itself cannot be derived deductively.

But we only understand that which we are prepared to understand, and perhaps only to the conscientiously introspective reader, the book may prove itself by offering ample opportunity to catch the mind performing one of its most insidious and pernicious feats: that of rendering to consciousness as erroneous, or incomprehensible, or meaningless, or trite, anything which it has evaluated *pre-consciously* as unpleasant or difficult. Whether or not these interpretations have some validity is not the point; the point is that they are all *autonomic,* literal instincts, generated *sub*-consciously.

Unless your faith is anchored in the dogmatic fundamentalism of any religion, or in secular humanism, radical behaviorism, or in your own objectivity (all of which are matters of faith), I believe your effort with this book will repay you, because, enlightened people tell us, as you come to an appreciation of the existence and the needs and powers of the "I", or Self, and an awareness of the machinations of the Love/Belief System, or heart, you'll begin to understand not only yourself, but all other people as well.

And assuredly, they say, if you persist, the day will come when you will partake of the thrilling discovery and realization of your True Self, your own immortal "I", and with it, the ineffable bliss of Free Being/Loving/Knowing, a state in which you will find yourself one with the Ultimate Nature of the universe, or what Christians believe is God, our Father.

Jesus said: If those who lead you say to you: "See, the Kingdom is in heaven," then the birds of the heaven will precede you. If they say to you: "It is in the sea," then the fish will precede you. But the Kingdom is within you and it is without you. If you will know yourselves, then you will be known and you will know that you are the sons of the living Father. But if you do not know yourselves, then you are in poverty and you are poverty.

—THE GOSPEL OF THOMAS

2
The Immortal "I"

A person is a social animal with few instincts, but endowed with a spiritual "I", or "Governor of the Being." To infer the "I", picture a healthy, hungry animal in a quiet room with a plate of food. One hundred times out of one hundred (unless he has been conditioned not to) the animal will eat the food. Only the human among the animals has the self-control to say, "I am hungry, but I am not going to eat." This self-denial brings two "I"'s into conflict, obviously only one of which can be the "I". Strictly speaking then, one should not say, "I am hungry;" but rather, "My stomach is signaling hunger pangs to my mind, but 'I' am not going to allow my impulses to eat to be enacted."

Therefore we see that the human, alone among the animals, has an "I", or Governor at the apex of her being. This Governor acts similarly to an air traffic controller, who responds with approval, denial, or alternate directions to the requests she receives from airplanes in the area.

> *What could begin to deny self, if there were not*
> *something in man different from self?*
> —WILLIAM LAW

The major thesis of this book is that any realistic or meaningful paradigm of person must be based on the following definition:

A person is a social animal with a spiritual "I".

As an animal, people have *physiological* needs:

1. For air, food, water, sleep, elimination, and in the winter latitudes, protection from the elements. These are the life needs, without which life is impossible.

2. For freedom from pain, discomfort, and fear/anxiety.
3. To explore their environment; the animal curiosity to know (lower case "k"), and to exercise and experiment with (resulting in development of) their physical capabilities.
4. For sex, erotic love (lower-case "l").

Taken all together, these are the basic animal needs. It will be seen that they are in a hierarchical order of importance to life.

But as a social animal, people share with all social animals additional *bio-sociological* needs:

As children:
5. For parental affection, protection, nurture.
6. Partially as a function of the needs 3, above, to seek physical pleasure in play.
7. To imitate their elders, siblings, associates.

As they mature:
8. To seek acceptance, belongingness, in the social group,
9. In the female, to protect and care for the young,
10. To establish as high a position in the pecking order as possible—to dominate others, to gain preference over others in satisfying their needs.[1]

Now needs 1-4 arise only periodically or circumstantially, and normally disappear when satisfied; they manifest themselves in the mind only intermittently. But needs 5-10 are more or less always operant as overall purposes; they exert a somewhat constant influence in the mind. I will therefore consider needs 1-4, unless operant, to exist substantially in the body, and, while recognizing their strong biological origins, consider needs 5-10 to exist primarily in the brain. This corresponds to the neurologists' distinction between old- and new-brain in the human.

---

[1]   But there are human societies and animal species, such as the langur monkey, which do not exhibit strong urges for dominance; providing excellent evidence that this need is either not innate in all social animals, or can be readily attenuated through social learning. If we are ever to gain any significant psychological insight into ourselves through a study of animals, the dominance drive certainly represents the most potentially rewarding field of study.

G

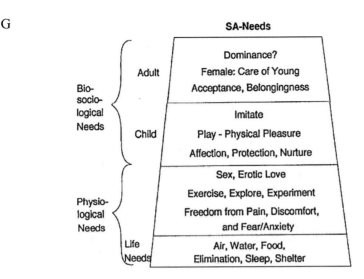

Figure 2 - The Social Animal Needs

These, then, are the needs people share with all social animals; I'll designate these needs, 1-10, as the "Social Animal Needs," or "SA-Needs."

Now the mix and degree to which each of the above needs exist in a given individual, together with her energy level, physique, and her gestation and perinatal experience (p. 41), largely determine her temperament: introvert or extravert, endomorph, mesomorph, or ectomorph, dominant or submissive, energetic or lethargic, etc. We are all born different. But the differences are attributable to differences in our inherent energy levels, physique, the measure and proportion of each the above needs, and to our experience in the womb. This gives the individual person and social animal what can best be described as a set of propensities, or a temperament.

There can be no doubt that the person has, except for a few minor instincts, all the physiological characteristics of a chimpanzee. After all, 99+% of our genetic material is identical to that of the chimpanzee. Which evolutionists said proved that humans are simply mutated apes, and that <1% of our DNA could account for all our differences. But now they are faced with a new dilemma: now they have found that most of this <1% DNA difference is primarily related to hair, skin, bones, blood, muscle, etc, hoisting them on their own petards. Our DNA is not *similar* to that of the chimpanzee, it is, to all intents and purposes, *identical*. So now, never at a loss for figments, they proclaim, "Aha! But we have *bigger* brains!" With the patently fatuous implication that a larger, but physiologically identical brain, can account for our infinitely greater capabilities. Shame on them! They have no clothes! Their blind faith in evolution as the genesis of all life makes them deathly afraid of the obvious conclusion that, since our DNA is practically identical,

> **We are now forced to infer one or more *non-physiological* elements in the human, if we are to account for the vast superiority of our capabilities to those of the chimpanzee.**

Can anyone logically conclude otherwise? The problem then, is to identify the human elements, faculties, and needs not shared with the social animal. Now we know that all God's creations exhibit both simplicity and economy in their design. Therefore, applying Occam's Razor (otherwise known as "Keep it simple, stupid"), the scientific question becomes: "What are the *minimum* elements, faculties, and needs we can hypothesize in the person, which, when added to those of the chimpanzee, can account for *all* human capabilities, motivation, and behavior?"

"Our" thesis, inductively derived from the research and experiences of scores of leading psychologists, psychiatrists, theologians, and philosophers, the teachings of Christ, and some of the many geniuses among the mystics/ saints/sages, and based on literally millions of their observations, is that the single element with which the person is endowed, and the social animal is not, the one element which differentiates us from the animal, and accounts for all our uniquely human capabilities, can only be described as follows:

1. The person is endowed with a spiritual "I", or *Governor of the Being.* This is the *Element* people do not share with the social animal.

2. This spiritual "I" is characterized by its Needs: 1) to Exist, 2) to Love, and 3) to Know. These are the *Needs* people do not share with social animals.

3. The spiritual "I" is capable of governing all functions of the being.[2] Enabling it to govern are its Faculties: 1) to Love, 2) to Know or Believe, 3) to Imagine or Ideate, and 4) to Decide. These are the *Faculties* people do not share with social animals.

---

[2]   Normally the "I" does not govern autonomic functions (but biofeedback proves it *can*), nor in extreme cases of need for elimination, sleep, food, water, or sex, and reactions to pain, fear, trauma, anger, desire, or ecstasy, when its powers can be overcome by its emotional, physiological or bio-sociological demands.

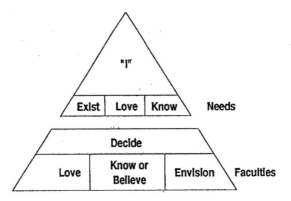

Figure 3 - "I" Needs & Faculties

These then, are the "I"-Needs: to Exist, to Love (capital "L"), and to Know (capital "K"), needs we do not share with animals; and the "I"-Faculties: to Love, to Know, to Imagine, and to Decide, faculties not shared with animals.

Now the mystics have been preaching realization of one's True Self, or "I", for centuries. For example, from *Thomas Merton on Prayer*, by John J. Higgins, S.J.:

For the present, it is sufficient to describe prayer in Merton's view as "a consciousness of one's union with God" or an "awareness of one's inner self." . . . As shall be shown later, the two descriptions are really synonymous. . . ! [18]

The Christian, then, has but one function in life and that is to be his real self, a son of God created in the image and likeness of God. To achieve this, he must search for the God Who is the source of his spiritual life. He shall find Him, . . . when he finds his own true self; for "He is nearer to us than we are to ourselves." [47]

"There is," says Merton, "no real love of life unless it is oriented to the discovery of one's true, spiritual self, beyond and above the level of mere empirical individuality with its superficial enjoyments and fears." Therefore, man cannot remain content to seek a self-fulfillment that fulfills nothing but this illusory self. Because man is made in the image and like-

ness of God; he is a spiritual or self-transcending being, and so, there is only one way for him to find out who he really is and that is by transcending his empirical self and finding within himself the true "I", the inner self, who is united to God in Christ. [59]

And from *Mysticism East and West* by Rudolph Otto:

Mysticism of the Soul:
To know and find one's self: to know one's soul in its true nature and glory, and through this knowledge to liberate and realize its divine glory; to find the abyssus, the depths within the self and discover the self as divine in its inmost depths; in short, "the canticle of the soul and the homo nobilis," has been rightly pointed out as the core and pivot of Eckhart' teaching. Absolutely parallel to this is the lofty atman faith of Sankara, and his "inner self." The wisdom of both is first and foremost Atma-bodhi.

. . . the inner atman of [Sankara] and the soul of [Eckhart] form very definite parallels:

A common antithesis between the "inward" and the "outward" in general, is characteristic of both masters. For both, deeply hidden "within" is something ultimate, pure, inward, entirely separate from all that is outward. This peculiar possession is absolutely different from all other elements that may be associated with it. It is a "SELF"—this expression occurs again and again with the same solemn significance in both mystics—as the spiritual center in a ring of ramparts and courtyards to which it is our task to penetrate. We have to know and liberate this self which is purely spiritual and gives forth its own light. This inward being is for Sankara the atman, for Eckhart the soul. . Both atman and soul, however vastly different from all the faculties they may be, however foreign and separate in the psychic life, are yet at the same time the stay and foundation of the faculties, without which they could not function.

The soul, like the atman is the "self." . . . [78]

I could quote hundreds of statements like this: the saints and sages continually exhorting us to a realization of our true selves, a realization which, they say, is always accompanied by a Knowledge of one's kinship with God.

But what is this true self, or "I", to which they so ardently refer? How do we relate this mysterious element in the person to what psychologists and neurologists tell us about the brain and human behavior? What functions does the "I" serve in the real world? Or is it just something like a wisp of smoke in the "psyche," known only to those who spend their lives in prayer and meditation in the desert or the cloister? Most saints are very vague about temporal functions of the "I". They say only enigmatic things like (above) "however vastly different from the faculties, however foreign and separate . . . [the soul] is the stay and foundation [?] of the faculties." Sts. Augustine and John of the Cross postulated three faculties of the soul: intellect, memory, and will, very similar the faculties of Knowing, Imagining, and Loving.[3] Only slightly more helpful is Dom David Knowles as quoted in *Understanding Mysticism*:

> *To the Christian, (and, . . . to many schools of philosophy) the human soul is an entity in its own right, directly created by God to "inform" the body, and to make up with it the human being. This soul, . . . a spiritual being, gives actuality [?] to all the powers and faculties of the body, but has also, of itself, intellectual and volitional powers which make it capable of rational knowledge of the universe about it and of free will to direct its activities and to control and direct its love . . . the Christian knows that his soul was created "in the likeness of God" in order that it might be raised, by means of what theologians call the potentiality of obedience, to a far higher and more intense knowledge and love, that of God as he is in himself.* [522]

But to my knowledge, none of these people saw the soul as the Goveror of the person, or identified it with what we call "I". Nor, of course, were they able to integrate the soul's faculties with the modern findings of psycholgy and neurology. Simply put, the saints seem to speak of the soul without temporal faculties, and most psychologists/psychiatrists seem content to study

---

[3]   About 1585 St. John of the Cross divided spiritual goods *". . . according to the faculties of the soul. Those dealing with knowledge are pertinent to the intellect, those referring to affection belong to the will, and others insofar as they are imaginary pertain to the memory."* Knowing, Loving, and Imagining ! ! [CW:273]

human faculties without reference to a soul, or Governor. Although many of the latter make vague references to an undefined "self," it seems that only Rank, Assagioli, and possibly Horney, saw intimations of its spiritual nature.

William James proposed the reductionism that the self was simply the passing thought. Freud hypothesized a sort of organic "I" (German *ich,* which his English-speaking counterparts mistranslated as "ego"; see p. 131), very similar to our spiritual "I", which he identified as the "Executive of Personality," with the faculties of perception, conscious thought, memory, learning, choice, judgment, and action. Jung also found it necessary to hypothesize a self, which he called the "God within us;" but then characterized it like one of his complexes, with the power to generate "inexplicable moods, nervous disorders, uncontrollable vices [!], to thwart *our* will." ? (See pps. 141-42)

The only psychiatrists who have helped in the development of a spiritual "I" are Karen Horney, who at least mentions a "real self, . . the central inner force, . . which is the deep source of growth, . . the spring of emotional forces, of constructive energies, of directive and judiciary powers;" and, most of all, Roberto Assagioli, who identified a "conscious self" (equivalent to what I call the Center of Consciousness), and a "higher self," very similar to our spiritual "I"—selves which could be merged through his practices of "psychosynthesis." But, like Horney, he did not identify its needs or faculties.[4] The great Maslow seemed comfortable studying people without reference to a self, but did identify a hierarchy of 20+ basic, prepotent, and meta-needs, (see p. 208) which I will show correspond well with the SA-Needs, the "I"-Needs, and some of the more common, self-adopted Needs and Values.

Allport recognized a human function of knowing, but denied any knowing entity, and refused to admit an element in people which did their choosing or Deciding, deciding that such an hypothesis would be unscientific. He seems to have carved in stone for most future psychologists his conclusion that the evidence for a "self" in humans is not sufficient to warrant its inclusion as a significant element in the development of personality. In his book *Becoming,* he argues:

> *. . . the danger we have several times warned against is very real: that a homunculus may creep into our discussions of personality* [a

---

[4]   Assagioli wrote: *"What we hope to see developed . . . is a science of the Self, of its energies, its manifestations, of how these energies can be released, how they can be contacted, how they can be used for constructive and therapeutic work."* [P:194] Would Dr. Assagioli have found this book a contribution to a "science of the Self"?

"creeping homunculus"? Ugh! !], *and be expected to solve all our problems without in reality solving any. Thus if we ask, "What determines our moral conduct?", the answer may be, "The self does." Or if we pose the problem of choice, we say, "The self chooses." Such question-begging would immeasurably weaken the scientific [?] study of personality by providing an illegitimate regressus.*

Apparently following Allport's lead, most psychologists today seem deathly afraid of indulging in any form of theorizing or hypothesizing, which real scientists do all the time, and to which practice they must attribute most of their progress. As one of my favorite psychologists says, "They're afraid they'd have to take off their white coats!" Or, as Allan Bloom explains in his excellent book, *The Closing of the American Mind*:

Psychology is mysteriously disappearing from the social sciences. Its unheard-of success in the real world may have tempted it to give up the theoretical life. As the psychotherapist has taken his place alongside the family doctor, perhaps his education now belongs to something more akin to the medical school than to the sciences, and the research relevant for him is more directed to the treatment of specific problems of patients than to the founding of a theory of the psyche. [!] The Freudian theories have been incorporated into some aspects of sociology, political science and anthropology, and it appears that the self alone had nothing more to tell the social sciences. This leaves open the question of what the solid ground is on which therapy stands, and where its newer ideas come from. Serious academic psychology is left with the segment that has to all intents and purposes fused with physiology. [361]

So psychologists, fearful of appearing "unscientific," and without the benefit of any serious theoretical research, have labored for a hundred years to understand human behavior without a self. But now, by offering them a self, or "I", with well-defined faculties and needs, I submit that they must begin to hypothesize such a *non-physiological* self in all their speculations about human motivation and behavior. The evidence now seems overwhelming that only a Loving, Knowing, Envisioning, Deciding "I", an "I" which programs, and thereby delegates much of its power to, a Love/Belief System, will enable them to explain all of their observations, neurologists' and physiologists' observations, *and* is compatible with what most mystics/saints/sages throughout the ages have discovered and told us about our potential.

So compelling is the psychologic, psychiatric, neurologic, philosophic, physiologic and theologic evidence supporting this hypothesis, and so illuminating its ramifications, I venture to predict that psychologists will not make significant progress in understanding and explaining human behavior, nor in the ability to help people attain mental health, until they recognize the existence, needs, and faculties of the "I", and the existence, constitution, and functions of the Love/Belief System, or "heart." (See Zimbardo, frontispiece.)

If our real scientists, the physicists, had half the evidence of a natural phenomenon that psychologists have of the "I", they would have hypothesized it long ago. Planets, positrons, neutrinos, quarks, and scores of other elements were discovered only after they were hypothesized and sought. But today, even physicists are being forced to learn to live with mystery. One said "the world is not only stranger than we have imagined, it is stranger than we can imagine." They have seen their most cherished and proven facts about the physical world dissolve right before their eyes. They have been forced to accept characteristics of elements of the material world like *spin* and *left-handedness* and *strings* (whose only dimension is length, too small to ever be seen, and which imply 10 or 24 space/time dimensions); then conclude that there are no elements, that the ultimate forms of our dear and solid material world have no physical representation which is susceptible to human visualization, and can only be explained in terms of mathematical formulae; that light, and now even matter itself, must be seen to exist both as wave and particle at the same time; that ethereal space somehow curves back upon *itself*; that a single electron can appear to be in two places at the same time!

Yet many psychologists, who pride themselves on being "scientific," will not accept anything which cannot be both seen and quantified; and they are dealing with the most mysterious thing in the universe: the human being.

Most major religions speak of the soul (as well as the heart). But one of the most important aspects of this theory is that the soul, or "I", is realizable empirically, or experientially, without religious considerations. Not only religious people, but atheists and agnostics too, have, on occasion, realized their "I"'s or True Selves. Therefore, the "I", or self, represents *the* element in the human which enlightened people of many faiths, as well as many non-religious philosophers, and now some few psychologists, are recognizing as essential to the understanding and explanation of human capabilities, motivation, and behavior. I will show that all the differences between the person and a social animal such as the chimpanzee, can be accounted for by an "I" in the person, an "I" which adds these three needs and four faculties to her being.[5]

This is the picture that struck me in 1978. Suddenly I saw that every percept entering our consciousness has first passed through a "black box," a computer/servomechanism, whose programs consist of our social animal needs, *and* all of our self-adopted Loves and Beliefs and their concomitant Desires and Fears; that the computer filters and modifies all our percepts *before* they reach our Centers of Consciousness; and that "above" the Center of Consciousness was the "I" which had adopted all these Loves and Beliefs. I saw that we don't *have* souls—we *are* souls. What we call "I" is a soul! Over the next few days it became clear to me that by simply positing a spiritual, Loving, Knowing, Envisioning, Deciding "I" as the single transforming element (like a diamond in the forehead) of a being which is otherwise just a very proficient social animal, all of these writers' observations and experiences, and most of their theories, would be reconciled.

Then I wondered, "If every child is conceived with a beautiful, sparkling, spiritual "I", what happens to it?" And the answer came, virtually shouting back at me:

**It starts Believing things,
and it starts Loving things!**

Like an octopus' tentacles, or an overflowing pot of glue, the child's "I" sends out "feelers" in all directions, seeking and adopting—both consciously and subconsciously—Loves and Beliefs by the thousands, until, according to current estimates, each mature person has acquired *hundreds of thousands* of Loves and Beliefs!

**All of our Loves, and those Beliefs with an emotional
or affective component, form a "Love/Belief System"
in the brain, a system which continuously monitors and
conditions all of our communications both to and from the
world, and can itself initiate responses to those communications.**

---

[5]   I refer those who decry this hypothesis as Cartesian dualism to *The Perennial Philosophy* (p. 70), by Aldous Huxley, who argues that non-dualism is not a condition one can assume or reason their way into. Rather it is a *state of grace* visited only on those who have first suffered the arduous *dualistic* spirit/flesh travail which has left them pure in heart and poor in spirit. Also, I have suggested that humans are not dual, they are triune. In Chapter 14, I'll show how the human trinity can be subsumed, i.e., graced with a true state of *non-dualism,* in the Trinity. The "dualism" which afflicts humanity is our separation from God.

With all its ramifications, it is virtually impossible to overestimate the importance of this concept to a full and accurate understanding of human capabilities, motivation, behavior, and personality.

Over the last 27 years of study and analysis, scores more details of this concept have come into focus, and found their place in a schematic diagram, a model or paradigm of the person, a relatively simple representation, which can illustrate and explain all human motivation and behavior.

I will show that the "I" acts as the Governor of the person, exercising her uniquely human:

> *Executive* powers (all too seldom) by a combination of Visualizing, Believing, and Loving (i.e., devoting, dedicating, committing her mind/body to the realization of) the Vision. Humans are *executives* and *creators*.

> *Legislative* powers by adopting Loves, Beliefs, Values, and Needs, which, because they modify her brain, become the *laws* of her life, and generate Desires and Fears additional to those arising from the SA-Needs. Humans *program* their brains.

> *Judicial* powers of rendering judgment and meting out punishment and reward by derogation or enhancement of her self-image, or her opinion and punishment of others, as she or they are perceived to break or keep her laws. The "I" enables humans to sit in judgment on themselves and others.

What then, is the "I"? Atheists and agnostics may consider it, with Freud, et al., as simply a part of the ill-defined "psyche" (from the Greek psyche: breath, spirit, soul, mind; now defined [?] as "the mental or psychological structure of a person, . ."), or, in spite of the DNA evidence to the contrary, simply as some aspect of the brain which will someday be located and circumscribed. But for the Christian, and for all theists, the "I" must be considered as spirit, the spirit of free Being, Loving, Knowing.

The "I" has never been discovered (and never will be) for the same reason that God has never been discovered: because they are not material entities. The "I" cannot Know itself, since the "I" is the subject of Knowing. (Nor can it Love itself.) Just as God, Spirit, dwells in the world, but is not of the world, so the "I" inhabits the mind/body, but is not *of* the mind/body. Like God, the "I" is spirit; it is not God, but it is *God-like,* and therefore, capable of communion with, a Loving/Knowledge of God.

Now the saints and mystics have made great lists of what God is not; because God cannot be defined in human or material terms. There are no words which will define God. Therefore we may assume that there are no words which will define the "I". Christians believe however, that among His characteristics are that God is Spirit, God is Love, and that He is the Creator of the world. In making humans in His likeness, in addition to spirit and love, did He also give us the power of creator?

All the evidence proves that He did. Millions of people have literally accomplished the impossible when they Visualized, Believed, and Loved (i.e., devoted, committed themselves, to) the results they wished to achieve (see page 87). Sometimes this has happened almost without effort on their part, though where necessary, their minds and bodies were almost always able to generate the effort required to actualize the vision. Is this not the power of creator? Dr. Maltz calls this our "Creative Imagination."

Whatever one Visualizes, Believes, and Loves,
becomes real in that person's life,
and comes into existence, provided only
that it does not conflict with her other,
or someone else's, Visions, Beliefs, and Loves.

From the millions of observations of the human and animal species, covering a span of more than three millennia of recorded history, the cumulative evidence for the existence of an "I", or self, in the person has now reached epidemic proportions. Although the "I" cannot be seen, since it is pure spirit, nor located in the person, since it is certainly non-local, the evidence is becoming conclusive that it is:

1. Spirit, therefore ageless, timeless, immortal—the same yesterday, today, and forever.
2. Ultimately unKnowable, but capable of being realized, intuited, experienced, and manifested (primarily, as we shall see, by exercising its powers of self-denial and unpossessive, unconditional Love.)
3. Capable then of communion with, a unitive Love/Knowledge of, God (or, if you prefer, Ultimate Being);
4. Endowed with Needs to Exist, to Love, and to Know.
5. Whose faculties are: to Love, to Know or Believe, to Envision, and to Decide.

I will show that these "I"-Needs and Faculties, when coupled with the social animal needs and faculties we share with all social animals, can explain one hundred percent of human capabilities, motivation, behavior, personality, and potential for enlightenment. This concept enables us to understand and explain all the psychologic phenomena, both normal and abnormal, which have been observed over the years;[6] and it also enables us to understand the mechanics, if you will, of what the saints and sages have been saying regarding the steps necessary to attainment of their particular form of Salvation, Liberation, Enlightenment, Nirvana, Union with God, or what Christ called "The Kingdom of God within you."

> *The soul shows its royal and exalted character, . . in that it is free and self-governed, swayed autonomously by its own will. Of whom else can this be said, save a king? . . . Thus human nature, created to rule other creatures was, by its likeness to the King of the universe, made as it were a living image, partaking with the Archetype both in dignity and in name.*
> —ST. GREGORY OF NYSSA

---

[6]   Excepting only, as noted earlier, most phenomena arising from chemical, genetic, or physical dysfunctions. This exception should be understood to apply throughout the book.

3
Human vs Animal Behavior

In this chapter I will summarize the differences in the determinants of human and animal behavior. A review of some simple diagrams will facilitate an understanding of this theory, and prepare the reader for the more detailed diagrams we'll be building on them in subsequent chapters.

A Person is a Social Animal with a Spiritual "I".

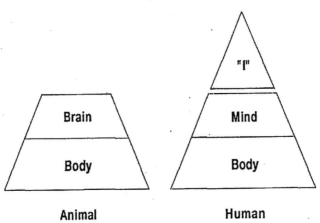

Figure 4 - A person is a social animal with a spiritual "I".

Since our DNA is, to all intents and purposes, identical to that of the chimpanzee, human and chimpanzee brains are physiologically and therefore, functionally, identical. Both contain a Reticular Activating System; but in the person it becomes a Love/Belief System, a "brain with a heart." Although this is the only significant difference between human and chimpanzee brains, it is important enough to justify calling the human brain a "mind." The faculties of the "I" enable it to transform the animal brain to a mind. Therefore I propose that we redefine mind as a *human brain*. This is the distinction used in the Figures above, and in the following text.

Figure 5 shows the animal's Stimulus/Response process. A sensory Stimulus, (S), which the RAS has selected as important, is processed by the brain (which, in this preliminary processing, can be seen to functionally consist of the Memory, the Reticular Activating System, and the Center of Consciousness). Having interpreted the Stimulus as important, the Reticular Activating System instantaneously 1) alerts the brain and suppresses "extraneous" stimuli (pg. 104); 2) compares and evaluates the Stimulus signal against all Instincts, Memories, and SA-Needs; and 3) initiates a vast search of the Memory for relevant information to identify—classify—the Stimulus, and to find appropriate precedent Responses to that Stimulus. The RAS then synthesizes all this information and forwards both Stimulus *and* Response signals to the Center of Consciousness. When the Stimulus signal is strong enough to cross the "Consciousness Level," the animal becomes aware of the Stimulus; when the RAS synthesized Response Impulse signal, R, is strong enough to cross the "Enact Level," it is sent back through the RAS and the Memory where it is translated into Neural signals, N, appropriate to that Response. These signals activate the motor neurons, and the animal acts.

When the animal is presented with signals not strong enough to cross the Enact Level, or two different Response signals, he freezes and the RAS focuses his senses on a search for additional Stimuli/Response signals until one becomes strong enough to cross the Enact Level. Also, obviously, these Stimuli signals do not make just one pass through the brain, but are continually coming in and being processed. Perception is an iterative process

So, for example, a bear will start to gorge himself when the fall weather Stimulus hits his hibernating Instincts, and a dog snarls at a cat if his Instincts tell him it's an enemy. And of course, Response Impulse signals are also generated by the Memory. Thus we see an animal retreating before a skunk, if he has a memory of a bad experience with a skunk.

Of course Stimuli signals can be internal as well as external. The SA-Needs for sex, exercise, food, etc., are continually generating Stimuli signals to the reticular formation, and their corresponding Response Impulse signals are instantly forwarded, with the Stimulus signal, to the Center of Consciousness. When any Response Impulse signal is strong enough to cross the Enact Level, the animal is forced to act.

In this Figure, we can also visualize habit, or conditioned response channels in the brain. When a Stimulus/Response sequence is repeated often enough, and with favorable results, there is a neural S/R hook-up, and the Response becomes a conditioned—almost an autonomic—Response.

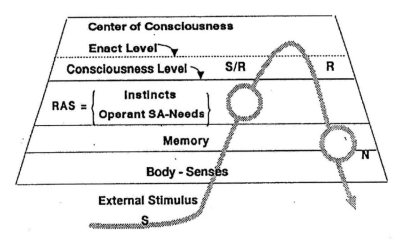

Figure 5 - The Animal Stimulus/Response Process

We can also visualize *anticipatory* conditioned Responses. When two Stimulus signals repeatedly follow each other, the perceptors of those signals are neurologically linked in the brain, so that the Response Impulse signal appropriate to the second Stimulus is now generated in response to the first Stimulus. Then, if the Response meets with acceptable results—positive reinforcement—the whole sequence becomes again the equivalent of an autonomic or conditioned response. (Does the name Pavlov ring a bell?)

Now here's one of the key concepts in the explanation of human behavior:

> **In the person, the SA-Need/Instinct section of the**
> **brain, the RAS, becomes a "Love/Belief System,"**
> **with the same SA-Needs, but where instincts are**
> **replaced with the person's Loves and Beliefs**
> **and their concomitant Desires and Fears.**

(See again, The Love/Belief System Programs, page 3.)

The stimulus/response elements of the human brain, or mind, can now be functionally defined as consisting of a Memory, a Love/Belief System, or RAS, and a Center of Consciousness.

Figure 6 illustrates the human Stimulus/Response system. For example, a child who sees a skunk will also get a Response Impulse signal, "Get out of here!" with his sensory impressions of the skunk, if he has been told about skunks and their defenses, and *believes* what he was told.

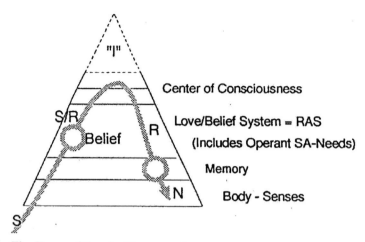

Figure 6 - The Human Stimulus/Response Process

Significant sensory Stimuli are selected by the Love/Belief System to be processed, i.e., compared and evaluated against all of his Memories and operant SA-Needs, but also against all of the Loves and, Beliefs, Desires and Fears, both conscious and subconscious, in his Love/Belief System, and appropriate Response Impulse signals are generated before the Stimuli signal has fully penetrated his Center of Consciousness.

**All Response Impulses are generated pre-consciously,
therefore *sub*-consciously.**

You may wonder how Response signals can be sent before the Stimulus signal reaches the Center of Consciousness. Most of us think our senses are reporting pure facts which are then evaluated against our Memories and Loves and Beliefs. But this is disproved by the well-known psychological repression, which is simply the shunting of unpleasant ideas and experiences into the subconscious, before they fully penetrate the Center of Consciousness. This is only one function of the inhibitory system, or RAS, in the mind, which is best described as a Love/Belief System.

The best (1998) computer could process a trillion "bits" per second. In mathematics, the computer is to the mind as a jet airplane is to a snail. But in cognition—perceiving, re-cognizing, and evaluating sensory data—the RAS is at least ten times as fast as the computer, processing the equivalent of ten trillion bits per second—some estimates go as high as 1,000 trillion bits per second! Cognitive psychologist George Sperling has identified this *iconic* memory: *"a very short-term visual memory of almost unlimited capacity."* (Watch for the discovery of similar auditory, tactile, etc., "memories.") So the computer takes 1 to 2 minutes to interpret a five-second utterance, while the human mind can do it in four seconds, before the statement ends.[1] But perhaps the best example of the mind's blinding speed is the instantaneous, involuntary, knee-jerk shift of our attention when our name is spoken even in a babble of sounds—or our spouse's name, or sex, or our current hobby, etc., etc. As we shall see, each of our brains has been neurologically modified—not just programmed, but actually "hard-wired"—to instantaneously force our attention to any sensory impression which is even remotely related to any of our operant SA-Needs, or any significant Love, Belief, Value, Need, Desire, or Fear.

Whether conscious or subconscious, each Love, Belief, Value, or Need a person adopts must have modified his reticular formation in such a way that it becomes a law of his being; a law against which all incoming (and outgoing) information is selected, evaluated, interpreted, and, most importantly and tragically, modified—emphasized, diminished, altered—to make it conform to that law, before it reaches his Center of Consciousness! Each of our Loves and Beliefs becomes a prejudice, biasing not just our decisions or opinions—it is our very *perceptions* which are biased, distorted, prejudiced, and therefore, often induce irrational and/or erroneous responses.

The second difference in the person is that:

The Center of Consciousness is "under" the "I",
which adds its Needs and Faculties to the system,
Faculties which enable it to act as an OBSERVER
and CONTROLLER of the signals going through it.

The "I" as Knower, Knows what is going through its Center of Consciousness,[2] and its Faculties empower it to act as a Governor, monitoring and

---

[1]   Current computers are faster than the brain, processing trillions of "ops" per second. But without our myriad sensory inputs, our Love/Belief System Elements, our database of millions of facts, the "programs" we'll discuss in Chapter 10, an output capable of an infinite combination of words and acts, and particularly, the "I"-Faculties of ideation and commitment, the artificial intelligence people seem to have taken on a "mission impossible"—animal responses, maybe; but *intelligence?* Never.

[2]   Cognitive psychologists have now recognized this uniquely human faculty, and aptly named it *metacognition.* [Merluzzi: 112]

controlling those signals. The "I" endows the person, in contrast to the animal, with a second, superior method of controlling the mind/body. It gives the child free will to either approve the Response Impulse signal "Get out of here," or deny it, by adopting a contrary vision/belief/commitment: "I will not run away; I will stay here." Or, in the case cited earlier, "My stomach is generating hunger pangs, but I am not going to eat."

> *Benjamin Libet of the University of California, recorded electrical signals generated by the brains of his experimental subjects and looked particularly at a signal called the "readiness potential" that always appears just before a movement. Using special timing techniques, he found that the readiness potential begins about half a second before a subject begins to move a hand. This is expected, since brain activity must begin before the brain issues a command to the muscles. What is surprising, however, is that the subjects do not become aware of deciding to move until only about two tenths of a second before the movement begins, some three tenths of a second after the brain activity began.*
>
> *. . . to Libet [this] says that the intention to act arises from brain activity that is not within our conscious awareness. [!] . . . the brain initiates the impulse to act and the conscious self [the "I"] sub-sequently becomes aware of it. Libet also finds that his subjects are able to veto the impulse to act during the few tenths of a second after a subject becomes aware of it. In this sense, consciousness [the "I"] becomes a gatekeeper for intentions generated by the brain, letting through only those that somehow meet an individual's criteria. [SM:13]*
> —KENNETH A. KLIVINGTON

The brains of people and animals are computers, processing information going through them in accordance with their "programs." In the animal, the programs consist of his Memories, the operant SA-Needs, and his Instincts. In the person the programs consist of his Memories, the operant SA-Needs, *and* all the Elements: the Loves and Beliefs, Desires and Fears, both conscious and subconscious, of his Love/Belief System.[3]

---

[3]   The pure "I"-Needs do not usually figure in Love/Belief System processing of stimuli—see pps. 66-68 and fn. p. 119.

The animal is simply a Stimulus/Response organism, whose Responses to environmental, physiological, and bio-sociological stimuli are determined by an autonomic processing/evaluation of that stimuli as they relate to his Memories, Instincts, and operant SA-Needs. When any Response Impulse reaches his Center of Consciousness with enough force to cross the Enact Level, the animal acts.

The person can also be seen to operate in terms of Stimulus/Response, but with three major differences:

1. The "I" provides humans with motivations additional to those attributable to the SA-Needs we share with all social animals; both directly, through its needs to Exist, to Love, and to Know; and indirectly, through its self-adopted Loves and Beliefs. The person is motivated to seek objects of "I"-Love/Knowledge, and then to seek fulfillment of the resulting Elements in the Love/Belief System. As a result of the "I"-Needs, one might even Love something as abstract as his "reputation." He is then motivated, without external stimuli, to undertake actions which will enhance it.

2. These self-adopted Loves and Beliefs in the person's Love/Belief System then affect his responses. The person's Response Impulses are determined by an autonomic processing/evaluation of stimuli as they relate to his Memories, his operant SA-Needs, *and* all the Elements in his Love/Belief System. The person who Values his reputation is impelled to defend it against circumstantial deprecation.

3. The third difference is that in the person, when a Response Impulse (always determined subconsciously or pre-consciously) enters the Center of Consciousness, it comes to the attention of the "I", which, if the Impulse is not too strong, or if it does not require immediate implementation, has the power to review, and alter or veto the Response. The "I" is the Governor of our being, with meta-cognizance of the Response Impulses entering the Center of Consciousness, and the ability to veto, modify, or change the Response, by visualizing, believing, and enacting, i.e., committing the mind/body to, another response. The person who Loves his reputation can choose to respond to a different Love, Belief, Value, Need, "I"- Need, or SA-Need.

The "I" is exactly like a pilot flying on autopilot (the RAS or Love/ Belief System). Any Response Impulse, (as determined by references to the Memory, the operant SA-Needs, and the Love/Belief System Elements) is brought to the pilot's attention. He can either allow that Response to be executed; or, if the Impulse is not too strong, he can override the autopilot and initiate a different response, using the same set of controls, with reference to conscious Love/Belief System Elements—but subject to the strong insidious influences of subconscious Elements—both used fully by the autopilot.

In the case of the animal, there is no pilot to review the responses; strange to say, the animal does not Know (metacognize) what is in its Center of Consciousness; therefore any Response Impulse strong enough to be enacted, is.

And this simple concept of the person as just a very proficient social animal, with the needs and faculties of all social animals; but endowed with a spiritual "I", an "I" with a will to Exist, to Love, and to Know, with faculties of Loving, Knowing, Imagining, and Deciding, can explain all human capabilities, motivation, behavior, and personality.

This theory immediately reconciles and explains all the successes and failures of the schools of determinism, psychoanalysis, behaviorism, psychosynthesis, cognitive, humanistic, and transpersonal psychologies; and provides an excellent foundation for the "still higher, Fourth Psychology," which Maslow envisioned.

4
Development of the Love/Belief System
Birth to Four

Now in the development of the infant's Love/Belief System, Stanislav Grof has proposed in *Beyond the Brain* that the infant starts developing her world view, her beliefs of what kind of a world she lives in, while still in the womb, and particularly during the "perinatal, " or birth experiences. This may help to account for the temperaments with which all new-born infants seem to be differently endowed. Certainly, however, the child starts acquiring beliefs very shortly after birth, long before she learns to communicate with others. Current research indicates that up to *100 trillion* synapses can be formed in just the first few months of a child's development. I am indebted to the brilliant R.D. Laing for the insight that even a parent's smile or frown can create synapses in a child's brain! Who knows how many non-verbal beliefs the child acquires before she learns to communicate?

But the first significant belief to enter the Love/Belief System must be that of her (the "I"'s) association with the body. As William James writes,

> *To have a self that I can care for Nature must first present me with some object interesting enough to make me instinctively wish to appropriate it for its own sake. . . . My own body and what ministers to its needs are thus the primitive object, instinctively determined, of my egoistic interests.*[1]

The first important thing the "I" learns is that the body is its medium of communication with the world. The body can generate feelings of pain and of pleasure; in turn the "I" can manipulate the body, and through the body, manipulate objects; through its vocal chords, manipulate her parents, and through them, her environment and her bodily pains and pleasures.

---

[1] As noted earlier, James decided that the object of the "self, I, me, my" to which he refers, was simply the passing thought: "the thought *is* the thinker;" ! just one more example of reductionism *ad nauseam*. [PP:319,324]

In a very important research study, Stanford anthropologist Suzanne Chevalier-Skolnikoff, has found that chimpanzees, gorillas, and orangutans develop behavior patterns during the first two years of life (i.e., through the first six stages of the Piaget model) that are identical to the developmental patterns of human infants. Therefore, we must assume that during this period the SA-Needs 1-7 (pps. 19-20) must predominate in governing the behaviors of both the animal and the human infant. After age two however, her studies showed that "early progress in vocalization provides human infants with the basic foundations of speech and language which, early on, become the principal mode of future learning and socialization." [Animal Kingdom, July '79]

The child's ability to learn a language is fully explained by her "I"-Faculties of Imagination and Knowing, and her SA-Need to imitate. Only the latter of these is available to animals, which is why their languages consist of just a few sounds, related only to the SA-Needs and instincts.

Of course when she learns to speak, her powers and efficacy of manipulation of her parents and her environment are expanded tremendously, and her ability to acquire beliefs is multiplied hundreds of times.

But the ability to communicate is both gift and curse. Because now her parents are able to instill in her the fallacy of all fallacies, the fallacious belief that has plagued humankind since Adam; indeed, the fallacy which could very well represent the fall of humankind:

You ARE your body.

They say, "You wet your diaper." "You spilled the sugar," "You are a good girl." "You are cute." "You are growing fast." "You are walking." And the child keeps saying, "Me? *'I'* wet my diaper? That's not *me*." Psychologists have known for many years the difficulty the child has in identifying herself with her body. Children Know intuitively that they are not their bodies. But parents, having also been raised to believe we are our bodies, insist, and eventually of course, they have their way.

> *The idea that one is one's body is what is called "hrdayagranthi" (knot of the heart). Of the various knots, this knot, which binds together what is conscious with what is insentient, is what causes bondage.* [36]
> —RAMANA MAHARSHI

> *We are dominated by everything with which our self becomes identified.* [P:22]
> —ROBERTO ASSAGIOLI

So the second major belief to enter the Love/Belief System is "'I' *am* my body." Later, she will include her mind: "'I' am my mind/body."

As her education continues, the child's belief, "'I' am my mind/body," is firmly cemented in place in her Love/Belief System. One of the major factors contributing to this belief is that she finds her parent's love is not love for "her," but primarily for what she does with her mind/body, and that their love is readily withheld when she fails to behave according to their wishes. They don't seem to care about *her,* only with how she looks and acts. When she spills the sugar bowl, mother says, perhaps in a kindly way, "You bad girl, you mustn't do that." To be met with the blatant reply, "'I' didn't do it, mommy;" meaning, "'I' only wanted to taste it; my hand spilled it." If she says this, her mother may infer schizophrenic tendencies, and rush her to the child psychologist, only to be told, "Don't worry about it; she'll outgrow it." (You bet she will!) But if she says she didn't do it, she is scolded for adding lying, the unforgivable sin to her mistake.

And now the child has acquired two more beliefs which will probably be with her all the rest of her life:

The only way she can get her parents' (or anyone's) affection, is through what they consider to be proper control of her mind/body.

There's something *wrong* with her. She is not intrinsically worthy of the affection each child, as a social animal, needs. And so is born a sense of unworthiness, i.e., guilt, or shame.

A profound anonymous letter published in the *American Journal of Psychoanalysis* reads:

How is it possible to lose a self? The treachery, unknown and unthinkable, begins with our secret psychic death in childhood—if and when we are not loved and are cut off from our spontaneous wishes. (Think: what is left?) But wait—it is not just this simple murder of a psyche. That might be written off,—the tiny victim might even "outgrow" it,—but it is a perfect double crime in which he himself also gradually and unwittingly takes part. He has not been accepted for himself, as he is. Oh, they "love" him, but they want him or force him or expect him to be different! Therefore he must be unacceptable. He himself learns to believe it [!] and at last even takes it for granted. He has truly given himself up. No matter now whether he obeys them, whether he withdraws, clings, or rebels,—his behavior, his performance is all that matters. His center of gravity is in "them," not in himself—yet if he so much as noticed it he'd think it natural enough. And the whole thing is entirely plausible; all invisible, automatic, and anonymous!

This is the perfect paradox. Everything looks normal; no crime was intended; there is no corpse, no guilt. All we can see is the sun rising and setting as usual. But what has happened? He has been rejected, not only by them, but by himself. (He is actually without a self.) What has he lost? Just the one true and vital part of himself: his own yes-feeling, which is his very capacity for growth, his root system [his "I"]. *But alas, he is not dead. "Life" goes on, and so must he. From the moment he gives himself up, and to the extent that he does so, all unknowingly he sets about to create and maintain a pseudo-self. But this is an expediency—a "self" without wishes. This one shall be loved (or feared) where he is despised, strong where he is weak; it shall go through the motions (oh, but they are caricatures!) not for fun or joy but for survival; not simply because it wants to move but because it has to obey. The necessity is not life—not his life—it is a defense mechanism against death. It is also the machine of death.*

From now on he will be torn apart by compulsive (unconscious) needs or ground by (unconscious) conflicts into paralysis, every motion and every instant canceling out his being, his integrity; and all the while he is disguised as a normal person and expected to behave like one! In a word, I saw that we become neurotic seeking or defending a pseudoself, a self-system [a self-image], *and we are neurotic to the extent that we are self-less.* [Read "I"-less]

Now not everyone becomes neurotic when people ignore their "I"'s. As the letter says, "'Life' goes on and so must he." People, like all social animals, are great imitators, conformers, and seeing all her significant others getting along without an "I", and getting only inane answers to her question, "Who am 'I', really?"—meaning, "What *is* this wonderful 'I'?" ("Why, you're my daughter, Sue. You are Susan Jones"—which is like telling her that she is really just the neighbor of the girl next door, just another mind/body), she begins to believe that she must be peculiar, wondering about "I"; that she must be imagining things, and had better learn to live like everyone else seems to be living, without an "I". In accepting the belief, "'I' am my mind/body," her "I" denies its own existence, and compounds its physical incarnation with what can only be construed as a suicidal cognitive incarnation. The child's innate, sublime, and *ennobling* "I"'s awareness of itself is suppressed, ignored, and, for 99+% of us, never recovered. The nagging question, "Who am I?" (meaning "*What* am I?") is never answered; but the subconscious search for a self-identity continues for the rest of her life.

And this is the spiritual blindness that enlightened people tell us afflicts the entire world. We have all been callously persuaded to ignore something every one of us as a child knew was the most important thing about us, the only thing which makes humans human: our spiritual "I"'s: our spiritual EYES.

Because almost every child's first major beliefs are:

1. "I" AM my mind/body.
2. "I" am not intrinsically worthy of love, acceptance.
3. "I" can only receive the affection and acceptance "I" need through appropriate use of my mind/body; a pretty face, a good build, a bright mind, a nice personality, proper behavior, are my only means of satisfactory relationships.

So she tries to manufacture, not a (whole) personality, or a character, but an artificial set of responses which will hopefully merit the affection and acceptance she, as a social animal, needs. But it is only a fragmented personality, a house of cards, and deep down, she Knows it.

In *The Denial of Death,* Ernest Becker calls character a "vital lie" (Sartre calls it "bad faith")—"a lie we need in order to live," but which "dooms us to a life that is never really ours." [2]

But now, in spite of these anomalies, and provided the child has been brought up with just a modicum of love and nurture, she arrives at the magic

---

[2]   When a person becomes extremely famous, her self-image becomes a public-image, and the sheer weight of this artificial superstructure of character and personality literally crushes the person. Judy Garland, Marilyn Monroe, Elvis Presley, John Belushi, were all "doomed [by other's expectations and their own need for continual acclaim in order to sustain and validate what they Knew was only an image, but still, the only 'self' they had] to [acting out] a life that was never really theirs."

age of FOUR.

At four, the child's behavior is fully differentiated from that of the social animal, a differentiation which can be fully accounted for by the needs and faculties of the "I". At age four the child has developed a full recognition and appreciation of the powers of her "I". In the following description of the child of four, you see a person completely enchanted with her magical powers of Loving, Knowing, Deciding and Imagining: *Ideating.*

> *For the most part, we have found the boy or girl of this age to be joyous, exuberant, energetic, ridiculous, untrammeled—ready for anything. . . If at times he seems somewhat voluble, boastful, and bossy, it is because it is so exciting for him to enter the fresh fields of self-expression"* ["I"-expression] *that open up at this wonderful age.*

> *. . . All of a sudden he discovers that the adult, though still quite powerful, is not ALL-powerful. He now finds much power in himself. He finds that he can do bad things, . . . and the roof does not fall in.*

> *. . . Four operates on the expansive and highly sure-of-himself side of life. . . Four . . . is an age when the child is characteristically in a nice state of equilibrium.*

> *. . . The typical Four-year-old LOVES* [based on his "I"-Need to Love] *adventure, loves excursions, loves excitement, loves ANYTHING new. He adores new people, new places, new games, new playthings, new books, new activities. No one is more responsive to the adult effort to entertain. He will accept what you have to offer with delightfully uncritical enthusiasm. So, it is a pleasure to provide [him] with new toys, books, clothes, experiences, information—because any of these things make his eyes sparkle so, because he is so wholeheartedly appreciative.*

> *. . . Four loves things that are NEW. . . Four has a lively mind, and new thoughts and ideas or bits of information may please him as much as do new toys. That is why it is so much fun to talk with him. His incessant 'whys'* [based on his "I"-Need to Know] *may sometimes pall, but . . . it is fun to inform somebody who so enthusiastically wishes to be informed.*

The key to the Four-year-old's psychology is his high drive combined with his fluid imagination. Four is, indeed, highly versatile. What can he not do? He can be quiet or noisy, calm or assertive, cozy or imperious, suggestible or independent, social, athletic, artistic, literal, fanciful, cooperative, indifferent, inquisitive, forthright, humorous, dogmatic. He is many people in one.

The typical Four-year-old is also speedy. Each thing he does, he does quickly, and he is also speedy as he moves from one interest to the next. For the most part, he does a thing once, and that's ENOUGH. He isn't interested in perfection; he is interested in getting on to the next activity. Behavior is fluid, and if he does stay with a single activity, that single activity may change so rapidly as to make your head spin.

A good example of the often quite remarkable fluidity of Four's imagination can be seen in his drawing. A Four-year-old in spontane-ous drawing may quite typically start with a tree, which turns into a house, which turns into a battleship. Or, . . . his person's "foot" grow so large that it develops large toes that turn out to be the back of a bird. And that turns out to be a roller coaster. And that turns out to be the BACK of the roller coaster. . . [YFYO:1-4]
—AMES & ILG

This description of the child of four is vitally significant to our study for two reasons: first, because it provides excellent evidence that it is the "I"-Faculties of Loving, Knowing, Imagining, and Deciding which fully differentiate the capabilities and behavior of the child from that of the social animal. The "I"-Needs and Faculties can explain all the differences in be-havior between the four-year old child and the social animal. Compare, for example, the strong innate desire of the child to Love and to Know, just for the sake of Loving and Knowing, as described above, with the animal's need for constantly repeated external positive or negative reinforcement before it can learn anything not related to a basic instinct or SA-Need.

Second, because it indicates that the child's discovery of the joy of utilizing her "I"-Faculties makes this the *happiest* period of most people's entire lives, a happiness the great majority of the human race never knows again. Bear in mind that the description above is how the child of four appears to the observer. But the observer cannot possibly know, and the child has no words to express her thrilling fascination with the simple application of her "I"-Faculties of Loving, Knowing, Imagining, and Deciding to the seemingly infinite number of wonders of the world. To her the world *is* so full of such wonder-full things, we ought all indeed to be happy as kings.

Ronald Havens, a psychologist using hypnosis to try to help people attain a semblance of "cosmic consciousness," reports in *The Journal of Humanistic Psychology:*

> *Another commonality between subjects, one that was unexpected, was that every subject responded to the initial suggestions to return to a place and time of calmness, self-assurance, and spontaneous participation by regressing to approximately the age of four. In addition, all subjects except two [13/15] emerged from this experience crying. Their tears were explained either by, "I had forgotten how beautiful life could be, and how wonderful I could feel," or, "It was so wonderful that I felt very sad when I realized I was back and it was gone." Afterward, subjects reported that this particular experience had changed their self-concept considerably and that they felt much more comfortable just being able to remember this aspect of themselves as a potential mode of functioning.* [Vol.22 No.1,1982:105]

As we shall see, we all began to lose this ability to enjoy life simply through an appreciation of the exercise of our "I"-Faculties at about the age of five, when we learned about old age, disease, and death; and the whole substance of the Perennial Philosophy is the art of recovering, as adults, a profound and mature form of that sublime state of Free Being/Loving/Knowing, realized only arduously and ardently by the mystics/saints/sages, and spontaneously and joyously by the child of four. Until we "mature" people are converted, and become like little children, we cannot *see* the Kingdom of God. [Mark 10:15, John 3:3]

Development of the Love/Belief System
Five to Twenty

And now is sprung the trap which we unwittingly set for our children when we teach them to believe they are their mind/bodies. Now, at five, the child learns that, someday, he will DIE. To adequately appreciate the horrendously traumatic thing it is for the child to learn that his mind/body, which he has just begun to accept as "I", will eventually become worm food, one need only read Ernest Becker's Pulitzer Prize winning *The Denial of Death*. He contends that most people never again in their whole lives face anything so terribly traumatic as the five-year old's confrontation with death. Becker presents a brilliant critique of Freud's theory that our primary repressions are sexual, the libido; and proves instead that the universal human repression is a "denial of death."

Now the child comes to believe that "he," who wants more than anything else to exist, will perish with the death of his mind/body. Even a five-year old can complete the syllogism, "I am my mind/body; my mind/body will die; ergo, 'I' will die." He may be told that he has a soul, and his soul will go to heaven when he dies. But that's like telling him he has an appendix, or a kidney, which will survive him. He doesn't care about an ephemeral soul; he's concerned about "I", which they have just spent three years convincing him is his mind/body. And now he learns that his mind/body will eventually be put in the ground and rot. Is it any wonder that this is such a horrendously traumatic experience for the child, whose greatest need is to *exist*?

In what must be considered one of the understatements of the century, Gesell et al., report, almost in passing, of the six-year old:

There may be a preoccupation with the appurtenances of death: graves, funerals, being buried in the ground. Children discuss these matters and may express dislike of the notion that their relatives or they themselves should be buried in the ground. ["Dislike?" I distinctly remember being horrified!] *Six often needs to be protected from death experiences.* [HOW?] *Pictures of dead children may haunt his dreams. Seeing a dead animal is an experience he does not forget easily. He asks, "How long does it TAKE to die?"* (emphasis added) [CFFT:124]

Can't you hear the terror in that question? But just as we cannot, as observers, fully appreciate the joys of the child of four, neither can we now appreciate, and the child cannot express, the numbing dread—not dislike, *dread*—that grips him when he learns about death and dying. His greatest need, the "I"-Need to exist, will inevitably be denied. Someday, sooner or later— maybe just around the next corner—he will have to face and accept the unacceptable, the worst thing he can contemplate, because it is the one thing he can not even imagine: *non-existence;* to be buried, lifeless, in the ground where he must lose forever his precious capacities to Love, to Know, to Imagine, and to Decide.

But again, as the letter says, "life goes on, and so must he." Having put his "I" out of consideration, and accepted the fact that he is his mind/body, he must now somehow integrate the fact of Death into his Love/Belief System. But it's impossible for a child, with no help from his elders, to rationalize the awful specter of Death. The only way to handle it is by repression. So he learns to deal with death the same way his parents are usually dealing with it: he refuses to think about it or talk about it. He tries to put it in a closet and forget about it (the same closet in which he has already put his "I"), and gets busy with his toys and games—as his parents are usually busy with theirs—so he won't have *time* to think about it.

But increasingly, as Becker shows, and, as we now know, because of the "I"'s immutable need to exist, his toys and games take on the form of a subconscious search for some form of immortality. Having accepted himself as just a mind/body, he must now accept its mortality. Now he finds it imperative that he *re-ground* himself in the only things left: the people and objects and specious Values of his society. And, as Viktor Frankl points out, he initiates a desperate, life-long "search for meaning" in a life which he knows must end.

Perhaps even worse than his denial of death, he has now learned the art of repression, and inaugurated his *subconscious*. The marvelous faculty of imagination enables him to suppress—"forget"—distasteful facts, and create barriers which prevent unpleasant aspects of reality from reaching his consciousness in their pure form, by the manipulations we'll review in Chapter 10. He has learned the spiritually fatal art of *deceiving himself*, literally blinding himself (see Blum, page 144), an art for which he will find dozens of applications as he matures. He has initiated the loss of his *Innocence*.

And now he understands why adults never enjoy simple living the way he does, and their obsessive concern for his physical welfare. He might die, and cease to exist. So he valiantly tries to suppress his Knowledge of death, But now, at the very heart of his Love/Belief System are planted the Elements the Love, Fear, and Desire, which will take absolute precedence in all his decisions, all the rest of his life. Based on the belief "'I' am my mind/body," the "I"-Need to exist now generates:

> A LOVE of his physical life, and a FEAR of death (because "I" will cease to exist); and,

> A repressed (because he is convinced it is impossible) DESIRE for survival, i.e., for immortality.

This is the (second?) fall of man. We have forgotten (or we never knew) what we *are*.

(Adam said, "I hid myself because I was naked," and God replied, "Who told you that you were naked?" But did He mean, "Who told you that naked body was *you*?")

This Love for his physical life, fear of death, and repressed desire for immortality, become the "roots" of what will grow into a gigantic "bush" of scores of other Loves and Beliefs, each of which will be adopted because of its apparent contribution to these concerns. This structure of Elements will occupy the supreme position and exercise the highest authority of all the Elements in his Love/Belief System. It will exhibit such autonomic influence over his life that many psychologists today still think of it as the human's "instinct" for self-preservation.

Now we can understand the profound psychological (existential) wisdom in Christ's maxim, "He who loves his life loses it, but he who disdains his life in this world shall find it, and shall keep it unto life eternal." What He is saying is that the overriding Love of one's life colors everything he sees, hears: experiences; and everything he does. By living each day only in the way which will most assure him of a guaranteed tomorrow, he fails to live in and Know the eternal Now. He is no longer able to perceive the beauty and the wonder of the world and his neighbor, nor is he able to respond rationally, i.e., graciously, generously, and creatively: Lovingly, to all the circumstances of life. It is not that he who Loves his life will lose it on some future day of judgment, or when he dies; he has lost it already; is losing it—forfeiting every day—the life he could be living as a child of God, a sibling of Christ and all people.

Ken Wilber seems to say it best:

Now on the Existential Level, man is . . . in flight from death. That is, he refuses to live without a future in the timeless Now; he wants a future moment as a promise that death won't touch him now. He doesn't want this timeless present alone, he wants the promise of yet another present ahead of him.

Thus he arranges for this present to pass on to yet another present, and he harbors the secret wish that all his moments will flee into future moments, forever. For precisely this reason, none of his present moments seem timeless, eternal, and complete in themselves. Rather, they seem to pass on, . . . seem to flee into, other moments. The eternal moment, which is always, therefore appears as a series of fleeing moments, a series of durations lasting a mere 2-3 seconds. . . the eternal Present appears as the . . . passing present.

Our most demoralizing fear is our fear of death, because it causes us to live our entire lives with one eye on tomorrow, and prevents us from seeing each moment of the eternal Now through the eyes of Love. Instead, we anxiously analyze and evaluate each moment of the eternal Now for its portents of the future. By living vicariously in our imaginary futures, we assume we have a future, and assuage our fear of death.

And our lives are shaped by the time frames in which we tend to live them. Of course the hungry person can only think in terms of his next meal; people in the ghetto tend to live their lives in terms of *mañana* or Saturday night, the businessperson lives in spans of months or years, and some philosophers think in terms of a lifetime. But most mystics/saints/sages, by the simple (but not easy) expedients of accepting death, and forsaking past and future, have freed their Love of life for Love of God and their neighbor, and are now able to live again as the four-year old lives: *sub specie aeternitatis,* under the aspect of eternity. But eternity is not an endless amount of time; it is a state of no time, or timelessness. Eternity is now or never. Truly enlightened people have learned to live their lives rationally, i.e., Lovingly, in the only eternity there is: the eternal Now. Until one has learned to live with the daily possibility of death, he has not yet learned how to live.

But in The Denial of Death, Becker also writes:

> *. . . we have today an excellent general theory of schizophrenia . . .*
> *Here I want only to mention the main characteristic of the syndrome*
> *—why it is that the schizophrenic is in such an extraordinary state of*
> *terror. It took a long time for us to understand this state because we*
> *were dealing with a phenomenon so strange it seems truly like science*
> *fiction. I mean the fact that human experience is split into two modes—*
> *the symbolic self* [I'm sure he means the non-symbolic "I"] *and the*
> *physical body, and that these two modes of experience can be quite*
> *distinct. In some people they are so distinct as to be unintegrated, and*
> *these people we call schizophrenic.*[1] *The hypersensitive individual*
> *reacts to his body as something strange to himself, something utterly*
> *untrustworthy, something not under his secure control.*
>
> *Right away we can see that the schizophrenic is burdened, like all of us,*
> *with an "alien" animal body.* [!] *What makes his burden greater is that*
> *he is not securely rooted in his body. In his early childhood . . . he did*
> *not develop a secure "seating" in his body: as a result his self is not*
> *anchored intimately in his neuro-anatomy. He cannot make available*
> *to himself the natural organismic expansion that others use to buffer*
> *and absorb the fear of life and death. He does not feel this natural*
> *animal plenitude.*[2] [DD:218]

Becker doesn't explain where this "natural animal plenitude" comes from, but baldly implies that those who are "securely rooted" in their bodies, who have "developed a secure 'seating' in their bodies," whose "self is anchored intimately in their anatomies," don't have problems. But the rest of his book is filled with descriptions of the psychopathologies the person under-goes—pathologies which I contend result primarily from being forced to identify his "I" with the "alien animal body"—the pathologies of anality, Oedipus complexes, denial of death, castration complexes, penis envy, sexual guilt, fetishism, existential anxiety, etc., etc.

---

[1] When they exhibit a profound love of God and their neighbor, they are also called saints. St. Francis' "distinction between his body and his 'symbolic self'" caused him to call his body "brother ass," like an animal he rode, but couldn't always control.

[2] In Chapter 10 we'll see how a malfunctioning RF can cause schizophrenia.

Apparently, it has been only Assagioli, among all the world's eminent psychologists, who has deduced that humans have a higher self, and that it is exactly society's blind insistence that the child identify his self, his "I"—what Becker later calls (in passing, and without defining) "his proud, rich, lively, infinitely transcendent, free, inner spirit," (!)—with his intractable, pain-riddled, bleeding, urinating, defecating, certain to be diseased and decomposed, body, that is at the root of most of our troubles.

The failure to recognize the spiritual element in humans, as distinguished from our minds and bodies, is the greatest psychologic tragedy of humanity, and it has come about primarily because James, Freud, Skinner, Crick, and others playing "Scientist," have thoughtlessly promulgated the reductionism that people don't have a spiritual element, a soul; that we are just another species of social animal. In so doing, they have taken all the meaning out of personhood; they have de-meaned the person. They have helped perpetuate our ignorance of our true nature, and unwittingly, but very assuredly, made a substantial contribution to the sum of "man's inhumanity to man."

> *By their own theories of human nature psychologists have the power of elevating or degrading that same nature. Debasing assumptions debase human beings; generous assumptions exalt them.*
> —GORDON W. ALLPORT

Instead of raising the child with the belief that he is his mind/body, we must learn to raise him with the knowledge that he is immortal Spirit, the Spirit of Free Being/Loving/Knowing, only temporarily associated with the mind/body of a very proficient social animal.

Then he can live a truly normal life, as a child of God, the life his "I" both requires and enables him to live: a life in which he could learn to love God with all his heart, soul, mind, and strength, and his neighbor as himself. He would not need, later in life, Assagioli's exercises in self-identification and dis-identification. As noted above, Assagioli proposed that "we are dominated by everything with which our self becomes identified." By identifying with our bodies, minds, or emotions, we subject ourselves to those elements. Therefore he developed his *Psychosynthesis* exercises, to repeat over and over to oneself: "I have a body, but I am not my body; I have a mind, but I am not my mind; etc." With our new understanding, we must modify Assagioli's thesis to read, "We are dominated by everything with which we identify our Selves; because (as we shall see) this is an act of "I-Love."

Most psychiatrists and psychotherapists (and unfortunately, many members of the clergy, too) are simply trying to help people relieve their anxieties by resolving some of the superficial conflicts in their Love/Belief Systems. But this is only rearranging the garbage in what can only be compared to Pandora's box, or a can of worms. As Freud so profoundly observed, "We cure the neurotic of his symptoms only to introduce him to the common misery of life."

As Becker has shown, the most common misery of life is death. Therefore as long as we continue to ignore our essentially spiritual natures, continue to believe and teach our children to believe, "'I' am my mind/body," just so long will the protection of our bodily lives, a possessive Love of our physical lives, remain at the heart of our Love/Belief Systems, supplanting our Love of God, usurping His place in our lives; and just so long will we suffer from the repression of a denial of death, and live all our lives with a proportionate, concomitant fear of losing that life.

This is why just rearranging our Loves and Beliefs is a waste of time. We need a major operation—*open-heart therapy*—on our Love/Belief Systems. We need to be born again; to root out the Love of our bodily lives, and replace it with the Love of God—or, if not God, certainly something more meaningful than the specious material and social values on which most of us squander our magnificent "I"-Faculties in a vain effort to gratify our "I"-Needs.

The only permanent cure, and the only happiness for the human race, lies in a re-cognition, and an appreciation, and a realization, of our essentially spiritual natures, our immortal "I"'s. To Assagioli's disidentification exercises, we must add an *identification* exercise: "'I' am spirit, the spirit of Free Being/ Loving/Knowing, associated with the mind/body of a highly developed and proficient social animal, from which 'I' will one day be separated." By identifying our true selves—our "I"'s—as Love, our lives tend, according to Assagioli's law, to be dominated by Love, and we begin to fulfill our destiny and our heritage, as children of God.

It is idolatry to Love our bodily lives. Loving our lives may prolong them, but destroys their *quality*. And most of our other possessive Loves, Values, and Needs are equally ephemeral, equally unprotectable, equally, at last, ungratifying, unfulfilling; yet each and every one of them generates its own set of fears, desires, worries, anxieties, and sorrows in our lives.

And the few and fleeting joys they provide are, say the saints, just a puff of smoke in comparison with the profound and permanent joy known only to those who have reorganized their Love/Belief Systems around the Love of God and their neighbor, restored the sovereignty of the "I", and come to *Know*, while they lived, their kinship with God.

The fear of death keeps us from living, not from dying.
—PAUL C. ROUD

But the child's belief that he is his mind/body, and its correlative denial of death, are only the most pernicious of his Loves and Beliefs; before he is twenty, he will have adopted thousands of other Loves and Beliefs, many of them completely irrational and/or erroneous.

For example, as his social life continues, he is perhaps told by the older kids that a Ferrari Matchbox car is worth two Datsuns, and that he would be very foolish to consider anything less in a trade. He may wonder about the ratio, but the question of Matchbox cars having some value never crosses his mind. After all, who is he to question the big kids, who are smarter and more experienced than he, and are *so sure of themselves*?

He has also learned from this advice that his reputation will suffer if he engages in unprofitable transactions.

Because conflicting Love/Belief System Response Impulses cause anxiety—cognitive dissonance—and because he soon learns that one of the greatest deprecations of his reputation occurs when he contradicts himself, he develops a tremendous desire for consistency among his Loves and Beliefs. As Drs. Lecky and Maltz have proved, this is one of the greatest forces in our lives, the desire for self-consistency: consistency of our actions with our Loves and Beliefs, consistency among our Loves and Beliefs, and consistency of our Loves and Beliefs with our versions of reality. This desire is so powerful that it will even cause distortions of our perceptions of reality and our actions to make them conform to our Loves and Beliefs, or, as Festinger has observed, modifications of our beliefs to make them consistent with our actions. "Oh, what a tangled web we weave, when first we practice to deceive"—ourSelves!

In short order, he also learns to value being liked or respected, fine clothes, a powerful car, a big home, an attractive wife, accomplished children, a high-level job. These come to be known as "his" car, "his" home, "his" wife (!), "his" children (!). Each of these possessive values generates a corresponding *desire* in his Love/Belief System, an *envy* of those who have it, a *temporary joy* and a permanent *fear* of its loss when he does attain it, and a *fear/hatred* of those who threaten it or his possession of it.

But perhaps the greatest challenge facing the child is the rationalization or reconciliation of the conflicts which arise between his SA-Needs for affection and acceptance and his "I"-Need to Love, with his SA-Need for dominance. In polite society, most children learn that their physical dominance drives must be suppressed, but they are then sublimated into dozens of other avenues or orders, symbolic of the pecking order. Such orders as income, accomplishments, reputation, possessions, physical, mental, or sexual prowess, etc. In other words, if, for social or physical reasons, I can't dominate you physically, then I will seek other orders in which I can be superior, e.g., "My old man can lick your old man." In our materialistic society, we come to believe that somehow, people on the higher end of these orders are better or happier than those lower down in the orders. We learn to evaluate everyone and everything in accordance with these orders. We learn the spiritually fatal practice of *comparing* everyone and everything with someone or something else, in order to determine their value, worth, or significance, in what we think of as the "real world." The crowning fallacy is when we begin to Love, or highly value, the things associated with higher positions on these artificial, sublimated orders.

Worst of all, we compare ourselves to everyone else, trying to determine our rating on these orders: our personality, our physique, our looks, our mentality, our abilities, our popularity, etc. We come to believe, "I am strong," or "I am weak;" "I am homely," or "I am handsome;" "I am smart," or "I am dumb;" etc. Of course negative characteristics are immediately subjected to our new-found skill of repression, becoming Jung's "shadow" (see Arieti, pg. 114); but whether conscious or subconscious, positive or negative, these self-image beliefs wield an absolutely dominating influence over our lives, as Dr. Maltz has so adequately proved.

Of course, the child's parents and teachers also convince him that he should be good, he should be careful, he should be honest, he should be polite, he should be clean, he should be ambitious, he shouldn't cry, or get angry, etc., etc. These values constitute Freud's "super-ego," Horney's "shoulds," the "parent" of transactional analysis, or what laymen call the conscience.

And so his Love/Belief System grows, willy-nilly, rapidly becoming stuffed with thousands of Loves, Beliefs, Values, and Needs, each of which is adopted because it came from a significant other, or because of its apparent contributions to the satisfaction of his SA-Needs, the "I"-Needs, or simply because of their apparent agreement with, or contribution to the fulfillment or assuagement of the Desires and Fears which arise from his other Loves, Beliefs, Values, and Needs—particularly of course, his major Love for his physical life, his repressed desire for immortality, his self-image, his need for acceptance, and the specious orders of Values which permeate his society.

The beliefs which constitute the self-image and each of his other Loves and Beliefs immediately find a very secure place in his Love/Belief System, where they become both the motivations and the laws of his life: the stimuli additional to the SA-Needs which impel him to action, and the standards against which all his perceptions, his actions, and the actions of others will now be *autonomically* measured and evaluated.

Current neurological research enables us to finally understand the power we bestow on our Loves and Beliefs. Dr. Gary Lynch of the University of California at Irvine has proved that *"learning involves a physical change in the circuitry of the brain,"* changes which can occur in as little as ten minutes. This should not surprise us, since every one of our millions of memories and "learnings" must have somehow modified our brains. But if a new fact can change the circuitry of our brains, I submit that adopting a Love or significant Belief, Value, or Need *must modify the circuitry of the reticular formation*. Loves and Beliefs are not facts or memories—they are not the *data* of the brain. They constitute the *principles* or the *programs,* which determine how all the data is handled, and therefore must have modified the reticular formation, the centralized, indefatigable, quintessential *Sentinel* of the brain. And it is this physiological modification, this hard-wiring of the reticular formation, which gives every one of our Loves and Beliefs a life and a will of its own.

All of our perceptions, cognitions, and Response Impulses are determned autonomically by the Reticular Activating System, based on our operant Desires and Fears, as determined by operant SA-Needs and all the significant Elements of the Love/Belief System. Because each of them has modified the reticular formation, these Elements become "Deputy-Governors," which act as eyes and ears and messengers and officers of the Governor, Deputy-Governors, which decide what he shall see and hear, in what form he shall see and hear it, and what his responses should be. They have the power to mobilize his entire being in the defense or enhancement of their objects, or the defense or enhancement of the Elements themselves. Whether conscious or subconscious, they are given a "power of attorney," are deputized to act for the "I", become in fact, surrogate "I"'s, unthinking bureaucrats, literal *instincts*, which can act automatically on the mind and body, without the approval of the "I", sometimes even in direct opposition to the "I"! In the final analysis, our self-adopted Loves and Beliefs act as the exact equivalent of the animal's instincts; the Elements of our Love/Belief Systems become a part of our autonomic response systems.

The shocking conclusion we must draw is that, in its totality, the Love/Belief System operates exactly like the U.S. government! Like the government, it is for most of us a vast and incredibly complex *bureaucracy*, consisting of a chaotic hierarchy of scores of bureaus, departments, and branches—whose responsibilities often overlap or conflict, and with very imperfect communications between them—staffed by thousands of bureaucrats; each competing for the "President's" attention, each mindlessly trying to enforce its own little set of rules and regulations, each continuously seeking to justify and expand its authority by bringing in only that data which validates its purpose, and suppressing that which does not—an appalling, but, unfortunately, a compellingly exact analogy.

**Whenever "I" adopt a Love, Belief, Value, or Need,
even subconsciously, my reticular formation
is modified in such a way that my mind/body will
always tend to act autonomically in accordance
with that Love, Belief, Value, or Need.**

**Our lives are inexorably *programmed* by our
conscious and subconscious Loves, Beliefs, Values,
Needs, and their concomitant Desires and Fears.**

For example, if "I" Love nature, then I am going to be impelled to react against people who impair the ecology. But I am also going to react to defend my Love of nature, since any derogation of this Love is an affront to my self-image as an intelligent person.

Of course, these reflex actions do serve many useful purposes. In an emergency, such as an imminent threat of physical harm, it is the Love/Belief System, or RAS, which rings the alarm throughout the person's entire system, alerting the brain, pumping adrenalin, etc., mobilizing all the faculties for a fight or flight activity.

However, we are seldom operating in an emergency. But unfortunately, as we know, the Love/Belief System also responds this way to a threat to any of its significant Elements. When someone criticizes "our" church, or "our" children, for example, the same adrenalin starts to flow, and we involuntarily lose our temper. This is because our Love for our church and our children is connected, related, to our suppressed desire for immortality, our most valued "possessions," our self-image, and who knows what else—all of our most significant Loves and Beliefs. Is it any wonder we lose our temper when they are deprecated?

But is it the RF which senses and generates Response Impulse to these circumstantial situations? Is the RF actually wired with our Loves and Beliefs? Well, if our Reticular Activating Systems can sense and initiate responses to any imbalance in our physiological or biological state, as well as to any sensory stimulus which signals a threat or opportunity for fulfillment of our SA-Needs, why would an efficient God (or Nature) find it necessary to create a different brain system to sense and engender immediate responses to circumstances representing a deprecation or affirmation of our church or our children?

This is the tragedy of the human race. The Love/Belief System, or RAS, is determining all of our responses to the circumstances of life, sometimes so instinctively and forcefully that "I" don't even enter into the transaction!

And obviously, even when "I" am in full control of my faculties, trying to make a rational decision, "I" can only choose among responses provided by, and on priorities or weights determined by, the conscious and subconscious Elements of my Love/Belief System.

And many, if not most of our Loves and Beliefs are subconscious. They were acquired by "osmosis," or by introjection, when we were two, three, four, five, etc. years of age. Many are unarticulated Loves and Beliefs—simply assumptions—which, if articulated, we would not adopt as adults. But they are wired in our brains and give rise to Response Impulses just as forcefully as our most solemn and considered commitments.

Sadly, even we "normal" people—like the psychotics described by Silvano Arieti in *The Will to be Human*—do not live; we are *being lived*, by the conscious and subconscious Elements in our Love/Belief Systems. We have all been blinded and devitalized by what has been so trenchantly described as "the hypnosis of social conditioning." As the brilliant R. D. Laing said, "We are are all living in a post-hypnotic trance, induced in early infancy."

We are all hypnotized by the Loves and Beliefs
acquired indiscriminately in childhood.
Until we restore the sovereignty of the "I", and recover our
ordained state of being as spirit: Lover and Knower,
our lives are being lived by proxy.

All of us then, born with few instincts, each create our own set of "instincts," made up, unfortunately, of the haphazardly selected Loves and Beliefs and the resultant Desires and Fears which, together with our Social Animal Needs, constitute the programs of the Love/Belief System, or the mental and spiritual "heart."

We have already seen, in the four-year old, the "I"-Needs to Love and to Know, and in the five-year old's denial of death, the "I"-Need to Exist. Now let's look at each of these needs in more detail:

The "I"-Need to Exist

> *Man cannot live without a continuous confidence*
> *in something indestructible within himself.*
> FRANZ KAFKA

René Dubos provides insight into this most vital of all our Needs:

About the experience of life, most people are under the illusion that they can be happy only if something especially good happens. . . . Oddly enough, there is only one phrase I know to express that life is good per se, that just being alive is good. Whenever one wants to say that, one uses the French expression—in all languages: one simply speaks of JOIE DE VIVRE. Joie de vivre simply means that just being alive is an extraordinary experience. It is totally immaterial what goes on, except for the fact that one is alive. It does not mean that you are very happy with the way you live; you can even be suffering. You can have lots of trouble, but just being alive is a quality PER SE.

Perhaps even more telling are Pitirim Sorokin's conclusions from his ordeals:

In 1918 I was hunted from pillar to post by the Russian Communist Government. At last I was imprisoned and condemned to death. Daily, during six weeks, I expected to be shot, and witnessed the shooting of my friends and fellow prisoners. During the subsequent four years of my stay in Communist Russia I underwent other painful experiences and observed, to the heart-breaking point, endless horrors of human bestiality, death, and destruction. Exactly in these conditions I jotted down in my diary the "observations of a cold intellect and plaintive murmurs of a saddened heart:"

Whatever may happen in the future, I know that I have learned three things which will remain forever convictions of my heart as well as my mind. Life, even the hardest life, is the most beautiful, wonderful, and miraculous treasure in the world. . .' [1]   [WPL:v]

"Just being alive is an extraordinary experience." Simple self-conscious existence—"I"-Consciousness, metacognition—is the greatest miracle and the most thrilling experience in the world. Every moment of self-conscious life, under almost any circumstances, is an exciting, precious, miraculous *event*. The difficulty we mature people have in appreciating simple existence is that there is too much to appreciate. If the stars only shone one night a year, on that night no human eye would close. If one only met another person once a year, she would prepare for that day as a bride prepares for her wedding. And imagine how even the most common things would appear to you if you had just recovered from six months of blindness!

> *Sense, feeling, taste, complacency, and sight,*
> *These are the true and real joys,*
> *The living, flowing, inward, melting, bright*
> *and heavenly pleasures; all the rest are toys;*
> *All which are founded in desire*
> *as light in flame and heat in fire.*
>   —EVELYN UNDERHILL

> *If your daily life seems poor, do not blame it;*
> *blame yourself; tell yourself that you are not*
> *poet enough to call forth its riches.*
>   —RAINER MARIA RILKE

---

[1]   His second discovery was *"fulfillment of duty . . . making life happy;"* the third was *"the only way toward a mental, moral or material millenium: the royal road of all-giving creative love."*

> *Life is not lost by dying. Life is lost minute by minute,*
> *day by dragging day, in small uncaring ways.*
> —STEPHEN VINCENT BENET

As we have seen in Chapter 4, all children, if they are fed and loved, know *joie de vivre*, and it is this simple enjoyment of life for its own sake, this "second naivete," as Maslow calls it, the innate human joy of Being, Loving, Knowing, which the adult can recapture only as the artist captures simplicity in her work: by great personal effort and self-discipline.

The primal thrill of simple "I"-Consciousness makes the thought of its loss absolutely unbearable, a thought which manifests itself as early as in the two-year old's fear of the dark (long before she knows about death), as explained by Bernard J. Boelen in his excellent book, *Personal Maturity*. The disappearance of the child's known world when the lights go out raises the fear that she might also disappear. In sleep, she loses her precious self-conscious existence; will it always return in the morning?

Animals, without an "I", have no "need to exist," or "instinct for survival," with which they have always been credited; only instinctual fears, and a fear of pain. Nor can they imagine their own deaths. And isn't it ironic, if our thesis is correct, that the "I", the uniquely human entity which enables us to imagine and fear our own deaths, is itself immortal?

The "I"-Need To Love

> *We must love.*
> —FÉNELON

Turning to the "I"-Need to Love, we all know what it's like to fall in love with a member of the opposite sex. This is SA-love, and although it is very similar to "I"-Love—and usually invokes "I"-Love—it is not "I"-Love. "I"-Love is an awe, and respect, and appreciation, and admiration; a fascination, enchantment, or entrancement, which is the equivalent of *worship*, of something for its own sake alone, because it is, in and of itself, worthy of our Love. This is unpossessive, unconditional Love, without any thought of self. This is the kind of Love most of us (unknowingly) spend our whole lives trying to find a worthy object for; and, unless we find God, fail to gratify, except only very sporadically and superficially.

Maslow describes "I"-Love, which he calls "B- (for Being) love."

1. *B-love is welcomed into consciousness, and is completely enjoyed. Since it is non-possessive, and is admiring rather than needing, it makes no trouble and is practically always pleasure-giving.*

2. *It can never be sated; it may be enjoyed without end. It usually grows greater rather than disappearing. It is intrinsically enjoyable. It is end rather than means.*

3. *The B-love experience is often described as being the same as, and having the same effects as the aesthetic experience or the mystic experience.*

4. *The therapeutic and psychologic effects of experiencing B-love are very profound and widespread. Similar are the characterological effects of the relatively pure love of a healthy mother for her baby, or the perfect love of God that some mystics have described.*

5. *B-love is, beyond the shadow of a doubt, a richer, "higher," more valuable subjective experience than D-love* [D for deficiency, i.e., a needing love] *(which all B-lovers have also experienced). . .*

6. *D-love CAN be gratified. The concept "gratification" hardly applies at all to admiration-love for (a) person's (or God's) admiration-worthiness and love-worthiness.*

7. *In B-love there is a minimum of anxiety-hostility. . . . There CAN, of course, be anxiety-for-the-other. In D-love one must always expect some anxiety-hostility.*

8. *B-lovers are more independent, . . . more autonomous, less jealous or threatened, less needful, more individual, more disinterested, but also simultaneously more eager to help the other toward self-actualization, more proud of his triumphs, more altruistic, generous and fostering.*

9. *The truest, most penetrating perception of the other is made possible by B-love. It is as much a cognitive as an emotional-conative reaction, . . . So impressive is this, and so often validated, . . that, far from accepting the common platitude that love makes people blind, I become more and more inclined to think of the opposite as true, that NON-LOVE MAKES US BLIND.* [emphasis added]

10. *Finally, I may say that B-love, . . . creates the partner. It gives him a self-image, it gives him self-acceptance, a feeling of love-worthiness, all of which permit him to grow. . . .* [TPB:47]

Wouldn't St. Bernard, who exclaimed "I love because I love!" have approved the corollary, "I love because 'I' am love"? (Also see Maslow's description of the effects of B-Value cognition—"I"-Love—in RVPE, p. 112.)

The "I"-Need to Know

All men by nature desire to know.
—ARISTOTLE

Turning now to the "I"-Need to Know, we see that just as humans have two ways of Loving, so too, we have two ways of Knowing. The first kind is relative, the second is absolute. As Thomas Goudge explains in his introduction to Bergson's *Introduction to Metaphysics*,

[Bergson's] *discussion opens with a contrast between the two ways of knowing anything. The first is characteristic of the intellect which approaches the thing externally from some point of view alien to it, uses symbols to express its findings, and yields knowledge that is relative. The second is the process of intuition, whereby we "enter into" the thing and identify ourselves with it by a kind of "intellectual sympathy"— much as we identify ourselves with a figure in a novel we are reading. Here no symbols are involved, yet the knowledge attained is absolute and perfect. The former of these two ways of knowing is the method of the sciences. The latter is the proper method of metaphysics. Bergson insists that we must not confuse intuition with mere feeling or emotion. Nor . . . as depending on some special faculty having a non-natural origin. Intuition is rather an act, or a series of acts, of direct participation in the immediacy of experience. It can be accomplished only by making an effort to detach oneself from the demands of action, by "inverting" the normal attitude of consciousness and immersing oneself in the current of direct awareness. The result will be a cognition of reality such as intellectual concepts can never yield.* [IM:11]

As we shall see, this "identifying ourselves with," this "intellectual sympathy," this "detaching ourselves, . . . immersing ourselves," is the act of "I"-Love, an act which always leads to the absolute kind of Knowing. This is Wilber's "direct, non-conceptual, and immediate" Knowing, the kind of Knowing George Leonard is referring to when he says education is ecstasy.

The "Aha! I understand!" insight is well-known as one of the most thrilling human experiences. Again, all we need observe is the barrage of questions put forth by our four-year old children, and their contented faces in sleep after a full day of living and learning.

As we all know, there is a great difference between knowing some facts about a subject or person (relative knowing), and Knowing the subject or person (absolute Knowing). Knowing someone's name and face is not Knowing the person, any more than knowing some formulas is a Knowledge of algebra, or knowing some phrases is a Knowledge of French.

The kind of Knowing the "I" seeks is best described as understanding, or Lonergan's *insight,* as exemplified by the child smashing the watch to get inside of it, to see and touch and Know what makes it run. Baudelaire sees metaphysical implications in this example of our need to Know.

> *Most kids want more than anything else to see the soul* [the "I"] *(of their toy), . . . it is the first turn toward the metaphysical. . . . The child turns his toy over and over again, he scratches it, knocks it against walls, throws it on the floor, . . . he starts its mechanical movements over again, sometimes backwards. The marvelous life of the toy stops. Like the people assaulting the Tuileries, the child makes a last effort; at last he opens it, he is stronger than the toy. But where is the SOUL?*

Of course his efforts are doomed to failure. The toy has no soul, and the only way to really Know anything is to devote oneself to it with care, concern, responsiveness, and respect—which is the act of "I"-Love—and Knowledge will follow. This is true of learning to Know French, it is true of learning to Know algebra, it is true of learning to Know a person, and it is true of learning to Know God.

> *The astrolabe of the mysteries of God is love.*
> —JALAL-UDDIN RUMI

The astrolabe of all mysteries is Love. We only come to really Know that which we first have Loved, i.e., devoted ourselves to, or identified our-

Selves with. It is erotic (SA-) love that is blind; "I"-Love is always 20/20. (See again, ¶9, p. 64)

Fulfillment of the "I"-Needs to Exist, to Love, and to Know, correspond to the Sat, Chit, Ananda—the Being, Knowledge, Bliss—of Hinduism; which some Hindus would change to Sat, Chit, *Bhakti*, Ananda: Existence in the Knowledge and *Love of God* = Bliss. With this modification it is also the state which Huxley calls the "unitive knowledge of God," and Christ calls "The Kingdom of God."

Now there are at least three major differences in character between the "I"-Needs and the SA-Needs. First, unlike the SA-Needs, the "I"-Needs to Exist, to Love, and to Know, must be considered to be incessant, i.e., always operant. They are of course superseded by stronger operant SA-Needs and Desires and Fears arising from Love/Belief System Elements, but the "I"-Needs are a strong constant "noise" in the Center of Consciousness, a noise which can only be stilled by gratification or by distraction, by keeping oneself occupied with gratification of (continually increased or varied) SA-Needs and our self-adopted Loves/Values/Needs: Desires; or the assuagement of our (mostly self-induced) Fears.

Second, unlike the SA-Needs and the Needs which constitute Love/Belief System Elements, the "I"-Needs to Love and to Know are, as Maslow says, and many mystics/saints/sages have confirmed, never sated, but when invoked, can be enjoyed continuously (see p. 8, and ¶2 & ¶6, p.64).[2] But this is true only of "I"-Loving/Knowing; not of the relative loving/knowing with which we continually try to satisfy these Needs, a love/knowledge which provides not gratification, but only a suppression of the "I"- Needs. Absolute Loving/Knowing is a rare experience for most of us, because it results only from an act of unconditional, unpossessive Love.

Third, even though the "I"-Needs are incessant and insatiable, they do not, like the SA-Needs, manifest themselves specifically, but are felt only as an emptiness, an incompleteness in one's life, only after the person's SA- Needs and major self-adopted Loves/Values/Needs are reasonably well-satisfied. While these (mostly specious) needs are unsatisfied, the "I"- Faculties (and therefore the Center of Consciousness) are fully occupied with, devoted to, the

---

[2] They are, therefore, sated in the first sense of **sate:** *1. to satisfy (an appetite, desire, etc.) to the full; gratify completely;* but not in the second: *2. to provide with more than enough, so as to weary or digust; surfeit; glut.*

gratification/assuagement of the person's Desires/Fears. Only when the SA-Needs and major Love/Belief System Elements are reasonably well grati-fied/assuaged, and she becomes jaded, do the pure "I"-Needs begin to be felt, but only in the form of the vague gnawing anomie, ennui, anhedonia, list-lessness, incompleteness, emptiness, the agonizing, insufferable boredom, the dreadful, awe-ful "nothingness," described by Maslow and many others.[3]

The most obvious way to alleviate this boredom is by ever-novel fulfill-ments of the SA-Needs and our self-adopted Loves/Values/Needs: Desires—by finding something new to "Love." The person who started out needing food, finds a temporary diversion of the "I"-Needs in, and therefore needs, gourmet food; who needed a car, now needs a Mercedes, then two cars; who needed acceptance, now needs admiration, popularity, fame, etc. As Vivekenanda says, "Desire is never satisfied by the enjoyment of desires; it only increases the more, like fire when butter is poured upon it." Because novel gratifications of the SA-Needs and our self-adopted Loves/Values/Needs do provide temporary distractions from the anxious ennui induced by the ungratified "I"-Needs, these SA-Needs and Elements are continually magnified and/or modified, until, as they must, they begin to pall. As Underhill says, "One after another these things either fail us or enslave us." Because the "I"-Needs are incessant, their tem-porary suppression by gratification of temporal needs—for power, or fame, or material possessions, the excitement of gambling, or the high of drugs, etc.—those needs always tend to become obsessive. Anything which, even momen-tarily, distracts us from the awful sense of nothingness invoked by the "I"-Needs becomes addictive. Conversely, addicts must now be seen to have found a temporary quiescence of the "I"-Needs in their habit.

And, *we are all addicted.* Those who are not intellectually addicted to something—or some multiplicity of things—must find a way to "numb" the brain through alcohol, drugs, etc. Haven's work (p. 48) proves that we all, in the deep recesses of our minds, remember the "state of being four." Perhaps all of our addictions are simply a reflection of our disappointment at the loss of that idylllic state. Therefore people whose SA-Needs are reasonably well-gratified must still always be into some-*thing* (I'm into art; he's into the

---

[3]   But this is Hilton's "essential nothingness" or "rich nothingness," which we must not flee, but rather enter into, or embrace, if we are to realize our true Selves, for the "I", like God, is no-thing. It has been said that if anyone Knew what was in this nothingness, they would leap into it. Unfortunately, for most of us it's not that easy. See page 157 and Appendices B and C. Also see Tolstoy's vivid description of the initial anguish of facing nothingness in Chapter 9 of *The Act of Will*, by Assagioli.

ecology: Pascal's "diversions;" Lilly's "simulations of God"), or *die* of what is known as "boredom," but which is really the plaintive voice of the "I", and can also be considered as the voice of God; a voice calling us, since we are essentially spiritual, home; home to the spiritual world above all created things, above all Desires and Fears; home to the Kingdom of God.

But artificial satisfactions (really only distractions or diversions) of the "I"-Needs are all most of us ever know. Only very late in life, if at all, for most of us, do we learn that the "I"-Needs are our most basic needs, and that they can only be fully and continuously gratified by Existence in the Love and Knowledge of God and our neighbor.

In these respects then, the "I"-Needs are the opposite of the SA-Needs, in that they are incessant, but do not manifest themselves specifically, and when invoked, are insatiable. The SA-Needs are desired only when they are ungratified, and disappear when gratified, whereas the "I"-Needs are only desired specifically while they are being gratified—their gratification fulfilling the person. But they are not desired specifically when they are ungratified.

There is this difference between spiritual and corporal pleasures, that corporal ones beget a desire before we have obtained them and, after we have obtained them, a disgust; but spiritual pleasures, on the contrary, are not cared for when we have them not, but are desired when we have them.
—ST. GREGORY THE GREAT

The "I"-Needs to Love and to Know are not manifest in the Center of Consciousness until the operant SA-Needs and major Loves/Values/Needs are gratified/assuaged (and then only nebulously, as an anxious boredom); the "I"-Need to Exist is represented in the Love/Belief System, but only indirectly and erroneously, as a Love of our lives, Fear of death, etc.

The fact that the "I"-Needs do not manifest themselves specifically explains psychologists' failure to identify the "I"-Needs to Exist, to Love, and to Know as the human's primary needs (as well as Maslow's speculation about what he called the person's nebulous "instinct remnants").

In closing this chapter, it's important to point out that saints and philosophers have found Love and Knowledge to be complementary, or even identical. For example, Huxley concludes that "love is a mode of knowledge." Sri Ramakrishna says, "There is no difference between pure Knowledge and pure Love." Polanyi says all knowledge is "personal" knowledge, and represents an "intellectual commitment," a commitment of oneself being, as we shall see, the act of Love. Fromm lists knowledge as one of the primary elements in all forms of love, suggesting that we don't really know someone unless we love them, and we can't really love them until we know (understand) them. Maslow (above ¶9 p. 64) says B-Love "is as much a cognitive as an emotional-conative reaction," and enables "the truest most penetrating perception of the other." St. Bernard writes, "What would knowledge do without love? It would puff up. And love without knowledge? It would go astray." Merton says, "Man is made for a loving knowledge of God." Also see Knowles conclusion on page 24.

In view of these observations, and since we only come to really Know that which we first have Loved, we must now conclude that:

**Love and Knowledge are two aspects
of the same reality, like energy and mass.**

The equivalence of Love and Knowledge explains why the great majority of our temporal Loves fade so rapidly. We lose interest in them because they soon fail to provide us with new Knowledge about themselves. They lose their worth-iness. The only temporal Loves which last for any length of time are those infinite subjects, like mathematics, or justice, or religion, or power, or fame, or golf, or bridge, or charity work, or social intercourse, or collecting things, or hopeless causes, etc., etc. But the only Love "Object" worthy of people is God. If, by faith, we devote ourselves to God, we come to Know something of God, and of course, to Know God is to Love Him, and so on. Since God is infinite, and infinitely good, growth in the Love and Knowledge of God is an endless beneficent circle.

From the fourth century, Abba Evagrius, the Monk:

*Faith is the beginning of love;
the end of love is knowledge of God.*

A verbal profession of faith may yield a posthumous "salvation;" but is only the beginning of a fulfilling spiritual life; only a first step on the long and arduous path to an ever-growing Love and Knowledge of God—the strait and narrow way of those who "seek first the Kingdom of God and His righteousness."

The "I"-Faculties

In this chapter I will examine the "I"-Faculties: to Visualize, to Know or Believe, to Love, and to Decide. I will propose that these faculties are each an essential ingredient in human will, in the person's powers of voluntary action, and therefore, in our ability to create. Human powers of action and creation derive, not from our decision to perform certain acts, but rather from the coordinated action of the four faculties of the "I", which are to Visualize, to Know (or believe), and to Decide to devote itself (which is the act of Love) to realization of the vision.

> **Human will is made up of a combination of**
> **the four faculties of the "I", to Visualize,**
> **to Know, and to Love: to Decide to devote**
> **its mind/body to the fulfillment of the vision.**

The "I"-Faculty of Visualization

The ability to visualize represents the power of imagination, or ideation: the ability of the "I" to *create* ideas and images; to occupy the Center of Consciousness with anything it wishes, even things it has never seen before. This is one of our greatest powers, the power responsible for all of our inventions, and an essential component of any successful human action. The child learns to move his finger from point A to point B by visualizing it at point B, believing it will get there, and devoting himself to getting it to point B. The youth best becomes an accomplished pianist by visualizing himself as an accomplished pianist, believing he will succeed, and devoting himself to doing so. The concert pianist believes he can, and devotes himself to, giving a memorable performance, and auditorizes, i.e., imagines, each note or series of notes just an instant before they are played, and long run, even auditorizes the applause he will receive when he concludes.

From Henri Bergson's *Creative Evolution*,

The function of the intellect is to preside over actions. Now, in action, it is the result that interests us; the means matter little provided the end is attained. Thence it comes that we are altogether bent on the end to be realized, generally trusting ourselves to it in order that the idea may become an act; and thence it comes also that only the goal where our activity will rest is pictured explicitly to our mind: the movements constituting the action itself either elude our consciousness or reach it only confusedly. Let us consider a very simple act, like that of lifting the arm. Where should we be if we had to imagine beforehand all the elementary contractions and tensions this act involves, or even to perceive them, one by one, as they are accomplished? But the mind is carried immediately to the end, that is to say, to the schematic and simplified vision of the act supposed accomplished. Then, if no antagonistic idea [Love or Belief] *neutralizes the effect of the first idea, the appropriate movements come of themselves to fill out the plan, drawn in some way by the void of its gaps. The intellect then, only represents to the activity ends to attain, that is to say, points of rest. And, from one end attained to another end attained, from one rest to another rest, our activity is carried by a series of leaps, during which our consciousness is turned away as much as possible from the movement going on, to regard only the anticipated image of the movement accomplished.* [325]

This ability to visualize a result also explains the quantum jumps in learning skills. In learning to type, for example, one first visualizes the location of the keys; then, as the neural connections are strengthened through repetition, he learns to visualize the letters appearing on the page, and his speed jumps; finally he visualizes whole words on the page, and again, his speed jumps.

The power of ideation is obviously unique to the human, and not a capacity of the social animal. The language of the brain consists of pictures and symbols, and, unlike the animal, "I" can create and manipulate pictures and symbols in my Consciousness; "I" can direct my attention. The animal's attention is always directed, his pictures created for him. His consciousness is only occupied by stimuli from the world, from his SA-Needs or instincts, or by the literal pictures and symbols from his memory. He cannot, as the person can, call up into his Center of Consciousness any factor, or combination of factors from his Memory and *think* about them. The animal must see a tree, or need one, to visualize it. The person can visualize a tree at will.

Again, from Bergson's *Creative Evolution*,

Thus, the recollection of the same spectacle probably modifies in the same way a dog's brain and a man's brain, if the perception has been the same; yet the recollection must be very different in the man's consciousness from what it is in the dog's. In the dog, the recollection remains the captive of perception; it is brought back to consciousness only when an analogous perception recalls it by reproducing the same spectacle, and then it is manifested by the recognition, acted rather than thought, of the present perception much more than by the actual reappearance of the recollection itself. Man, on the contrary, is capable of calling up the recollection at will, at any moment, independently of the present perception. He is not limited to playing his past life again; he represents it and dreams it. [198]

Finally, since ideation is the process whereby the "I" brings words, ideas, pictures, symbols, into the Center of Consciousness, this faculty alone would explain the person's transcendence of the animal's capabilities, since this represents our ability both to *think* and to *create*.

But people have three more unique and equally significant powers:

The "I"-Faculty of Knowing

This is where we derive most of our power, experience many of our greatest satisfactions, and suffer one of our gravest errors, in our capacity to Know. All "I"-Knowing is metacognition (p.37); it is Wilber's "direct, non-conceptual, immediate" Knowing. It is seemingly *inerrant* Knowing.

The power in the "I"-Knowing faculty lies in the fact that every act of "I"-Knowing creates a corresponding wiring of my reticular formation, and becomes a "fact" or a self-fulfilling prophecy. The problem arises because in my need to Know, "I" eagerly attribute "I"-Knowledge to—i.e., believe—many things "I" don't Know; and each of these beliefs also becomes a fact or a prophecy. Most of the problems in our lives arise not from what we Know, but from what we think we Know, i.e., what we believe.

Now beliefs come in two categories:

We believe certain things are true; and,
We believe certain things will happen.

The first are *static* beliefs, the second are *dynamic* beliefs. Let's look at each type in turn.

Static Beliefs

Static beliefs are those which reside in the Love/Belief System as "facts," and represent the laws of our life, the programs which shape our percept selections, evaluations, and judgments, and in the mature person, their numbers are astronomical. The "I"-Need to Know causes it to soak up static beliefs like a sponge, or a vacuum cleaner—the Love/Belief System is its bag. The "I" draws static beliefs into the Love/Belief System by the thousands, until it contains, according to Rokeach, possibly hundreds of thousands of beliefs. Think of it: to acquire 100,000 beliefs requires adding 14 beliefs a day for 20 years! Polanyi points out that even doubt is a belief, and the only way one can stop believing is to stop thinking. Even the disbeliefs which Rokeach has noted are automatically and unconsciously adopted with every belief—disbeliefs which are not simply a mirror image of our beliefs: our belief in democracy engenders disbeliefs in communism, socialism, monarchy, etc.— these too are beliefs. So we can see the tremendous rate at which static beliefs, including doubts and disbeliefs, pour into our Love/Belief Systems.

This avaricious acquisition of beliefs led Joseph Jastrow to conclude that "the mind is a belief-seeking, rather than a fact-seeking apparatus." But of course it is the "I" which is seeking—the mind is only its store-house and computer. And the "I" is seeking facts or knowings, but confuses them with beliefs. To the "I", firm beliefs are facts; and in its need to Know, the "I" does become a "belief-seeking apparatus."

It seems obvious, however, that the "I" is not trying to store up facts or beliefs. The satisfaction to the "I" is in the Knowing, or discovering, or belief-acquiring act itself. For the "I", education *is* ecstasy.

It is also obvious that the "I"'s selection of its static beliefs is neither entirely voluntary nor rational. Many of our beliefs were adopted long before we could even communicate, let alone reason—therefore never even verbalized; some beliefs are forced on us; some are accepted simply because they come from significant others; a great many are accepted without a full understanding of their ramifications; and many represent gross generalizations—we take in the bath water with the baby. This is especially the case with our unacknowledged doubts and disbeliefs. And many are adopted simply as a result of a temporary circumstantial pleasure or pain. Mentally or physically abused or neglected children, for example, must adopt many erroneous beliefs simply to survive their childhood without insanity or suicide; but the beliefs are wired and their effects persist long after they have served their purpose.

However, in spite of the above, there is some logic in the "I"'s selection of most of its beliefs. Their acceptance often results from our interpretations of our experiences, or, where direct experience is lacking, because of their apparent agreement with, or contributions to, the satisfactions or prevention of deprivation of the SA-Needs, or because of their compatibility with other Elements already present in the Love/Belief System. Inconsistent or conflicting beliefs are rejected because they give rise to cognitive dissonance, one of the major causes of anxiety. Thus, to preserve the consistency of our Love/Belief Systems, erroneous beliefs beget other erroneous beliefs, and prevent the acceptance of more valid beliefs. When incompatible beliefs are forced on us, they must either be repressed, or they must be *isolated*.

Therefore in spite of the "logic" involved, many of our beliefs are not very rational. Unfortunately, there is almost no limit to which we can stretch the Love/Belief System to accommodate beliefs which, even by the remotest stretch of the imagination, can be seen to somehow contribute to our SA- Needs, or to be consistent with other, even subconscious, Elements in the Love/Belief System, and to reject beliefs which are not consistent with those Elements.

Now although our static beliefs number in the thousands, most of them are inconsequential beliefs, and therefore do not seriously affect our judgment or our behavior. Only those beliefs with an emotional or affective component find an influential place in our Love/Belief Systems.

Specifically, our most significant static beliefs are, 1) those which constitute the self-image, our roles, our beliefs about what we are, the "I am _____" beliefs. As Maltz and Assagioli have proposed, our lives are dominated by our beliefs about ourselves. (It is then, by changing these beliefs, that we can most significantly alter our lives.)

Other significant beliefs are, 2) those related to our major Loves: Love of our lives, our families, our countries, etc., 3) beliefs which constitute our world view, our cosmology, our religion, 4) beliefs about significant others— parents, siblings, spouse, etc., 5) beliefs about people in general, 6) beliefs about the SA-Needs: dominance, acceptance, sex, erotic love, etc. 7) beliefs about life and death, 8) beliefs about the future, what we expect, (static beliefs about the future, what we expect, tend to act as dynamic beliefs; which is why they become self-fulfilling prophecies), and 9) beliefs about God.

In general terms then, the only significant static beliefs, doubts and disbeliefs are all of those—but only those—which are related to our SA-Needs or our major Loves, Beliefs, Values, Needs, Desires, or Fears. Beliefs not so related must be considered as unimportant or inconsequential.

Since every significant belief is related to the SA-Needs or one or more of our significant Loves, Beliefs, Values, or Needs, this helps explain why we are so compulsive about maintaining our beliefs.

The reason for the compulsive defense of our beliefs—the "hardness of our hearts"—is that the Love/Belief System must be seen as a series of structures or clusters, each significant belief being interrelated to as many as hundreds of others. For example, our Love of our bodily life is only the root of a gigantic "bush" of beliefs, which grows hundreds of branches, as it acquires throughout its life, beliefs which appear either to help protect our lives, or are compatible with beliefs which protect our lives. Belief in diet, exercise, regular check-ups, safety first, etc., etc., are just a few of the beliefs we acquire which are ancillary to, or supportive of, our Love of our physical lives. So too, our other major Loves and Beliefs each generate hundreds of related beliefs. An attack on any significant belief threatens the entire structure of Elements to which it is related. It is a rare belief that doesn't have some connection with protection of our lives, our self-image, our reputation, or something equally important, and which therefore must be defended at almost any cost. If the structure threatened is significant enough, our "world" is in jeopardy and our sanity is at stake. It is no wonder then, that we come to rigidly protect the status quo in our Love/Belief Systems.

As we have seen, every belief, doubt, and disbelief is taken for fact, and actually modifies the brain—rewires the reticular formation—to interpret all communications autonomically in accordance with that belief. Each belief becomes a *law* of our existence, with a life and a will of its own. Its interpretations of our perceptions become part of the very fabric of our lives, the furniture and woodwork of our habitats, bits and pieces of the *ground* of our world.

Therefore, as we shall see in chapter 10, each time "I" adopt a significant static belief, "I" am, in effect, appointing a Deputy-Governor in my Love/Belief System, a Deputy-Governor with both the responsibility and the capability 1) to pick up on all relevant percepts; 2) to repress those contrary to the belief and to speed those compatible with that belief to my Center of Consciousness, and 3) to generate mental and physical Response Impulses to all external and internal stimuli, responses "appropriate" to that belief.

By the time the "normal" person reaches maturity he has adopted hundreds—perhaps thousands—of significant conscious and subconscious beliefs, doubts, and disbeliefs, thereby automating the great majority of his thoughts, actions, and emotions into conditioned responses, and eliminating 99+% of the world's stimuli from his consideration.

> *For this people's heart is waxed gross, and their ears are dull of hearing, and their eyes they have closed; lest at any time they should see with their eyes, and hear with their ears, and understand with their heart, [!] and be converted, and I should heal them.*
> —MATTHEW 13:15

Dynamic Beliefs

These are beliefs about the future, something which will happen, and are the means by which we act. As Bergson intimates (p.72), "I" do not will the action; "I" visualize, believe, and commit myself to a result, in order to act.

Perhaps the best way to prove this is by the example of post-hypnotic suggestion. For example, the hypnotist plants the belief that one hour after coming out of hypnosis, I will feel chilled and put on my coat, and this dynamic belief forces me to do exactly that.[1]

Now it is neatly apparent that "I" act the same way, only "I" plant the belief myself. The mental activities which result in action are not represented by the words, "'I' will to go to the store;" but rather, "'I' believe I will be at the store." When this belief is accompanied by a vision of myself at the store, and a commitment to get there, my mind/body then follows through automatically with all the necessary actions to get me there, to fulfill, or actualize, the vision/belief/commitment. Human powers of action derive, not from our will to do something, but rather from the "I"'s ability to visualize a result, to believe it will be realized, and commit oneself to its attainment.

Static beliefs then, powerfully participate in the RAS determination of Response Impulses to external or internal stimuli signals traveling "up" to our consciousness, as well as to the evaluation and modification of those same Response Impulses, or acts of will, traveling "down" to the muscles which will enact them. Dynamic beliefs, on the other hand, are those planted in the Love/Belief System, by the RAS Response Impulses and/or the "I" (or the

---

[1]   Incidentally, we see here that a belief can be more powerful than a commitment. In this example, the belief that a certain result will obtain engenders the commitment (is the commitment?), whereas a commitment contrary to a significant belief will always tend to be thwarted in its accomplishment.

hypnotist), which generate their enactment.

This explains why we fail to accomplish so many things we try to do. Our creative dynamic beliefs are opposed by conscious and subconscious Loves and Beliefs already firmly in place in the Love/Belief System, and somehow, it just doesn't get done. Our intentions are *displaced*.

Since belief in anything with which we have no direct experience requires language, it is obvious that, except in the case of instinctive languages, e.g., the bee's ability to communicate the location of nectar, the social animal's "beliefs" consist only of his memories. The animal is not capable of inferring beliefs from his experiences; his memory contains only the raw experiences. The human's ability to generalize and infer beliefs from his experiences, thereby adopting beliefs which arise solely from his imagination, or from the reports of others, is one of his greatest and most consequence-laden powers.

The "I"-Faculty of Loving

Now "I"-Love, defined as a function, is not an emotion or feeling; rather it is a *decision* to devote one's time, energy, attention, etc., to a purpose, activity, or person. Therefore "I"-Love can also be seen as a dedication, or a commitment, or an investment, of oneSelf. All the saints agree that the true act of Love is not an emotion, but a decision to devote, dedicate, commit, or invest, one's time, energies, and concern to a person or a purpose. If "I" devote myself to another's welfare, that is an act of Love; but if "I" devote myself to his downfall, that is also an act of Love. But now "I" don't Love him, "I" Love the idea of his demise. In short then, any devotion, dedication, commitment, or investment of our time and concern to any person or purpose, is seen to be an act of "I"-Love.

In *The Art of Loving*, Erich Fromm enumerates the common elements in all forms of love as care and concern, responsiveness, respect, and knowledge. These are the characteristics of true, unpossessive, unconditional Love, and can readily be seen to require a devotion or dedication or a commitment of oneself. This is obviously not the type of love experienced when one "falls in love" with a member of the opposite sex. As M. Scott Peck says in *The Road Less Traveled,* the human propensity to fall in love is a biological trick (now thought to be a combination of lust and dopamine) nature plays on all social animals in order to perpetuate the species. Observing social animals during the mating season, it is obvious that they almost certainly experience the same basic emotions and drives that humans do.

But—and here's my candidate for one of humankind's greatest problems—in the person, SA-love always invokes, and is compounded by, "I"-Love. It is innately and uniquely human to Love the experience of biological falling-in-love. Everyone Loves love. (And, since erotic love is always possessive, expects that "possession" of the loved one will certainly provide them with lifelong happiness.)

But if "I"-Love consists of care and concern, responsiveness, respect, and knowledge, then, conversely, we must be said to Love things with regard to which we exercise those attitudes. Therefore, the person who devotes himself to everything connected with professional football, must be said to *Love* football. He literally gives himself to the game. And this is "I"-Love, different from biological falling-in-love. It is not an emotion, but rather a decision (albeit perhaps, an unconscious, even involuntary, decision) to give, commit, devote oneself, to something beyond, or outside of, oneself. It is not a needing love, it is a giving Love—in Maslow's terms, B-love, not D-love.

As noted, all female social animals have an instinctive "mother-love," to care for their young unpossessively and unconditionally; but this too, is a biological trick nature plays on us in order to perpetuate the species: a release of large amounts of prolactin and oxytocin in the mother, hormones which it has been said would cause the wildest animal in the jungle to start mothering everything in sight, including a rock![2] But the ability to Love something other than one's own child unpossessively and unconditionally, must be a uniquely human power, a power of the "I".

So pure "I"-Love represents a devotion of oneself to a person or a purpose. Unpossessive Love consists of care and concern, responsiveness, respect, and knowledge exercised on behalf of the purpose, without regard to possessing the love-object, or for any return which might result from the exercise of that Love. Unconditional Love is Love exercised without regard for the merits or response of the Love-object.

Unpossessive, unconditional Love represents a decision to devote oneself to exercising care and concern, responsiveness, respect, and knowledge toward a person or a purpose, without concern for its merits, or any expectation of reward or response for that Love. Obviously, if we really understood all the ramifications of these attitudes, and were honest with ourselves, most of us

---

[2]   But when the hormones wear off, female social animals raised without mothers refuse to mother their offspring, proving that continuing mother-love is due to social learning, and in the human, to social learning *and* "I"-Love towards the child.

would have to admit that we really have very few unpossessive, unconditional Loves—and many of those we do have are not beneficent, but simply the addictions referred to earlier, e.g., professional football! And yet it is only in the exercise of this kind of Love that the human finds fulfillment.

From Thomas Merton:

> *The freedom that is in our nature is our ability to love something, someone besides ourselves, for the sake, not of ourselves, but of the one we love. There is in the human will an innate tendency, an inborn capacity, for disinterested love. This power to love another for his own sake is one of the things that makes us like God, because [it] is the one thing in us that is free from all determination. It is a power which transcends and escapes the inevitability of self-love.* [UMSSM]

And the beautiful argument of the saintly Fénelon:

> *You know by practical experience what it is to waste away for lack of an inner life fed by love. A man becomes lifeless and without heart directly that he is without the indescribable something which sustains, upholds, renews him hour by hour.*
>
> *All that which the mad lovers of this world say in their frenzy is literally true after a fashion. To be without love is not to live, and to love feebly is rather waste than growth. All the wildest passions by which men are led away are but true love which has strayed from its rightful sphere. God has made us to live through Him and His love. . . .We must love.*
>
> *But then, what will you love? That which does not really love you, which is not loveable, which you can no more grasp than a shadow? What will you love in the world? Men who are jealous, and fume with vile envy if you are satisfied? What will you love? Hearts as hypocritical in things of this world as the devout are accused of being in religious things? What will you love? A worldly dignity which may slip from you, and can give you no real comfort if you obtain it? . . . What will you love? This body of clay which fetters our reason, and subjects the soul to present sickness and approaching death? What then? Will you love nothing? Will you drag on a lifeless existence rather than love God Who loves you, Who seeks your love, and would have you be wholly His, only*

that He may give Himself to you? Do you fear that you should lack
aught, possessing such a treasure? Do you not believe that the infinite
God can fill and satisfy your heart? [LMW:117]

Our need to Love, to give ourselves, explains our susceptibility to the
demands of the cults; why most women have willingly accepted subordinate
positions in marriage, then given themselves to their children, then to religion
(or to God); and why men, relegated to the dominant role, must always seek
causes, even those involving risk of life itself—we need absolute causes. I read
about a man who never had a happy day until Germany declared war on the
United States. He had finally found something absolute to Love, an impeccable
cause to which he could devote himself.

So Becker concludes that "our central calling is the heroic." It is not.
Our central calling is what Becker himself calls (but seems to disregard) our
"universal motive of Agape-merger." Even cult- and mob-psychology are acts
of "I"-Love: a conviction that the group's purposes represent an absolute cause
to which one can give himself wholly, often sacrificing his deepest sensibili-
ties—even, as in Jonestown, his life. As Keith Harrary, who interviewed cult
members, includ-ing some Jonestown survivors, reports:

> . . . *although the specific details of their belief systems and activities*
> *varied considerably, those who became involved in cults had a fright-*
> *ening underlying commonality. They described their experiences as*
> *finding an unexpected sense of purpose, as though they were becoming*
> *a part of something extraordinarily significant that seemed to carry them*
> *beyond their feelings of isolation and toward an expanded sense of*
> *reality and the meaning of life. . . Most of us don't think of ourselves*
> *as the kind of person who could ever possibly become embroiled in a*
> *cult like the Peoples' Temple. We are not at all correct in that assump-*
> *tion.* [Psychology Today, Mar. 92]

But if giving ourselves is a major need, why are we so chary of doing
it? Probably because each of us, early in life, has met with the negative and
embarrassing experience of giving ourselves to someone—which we experience
as placing a part of our very Selves at their disposal—expecting that such a
great gift, if not reciprocated, would at least be appreciated, only to find that
it wasn't. But this part of our Selves is not recovered—it has been *discarded.*
Or, we give ourselves to causes that proved unworthy or unattainable and come

to believe that a "total giving of ourselves" leads only to humiliation or disappointment. So most of us seek things which are "safe" to Love, or find our fulfillment elsewhere.

But some become psychopaths,[3] developing a bitter hatred of people because their Love—however misguided or crudely expressed—has been spurned. All hatred is the result of frustrated Love. Hell, indeed, hath no fury like a person scorned: whose possessive Love for a person or thing—like the Bible or the Koran—has been discarded, demeaned, or its object threatened.

So "I"-Love, expressed as a possessive Love, or with the expectation of being appreciated or requited, is a perversion of the "I"'s natural need to Love unpossessively— "true love strayed from its rightful sphere." Many who cherish their reputations as loving persons love possessively or expectantly, and are not Loving at all. (The pertinent question asked of wannabe volunteers at Pace Institute [pps. xi,87] is: "Do you see yourself helping others, or just others being helped?")

Also, by virtue of our SA-Needs and our materialistic society, our multiplicity of sublimated orders of superiority, we all tend to confuse the Joy of Loving something with the joy of possessing it. The "I" is capable of Loving anything, God, people, things, even ideas. What happens is that "I" learn to Love (devote myself to) possessing things or people who appear to contribute to the satisfaction of my SA-Needs or my other Loves, Values, and Needs. And it is these possessive Loves that generate most of my emotions or feelings.

> **Every possessive Love gives rise to a *desire* for**
> **the Love-object when we have it not, an *envy* of**
> **those who have it, a temporary *joy* when we attain it,**
> **coupled with a *fear* of its loss, and a *fear* and/or *hatred***
> **of those who threaten it or our possession of it.**

Possessive Love is an oxymoron—it is not Love at all. It is a perversion of the "I"-Need to Love unconditionally, unpossessively. Its care, concern, responsiveness, and respect for the Love-object are dependent on possessing it. When our Love is diminished because the Love-object is no longer ours, we can be sure that it was a possessive Love, or a desire. The O. J. Simpson

---

[3]   **Psychopathology**: a mental disorder in which an individual manifests amoral and antisocial behavior, *lack of ability to love or establish meaningful personal relationships,* extreme egocentricity, failure to learn from experience, etc.

case is a classic example of the manic hatred which can result from the loss of a strong possessive Love. After he was acquitted, Simpson said, "Even if I did this, it would have to have been because I loved her very much ..." !

Thomas Merton explains,

The image of God in man—the openness to love, the capacity for total consent to God in Himself and in others—remains indestructible. But it can be buried and imprisoned under selfishness. The image of God in man is not destroyed by sin but utterly disfigured by it. To be exact, the image of God in man becomes self-contradictory when its openness closes in upon itself, when it ceases to be a capacity for love and becomes simply an appetite for domination or possession: when it ceases to give and seeks only to get. . . In monastic terms: the inclination to love, which is at the core of man's very nature as a free being is turned in on itself as its own object and ceases to be love. [MTAR:x]

So every possessive Love is an *attachment.* The "I" is identified with, and therefore attached, to the objects of all of its possessive Loves, and those of all of its other Loves, Values, or Needs which are related to those Loves. Each possessive Love has modified the reticular formation, and thereby acquired a life of its own, and a will of its own. And it is these collective attachments which prevent the "I" from soaring to communion with God.

The soul that is attached to anything, however much good there may be in it, will not arrive at the liberty of divine union. For whether it be a strong wire rope or a slender and delicate thread that holds the bird, it matters not, if it really holds it fast; for, until the cord be broken, the bird cannot fly. So the soul, held by the bonds of human affections, however slight they may be, cannot, while they last, make its way to God. [CW:97]

—St. John of the Cross

Therefore, the "I" is best seen as a seeker of objects, people, or even ideas, which it can Love unpossessively, unconditionally. Possessive or conditional Love is a perverted Love which generates corresponding desires, envies, temporary joys, and permanent fears and hates. But the Bible tells us, "perfect love casts out all fear." It also casts out desire, envy, and hatred.

In the final analysis, "I"-Love, directed toward God and our neighbor as unpossessive, unconditional care and concern, responsiveness, respect and knowlege, is as we have seen, not an emotion, but an attitude, or "way of being" in the world. But practiced not to improve our image or our self-image, but because it is the *only completely fulfilling human activity.* The practice of perfect "I"-Love is, like Virtue, its own reward.

In the perfect Love of God and our neighbor, the saints are urging us to ascend with them into "The Freedom of the Will of God," the freedom Christ promised His followers, the freedom of the Kingdom of God, above all Desires and Fears, into the "peace which passes understanding."

Again, the power of self-commitment—"I"-Love—is a uniquely human faculty, one not shared with the social animal. The animal is committed by any Response Impulse strong enough to cross the Enact Level; an impulse which is always the autonomic resultant of external, physiological, or bio-sociological Stimuli acting on his Instincts, Memories, and operant SA-Needs. But the person can commit himself; as noted earlier, even the simple act of postponing a meal when one is hungry is a commitment enacted by the "I", a commitment impossible to the social animal.

The difference between the commitments of a child and a social animal can be clearly seen, for example, in the case of reaching for an object and being restrained by the mother from completing the act. The animal's "commitment" is an autonomic Response Impulse, and is simply replaced by another stronger signal to stop the action. He has no investment in the act. (There is no investing "he.") As a result, he is simply puzzled by the conflicting signals. But the child's "I" is invested in the act. His "I" has enacted a commitment to pick it up, and it is the (Gestalt) *interruption* of this Self-commitment which causes the rage and angry tears so often seen in frustrated children, emotions never, to my knowledge, manifested in any young social animal.

This "I"-Need to exercise the faculty of Love, to commit ourselves, and fulfill those commitments without interference from others, causes many of us to consider freedom as our primary value, even ahead of happiness (p. 98).

The "I"-Faculty of Deciding"

The determinists and behaviorists have been trying to explain away free will for centuries and have failed. Granted, most of us make what we grandiosely call our "decisions," from an artificially restricted number of options, since we are obviously limited to Response Impulses generated by our Love/Belief Systems, or "I"-initiated responses based on a consensus of the Elements in our Love/Belief Systems. Therefore our behavior does tend to consist of rubricized, habituated, or conditioned responses. But "I" can control the SA-Needs, and choose the Loves and Beliefs which determine my thoughts, emotions, and behavior, and therefore, in the final analysis, have free will.

This new paradigm at last resolves the age-old question of free will. The answer to the question "Do we have free will in the determination of our thoughts, emotions, and behavior?" depends entirely on whether we are speaking of short-range or long-range. As we have seen, our immediate Response Impulses are determined pre-consciously by the RAS with reference to the Memory, the operant SA-Needs, and all the Elements in our Love/Belief Systems, usually subject to only a cursory review by the "I". And even our considered, thoughtful, willful responses can only be determined by a consideration of the conscious Love/Belief System Elements—subject, of course, to powerful insidious influences from subconscious Elements.

Therefore most of us have little or no free will over our immediate responses, except in those rare cases when the Love/Belief System resolution of a given stimulus is equally balanced between two or more alternative responses, and "I" can choose between them. Long-range, however, people do have free will in their ability to bring the SA-Needs under control of the "I", and to change, adopt new Loves and Beliefs.

The behaviorists are correct in considering humans as stimulus/response organisms. But what they don't seem to understand is that what we respond to and how we tend to respond, are determined by the RAS with reference to our memories, our operant SA-Needs, and all of our self-adopted Loves and Beliefs and their concomitant Desires and fears. Thus they disregard both the programs and the programmer. Granted, we have no free will in the determination of our immediate mental, emotional, and behavioral Response Impulses. But that does not mean we do not have free will; it only means that our free will is one step removed from our thoughts, actions, and emotions in the decision-making process. It lies in the power of the "I" to control the SA-Needs, to abrogate or modify our Response Impulses, and, more basically, to choose the Loves and Beliefs which are determining our Response Impulses and most of our thoughts, emotions, and behavior.

Putting it another way, except for the SA-Needs and the "I"-Needs, the only factors inhibiting the free person's free will are the Loves and Beliefs in his Love/Belief System, each of which represents a previous exercise of the "I"'s free will in adopting that Love, Belief, Value, or Need. Once chosen, each of our Loves and Beliefs severely restricts—practically negates—the "I"'s powers in future decisions on matters relevant to its object. But we do have free will in our ability to bring the SA- Needs under control of the "I", and to change the Loves and Beliefs and their concomitant Desires and Fears which are determining our thoughts, behavior, and emotions. We must simply devote ourselves, not to changing our behavior or superficial beliefs, as the behaviorists and cognitivists would have us do, but to changing the fundamental Loves and Beliefs which determine our cognitions and our behavior (see pps. 159-160). At least potentially in each person, the "I" can recover its sovereignty, and with it, his free will.

I'm not underestimating the difficulty of controlling the SA-Needs, or changing one's Loves and Beliefs; we simply must learn how to harness the awesome powers of the "I" in doing it. And anyway, the difficulties should not dissuade us from concentrating all of our attention on the *causes* of our psychological, sociological, and spiritual aberrations, rather than studying such extraneous things as our dreams, or our childhood experiences, or our feelings (except of course, as a means of identifying, by tracing them back to, the Loves and Beliefs which cause them). It seems to be the inherent nature of people to give up almost all of their decision-making power, and therefore their free will, to the self-adopted conscious and subconscious Elements in their Love/ Belief Systems. But each child is born with free will, and adults can, by gaining control over their SA- Needs, and by eliminating or changing Elements in the Love/Belief System, recover it.

So all human actions can be seen to be of three kinds, or combinations thereof: 1) Autonomic physiological responses; 2) "Conditioned" Response Impulses generated by the Love/Belief System, Response Impulses either assented to by the "I", or which are so powerful they are enacted autonomically, without the approval of, or even in opposition to, the "I"; and 3) Conscious willful, deliberate, *executive* actions, initiated by the "I"-Faculties of Visualizing, Believing, and Loving—deciding to commit its mind/body to the fulfillment of the Vision.

Obviously, the great majority of our reactions: thoughts, behavior, and emotions, are the result of the second method—the "I" thoughtlessly assenting to Response Impulses emanating from the Love/Belief System. Very seldom are most of us operating in our creative capacity, visualizing, believing and committing ourselves to a significant accomplishment or a change in our lives.

But in our voluntary acts, we have many *levels* of devotion or commitment. If I commit myself to going to the store, but a better idea occurs to me en route, I immediately change that commitment. Every commitment we make has implicit limits beyond which we feel free not to honor it. Those limits are determined in each case by the Love/Belief System, which continuously monitors our actions and environment, and, operating with hundreds of instantly *self-actuating priority interrupts,* automatically shifts our focus whenever an operant SA-Need or significant Love/Belief System Element is being placed in jeopardy or offered an opportunity for fulfillment or enhancement. (Thus Babe Ruth is said to have left his stalled car standing in the middle of the street when a passing female motorist offered him a ride to her apartment.)

But it is in our power of *unlimited* Love, to devote, or dedicate, or commit ourselves without reservation, as in, "I'm going to do this if it kills me," that we move into the capacity of creator. As stated earlier, "Whatever one Visualizes, Believes, and Loves, becomes true in that person's life, and comes into existence, provided only that it does not conflict with something else that he or others Visualize, Believe, and Love." Many books have been written on the power of human belief; and, more and more, psychologists are becoming aware of the power in visualization of a result. But many proponents of these principles have ignored the third, and also essential ingredient in human creative powers, the faculty of Love, the necessity of devoting or dedicating or committing oneself, of making a decision to be willing to do whatever is necessary to bring about the desired result.

It's often said that the great majority of us live our entire lives using only about ten percent of our total mental and creative powers. The reason, we see now, is that we are not committed to anything, or we are concurrently committed to a hundred incompatible things just as strongly. When we do commit ourselves to a single purpose, clearly visualize, and believe in the result, we become physical, mental, or social giants in that endeavor.

Item: Reverend John R. Erwin committed himself to spending the rest of his life if necessary to get the support he needed to build a school for inmates inside Chicago's Cook County Jail, and two years later, against impossible odds, the famous Pace Institute was opened.

Item: Earl Nightingale dedicated himself to earning enough money to retire at age 35, and was able to do so.

Item: A Michigan man saw a boy who was pinned under an 1800 lb. culvert pipe, committed himself to saving the boy's life, and, as he said later, "went over and picked it up," (one end = 900 lbs.) high enough to free the boy!

Item: In March, 1955, having earned only $450, I dedicated myself to earning $9,000 that year, and it took my Deputy-Governors six weeks to show me how to do it. I earned $9,238.88. (And, in 1940 I vowed to someday put together an encyclopedia of human irrationalities, initiating the life-long search which led to this book.).

Another instructive example of this power is Barbara B. Brown's discovery of the individual's ability to control the firing of a single nerve in his body, by simply willing its distinctive trace to appear on a cathode ray tube to which it is connected; a feat which she says is completely beyond the realm of any known physiological capability, and which, she admits, perhaps restores perforce to psychology the concept of "will." [NMNB:Ch.5] (Well duuuh!)

Again, one day "I" made up my mind that I was going to fix an electrical outlet in the house, a job I had been putting off for weeks, mainly because I didn't know how to do it. I was a little angry at myself, and swore that if I didn't do anything else that day, I'd get it fixed before the sun went down. Then I had breakfast and relaxed for a few minutes, but within an hour from making that decision, I found myself with a book in my hand, open to the page that showed how to do the job.

Hypnosis proves that our subconscious retains practically everything we've ever seen, heard, or even thought about. For example, subjects under hypnosis can actually "read off" the license plate numbers of a car with which they were involved in an accident—obviously something they don't consciously remember. But when we make a decision, i.e., adopt a belief that something will happen, clearly visualize the result, and mentally commit ourselves to being willing to do whatever is necessary to make it happen, then, provided it is not in conflict with any of our static Loves and Beliefs, all of our Deputy-Governors, conscious and subconscious, go to work automatically— literally make us into a one-purpose automaton—to bring about the desired result in the quickest and most efficient way.

In this sense, American science and industry visualized, believed, and committed themselves to putting a man on the moon, obviously starting with the visualization of a man walking on the moon with the means to return to earth, then working backwards to develop the necessary components to fulfill the vision. Hitler visualized, believed, and devoted himself to a thousand year Reich, and almost conquered Europe. Amundsen visualized, believed, and dedicated himself to being the first to the South Pole. And Christ visualized, believed, and consecrated Himself to doing the will of God.

The examples could be multiplied infinitely. We only unleash our magnificent (omnipotent?) powers of mind and body when we commit ourselves to a purpose. As the great Goethe said, "When one commits oneself, even Providence begins to move." But the commitments of the normal person —commitments to longevity, to pleasure, to freedom from any mental or physical pain, discomfort, or, in many people, even effort, etc., etc., etc., are so strong and so numerous, that he has lost his power to make other serious commitments without dozens of implicit limitations, thereby rendering them completely ineffectual.

We must conclude that the complementary exercises of clear visualization, firm belief, and unlimited Love (commitment), provide the creative power in God and people. Underhill referred to this power when she said of the saints, "By such love, they think, the worlds themselves were made."

Conversely, failure to clearly visualize the result we seek, or to believe it will be achieved, *or* to make the decision to commit ourselves to its attainment, almost always results in failure to achieve the goal.

Here then, is one of the most significant conclusions to be derived from our theory:

> **People act and create best, not by willing the action,**
> **but by Visualizing, Believing, and Loving,**
> **Deciding to commit themselves to,**
> **the *result* they seek to achieve.**

So, for example, if one wishes to lose weight, he should not try to eat less, but first of all work on changing his beliefs about fat and thin and eating. He should adopt the static beliefs: "I have a tendency to overeat;" and "Fat is bad, thin is good," with all the appropriate evidence he can find; and the dynamic belief, "In the very near future, I will be slim, whatever the cost." He should carry a timer which beeps hourly to remind him to visualize a slender self, repeat his litany of beliefs, and reaffirm his commitment. When these beliefs are accepted into his Love/Belief System, one day he will find himself saying, "Today is the day," and he will discover that living on a diet has become a most natural thing to do.

Of course with our new paradigm, we can see that this exercise does not remove the *cause* of his tendency to overeat, which could be due to a denial of death, an acceptance anxiety, a self-image complex, or perhaps a way to induce a "psychic numbing" of the brain in an effort to relieve the emptiness of a life without worthwhile objects of "I"-Love/Knowledge. He might find that being slim is not all that great, that his life still lacks meaning, and the basic cause might then reassert itself in a now virtually immutable tendency to over-eat, or other, possibly much more deleterious, tendencies—the last state of that man being worse than the first. Taking off weight is just one of the superficial patchwork-cures of the human malaise referred to on p. 55.

So, whether it's taking off weight, visiting someone sick or in prison, putting a man on the moon, or seeking the Kingdom of God and His righteous-ness, we see that all human creative actions are accomplished by the exercise of the "I" faculties of Visualization, Belief, and Love—a commitment of oneSelf.

But it's important to realize that Visualization, Belief, and Love do not effect the result; more often they yield only the *means* of achieving the result. Once we have visualized, believed, and committed ourselves to a goal, we must not look for the result to magically occur, but be alert for the appearance of the means of attaining the result; means—often in bits and pieces—which our Love/Belief Systems will now *autonomically* select from our memories or the environment!

All the positive thinking and positive mental attitude books boil down to this: to unleash all our powers in any endeavor, we must learn to visualize, believe, and devote ourselves. In short, Visualize, Believe, Love: Create.

I have brought myself, by long meditation, to the conviction that a human being with a settled purpose must accomplish it; and that nothing can resist a will which will stake even existence for its fulfillment.
—BENJAMIN DISRAELI

8
A New Paradigm of the Brain

Any study of the human brain must begin with where the action is, the battleground of the human mind, the Center of Consciousness (hereafter designated as C.C.) The C.C. is best thought of as the "container" of our current thoughts. Many writers believe the C.C. *is* the "I", but since "I" can control what comes into and stays out of my C.C., or even empty it entirely, the two cannot be one and the same.

Nor can the "I" be just pure consciousness, as some believe, since animals too, have consciousness. But the "I" is an *observer* of its consciousness. The person not only has concepts and percepts passing through her C.C., she Knows, can observe, those concepts and percepts (see *metacognition,* p.37).

But where in the brain *is* our consciousness? Is it localized? Or, as some believe, does the whole brain contribute to consciousness? Although researchers have been zeroing in on the reticular formation as the location of consciousness (p. 187), recently several renowned psychiatrists, psychologists, biologists, neurologists, even physicists and mathematicians, have begun promulgating the figment that, because a larger cortex is the only brain difference between humans and chimps, the cortex must be home to consciousness (chimps aren't conscious?), and also represent the "thinking" and "decision-making" portion of the brain. These speculations, coupled with brain research which is limited of necessity to analysis only on neuronal, molecular, and small segmental levels, leaves them with nothing to say about the etiology of human motivation, behavior, or the vast array of well-known psychologic phenomena which can only be attributed to the activity of the brain.

Look at it this way: if beings from another planet were smart enough to get to our earth, and simply observe an automobile for a day or two without raising the hood, but listening, examining the gas, the exhaust, etc., they would undoubtedly be able to tell, *without a design of each part*, exactly what components were at work inside the car. They would know that the fuel must be vaporized, ignited, the explosion contained, and the energy transmitted to the wheels through a variable power train to the wheels. They would know that the accelerator must increase the rate of fuel vaporization and combustion, that the brake must put pressure on the wheels to slow their rotation, and so on, and so on, and so on.

Now we have been observing human behavior for three thousand years, and apparently no one seems to be trying to analyze the brain from a systems standpoint, and postulate what components must be at work "under the hood." Why? To understand their problem, just imagine the difficulty our space travelers would have in figuring out the automobile if they couldn't see the driver. They too, might arbitrarily insist there couldn't be one.

This is exactly the problem facing our evolution-theory-bound scientismists. They dogmatically insist there cannot be "a ghost in the machine," a non-physiological element in the human, a homunculus, a spirit, a soul; that we are just neuronal machines; and apparently assume that once they have mapped all the neurons and synapses that make up the brain, they'll understand all human behavior; exactly as our handicapped space travelers might assume that once they took the car apart and examined every piece of it, they'd understand how it consistently navigated its way through traffic.

Practically all of our contemporary brain scientists, fascinated with their fMRI and PET scans, seem to be exclusively concerned with identifying the functions of each element of the brain, as though they operate independently. They proclaim for example, that the limbic area is the "seat" of our emotions (whatever that means), physical actions are initiated by motor neurons, sensory neurons interpret our percepts, "thinking" and "decision-making" occur in the cortex, etc. But they ignore the reticular formation, which, as we shall see, is the brain's "command and control center;" the *manager* of the brain.

Looking at the brain from a systems standpoint, we all know that every complex mechanism, made up of more than two or three sub-systems—a mechanism whose sub-systems can operate in unison in a coordinated way, enabling the mechanism to accomplish a number of different tasks, like a battleship, for example—must have a "command and control center" which coordinates the functions of the sub-systems. But of course this command and control center must have immediate access to all incoming information, and immediate two-way communications—for control and feed-back—with all of the sub-systems.

Now the human body is a complex mechanism with scores of sub-systems, and its obvious "command and control center" is the brain. But the brain itself is a very complex "mechanism" with scores of subsystems. It too, must have a command and control center.

As a boy, running across the street, I was surprised by a car coming right at me. The driver said I made a leap which would have won an Olympic medal—but "I" didn't make the leap. It could only have been accomplished from a command and control center which had access to all the information available, AND access to all the muscles and body chemistry which would carry out its directives. Only a very efficient command and control center could have correctly assessed the situation, and accessed *all* the faculties of my body to generate the adrenalin, calculate the best direction to jump, plant my foot, orchestrate the actions of all the motor neurons essential to the leap, and do all this in a fraction of a second. "I" merely assented to the action.

An even more instructive example is Willie Mays' unbelievable catch over his head, running away from the ball, in the 1954 World Series. From the instant the ball left the bat, Mays became an automaton with one purpose: to get his glove to the exact place in the field where the ball would be a foot or more off the ground. Some might say that Willie Mays had programmed himelf to catch fly balls; but he was never programmed to catch *that* fly ball. That catch required the continuous, collective, graded, coordinated firing of hundreds of motor neurons, hundreds of times, with continual corrections as his eyes reported the trajectory of the ball—actions I submit, which could only have been accomplished with instantaneous control from the area where the information was being received and evaluated.

So the brain too, must have a command and control center, if it is to respond instantly in a coordinated way to the various exigencies of life. Now the reticular formation has been compared to a good secretary, who lets only important information through to our consciousness, shunting the trivial aside (pg.186). This could only be true if the "secretary" has access to *all* incoming information *before* it reaches our consciousness. And it is only the reticular formation which receives all incoming information, AND has access to all of the motor and sensory neurons (for control and feedback) to implement its responses. Only the RF could serve as our "command and control center."

The evidence is compelling that it is the reticular formation, operating through its vast two-way communications network, which evaluates and interprets our percepts, "tells" the sensory neurons which of their percepts are important (pg. 192), generates our emotions, focuses our consciousness, alters the chemistry of the body, "plays" our motor neurons like hundreds of piano keys, each with infinite gradations, etc. It is the reticular formation which operates, manages, runs the brain.

This is one of the most important conclusions of our theses, a new paradigm.of the brain:

In all sentient organisms, the reticular formation is the brain's command and control center, the *manager* of the brain. All the other elements of the brain are only its "tools;" their major functions lie in their service to the reticular formation.[1]

But where does that leave "consciousness"? Could consciousness still be centered in the cortex? Well, we know that all God's creations are marvels of efficiency and economy of design. Ideally then, our consciousness should be located as close as possible to the RF, where information first comes in and is interpreted. Is it reasonable to assume that if information comes in which is evaluated by the RF as pertinent to the person's concerns, it has to transmit an alarm all the way to the cortex? Or does it make that information immediately available to our consciousness because consciousness is in the reticular formation? When I saw a car coming at me, I can't believe my RF had to send a signal all the way to the cortex to tell me I was going to get creamed.

Of course all stimuli also go to the cortex, but the signals are scattered over the sensory neurons. Unless some segment of the cortex had access to all stimuli, and two-way access to *all* the motor neurons (the famous "binding problem"), it could neither "think," reach a "decision," nor initiate and maintain coordinated responses to the stimuli. If some area of the cortex were to reach Response "decisions," they would have to go back to the reticular formation to be implemented—a very unlikely, because inefficient, arrangement.

Consciousness must reside in the reticular formation, and therefore so does "thinking" and "decision-making."[2] (See www.HowOurBrainsWork .com)

Locating consciousness in the reticular formation, we can see that our thoughts are moved by the "I", by Stimulus/Response signals, or by association, into it: that Stimulus/Response signals come "up" through the Love/Belief

---

[1]   And indeed, since I reached this conclusion more or less independently, I was pleased to learn that two (unidentified) neuroscientists have stated: *"From modern neuroanatomy, it is apparent that the entire neocortex of humans continues to be regulated by the paralimbic regions from which it evolved."* [Lewis, et al., GTL:33]

[2]   I am deeply indebted to Professor Sebastian Grossman, Emeritus Chair of Bio-Psychology at the University of Chicago, who responded to the above argument: *"Your analysis is quite cogent and logically impeccable - 20 years ago, the only counterargument would have been the neuropsychologists' proclivity to 'localize' complex functions such as consciousness in the part of the brain that has undergone the most obvious evolutionary change. To this I would add that the reticular formation has been sadly neglected by contemporary neuroscientists, . . "*

System to the C.C.; and that "I" can call "up" ideas from the Memory and the Love/Belief System into the C.C., and "I" can send action instructions from the C.C. "down" through the Love/Belief System, to the body.

The Center of Consciousness is therefore best thought of as our "Command and Control Center," adjoining the "I"'s private office (since "I" *can* close the door), a Command Center into which her Deputy-Governors are continually sending pictures of recommended actions; and where she originates and transmits pictures to them. I'll develop this analogy further in Chapter 12.

Common introspection also teaches us that the C.C.'s purview consists of a field, similar to our field of vision. Our eyes usually focus on one aspect of the field, but peripheral vision gives us some sense of all the surrounding scenery. In the same manner, the C.C. can hold perhaps a dozen thoughts or ideas at one time, but focusing, as the eye does, on only one of them at a time.

We can also visualize the well-known "stream of consciousness" as a chain of memories, ideas, pictures, or symbols, each one entering the C.C., and pulling the next associated thought behind it, into the C.C.

Now many things go on in our mind/body systems, which never reach the C.C. Hundreds of external stimuli are responded to by the body's autonomic nervous system without recourse to the C.C. On the other hand, when the autonomic system can't handle a given stimulus, it eventually breaks through the Consciousness Level in the C.C. and we then become aware of it.

For example, if the temperature drops while I'm reading an interesting book, the autonomic system increases my blood circulation without my knowledge in order to maintain my body temperature. When the autonomic system is no longer able to sustain the body temperature, the cold signals eventually break through the Consciousness Level into the C.C., and "I" become aware that I am cold. And, as indicated earlier, by the time this Stimulus does penetrate my C.C., the Love/Belief System has already attached the Response signal, "Turn up the thermostat," to the cold signal. "I" no sooner get the cold signal, than the Love/Belief System tells me what to do about it.

We must also assume an *Enact Level* in the C.C., such that, when any S/R signal reaches a given intensity or force, it crosses the Enact Level, and the indicated Response is enacted. This is why the C.C. must be considered as a battleground. It is here that the "I" battles the S/R signals trying to cross the Enact Level. A person holding her breath, postponing a meal, or trying to resist the need for a cigarette, can be seen to be an "I" conducting a battle with the S/R signals at the Enact Level.

Now many signals reach the C.C. without crossing the Enact Level

Particularly we see this to be the case when there are multiple, differing Response signals. They are then brought to the attention of the "I" for a decision. Also, "I" can visualize many things in my C.C. without making a decision to implement them by pushing them across the Enact Level. But, by definition, when a Response signal does cross the Enact Level, my body acts.

As indicated earlier, many S/R signals have been through the senses, Memory, Love/Belief System, and the C.C. so many times that they have worn a hard-wired path—a habit or conditioned response channel—through the system, which they are now allowed to traverse almost autonomically, almost subconsciously. The "I" in this case can be compared to a guard at a gate, who, seeing the same person come in at the same time every day, eventually allows her to pass without really noticing her; may find an hour later that she doesn't remember her coming in at all.

For example, if an "itch" Stimulus and its associated "scratch" Response Impulse reach the C.C. while "I" am reading a good book, those signals must be considered to have worn a groove so deep in the Love/Belief System and C.C., that they traverse them, crossing the Enact Level, and I am forced to scratch the itch. But "I" hardly noticed the transaction.

Most of our actions must be seen to be habitual or conditioned responses. The Love, Belief, Value, Need, Desire, or Fear, which once may have served a useful purpose, and which originated the action, may have long since outlived its usefulness, but the conditioned response channel has been worn so deep that the response has become autonomic.

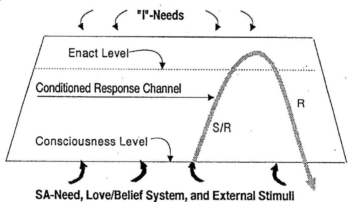

Figure 7 - The Center of Consciousness

With this brief systems analysis of the brain, we will now turn to the POWER in our lives: the Love/Belief System.

9
The Love/Belief System

Location

Taken all together, the SA-Needs and our self-adopted Loves and Beliefs, and the resultant Desires and Fears constitute the Elements of the Love/Belief System. Since the Love/Belief System can suppress and alter signals from the senses to the Center of Consciousness, and alter signals from the Center of Consciousness to the body, we must assume that the Love/Belief System resides in the mind, between the senses and the Center of Consciousness (see Figure, page 36). This corresponds to the centralized location of the reticular formation, and will enable us to explain human physical, mental, and emotional behavior.

Programs

In the following description of the "programs" of the Love/Belief System, it should be understood that all Elements in the Love/Belief System can be either conscious or subconscious, the latter including both repressed and forgotten Elements.

Although I will be listing the Love/Belief System Elements in a more or less hierarchical order, it should also be understood that almost any significant Love, Belief, Value, Need, Desire, or Fear can, at any given time, assume complete dominance over all other Elements, SA- Needs, and "I"- Needs. Most of us have a very democratic, unstable "hierarchy" of needs.

Turning now to the programs of the Love/Belief System, I have already postulated that at the very heart or base of most everyone's Love/Belief System is the Love of one's physical life, and that this is not an innate or instinctive Love, but is adopted as a result of the "I"'s will to exist, and its identification with the doomed mind/body.

In most people we would also find Love of their loved one's lives occupying a place of equal importance in their Love/Belief Systems.

Next, let's consider some other typical Loves, and here there are thousands of possibilities. One can Love anything in this world, from God or a spouse or a friend, to such things as football, sex, good (or bad) books, fame, money, power, mathematics, the idea of being first to the South Pole, one's country or political party or religion, and of course, any of an infinite combination of things.

However, it seems obvious that the most natural Loves for the "I" to adopt are those related to the SA-Needs, the self-image, the Fear of death, and the sublimated orders of Values which dominate our society. All the saints and sages agree that this is the most common dis-ease of mankind: trying to satisfy the "I"-Need to Love by devoting it to transient and temporal things.

Thus we have the "life" Lover, the food Lover, the sex Lover, the physical, or social, or political, dominance or superiority Lover, the acceptance Lover, the fame lover, the play Lover, the possessions Lover, the falling-in-love Lover, the spouse Lover, the professional parent or grandparent, the territorial Lover, the money Lover, the (narcissistic) self-image Lover, the fun Lover, the knowledge Lover, the prestige Lover, etc. Because any momentary gratification of these Loves does provide a temporary suppression—not a gratification—of the incessant and insatiable "I"-Needs, and because the gratification provided by indulging these Loves tends to wane, they usually become greatly magnified, become consuming Desires, passions, rather than just nominal Needs and Values which, when satisfied, disappear. People are the only animals which, by virtue of "I"-Love, can compound, make obsessions of, the SA-Needs, as well, of course, of any of their self-adopted Loves, Values, or Needs.

Aldous Huxley gives us a profound description of the effects of the typical person's haphazard Love-adoption or self-identification process:

> *The will is free and we are at liberty to identify our being with* [Love]
> *our selfness and its interests, regarded as independent of indwelling*
> *Spirit and transcendent God-head (in which case we shall be passively*
> *damned or actively fiendish), or exclusively with the divine within us and*
> *without (in which case we shall be saints), or finally with self at one*
> *moment or in one context and with spiritual not-self at other moments*
> *and in other contexts (in which case we shall be average citizens, too*
> *theocentric to be wholly lost, and too egocentric to achieve enlighten-*
> *ment and a total deliverance). Since human craving can never be*
> *satisfied except by the unitive knowledge of God and since the mind-*
> *body is capable of an enormous variety of experiences, we are free to*
> *identify ourselves with* [Love] *an almost infinite number of possible*

objects—with the pleasures of gluttony, for example, or intemperance, or sensuality; with money, power, or fame; with our family, regarded as a possession or actually an extension and projection of our own selfness; with our artistic or scientific talents; with some favourite branch of knowledge, some fascinating 'special subject'; with our professions, our political parties, our churches; with our pains and illnesses; with our memories of success or misfortune, our hopes, fears and schemes for the future; and finally with the eternal Reality within which and by which all the rest has its being. And we are free, of course, to identify ourselves with more than one of these things simultaneously. Thus a man can be at once the craftiest of politicians and the dupe of his own verbiage, can have a passion for brandy and money, and an equal passion for the poetry of George Meredith and under-age girls and his mother, for horse-racing and detective stories and the good of his country - the whole accompanied by a sneaking fear of hell-fire, a hatred of Spinoza and an unblemished record for Sunday church-going. [PP:40]

Add the ubiquitous denial of death and the self-image, and what honest person cannot see something of himself in this description? And each of these self-identifications (Loves) exercises its own dominating influence over our lives. In this insidious way we all fractionate and dissipate our lives, break them up into inconsistent pieces, and lose all possibility of realizing "the peace which passes understanding."

Surely it's safe to say that most people, in addition to their Love of their physical lives, have at least ten to twenty other significant Loves.

Next let's consider the category of "Values-Needs." It is not necessary to set up separate categories for our self-adopted Values and Needs. Of course we may Value some things we don't consider as Needs, so Values and needs are not identical in their nature. But they do seem to be identical in their effect on our lives, and therefore can be included in one section of the mind, identified as Values-Needs. One of my authorities for combining them is Maslow, who identified the B-Values as meta-needs. (Incidentally, Milton Rokeach perceptively notes that values can also be considered as beliefs.)

"Value" in the sense we're using it here means, "that which is held to be desirable or worthy of esteem," or which represents one of "the social principles, goals, or standards held or accepted by an individual, class, society, etc." Earlier I described the sublimation of the dominance need into dozens of other orders, symbolic of the pecking order; such things as personality, looks, physique, wealth, etc. These form many of the principles, goals, or standards of our society, and therefore represent our inherent values. The "I" gives humans the ability and the propensity to acquire, adopt, scores of values from literally thousands of possibilities.

Leonard Gordon has developed measurements of one's "personal" and "interpersonal" vocational values. The interpersonal values are: intimate support, conformity, recognition, independence, benevolence, and leadership; his "personal" values are practical minded, achievement, variety of tasks, decisiveness, orderliness, and goal orientation.

Sociologist Milton Rokeach has identified 18 "terminal" values commonly held in civilized societies. In order of importance among American college students for example, they are: freedom, happiness, wisdom, self-respect, a sense of accomplishment, mature love, family security, true friendship, inner harmony, a world at peace, a comfortable life, an exciting life, equality, social recognition, pleasure, salvation, national security, a world of beauty. The rankings vary, of course, by culture, age groups, etc. [NHV:89]

Rokeach has also identified eighteen "instrumental" values, personal characteristics which people feel are desirable, or conducive to the attainment of the terminal values. Among American college students, these are: honest, responsible, ambitious, broadminded, capable, independent, logical, courageous, intellectual, self-controlled, loving, forgiving, imaginative, helpful, cheerful, polite, clean, obedient. [NHV:90]

To which we might safely add: fair, refined, shrewd, adventurous, poised, generous, cool, competitive, consistent, tough, conscientious, etc.

Rokeach's terminal values all seem to represent ideal states or conditions, and his instrumental values represent ideal character traits. But what about the personal values which are paramount in most people's lives? Don't most people value good times? Money? Longevity? Fun? Sex? Getting even? Nice things? Winning? Good health? Popularity? Good food? Their rights? The finish on their new car? After all, anything to which one devotes much of his time, or to which he responds emotionally, must be considered as one of his values; and the list of different values for different people is endless.

And what about our possessions? Doesn't everyone value most of the things he owns? His home, his car, his job, his reputation, his Grandfather clock, his furniture, his golf clubs, his clothes, etc.? Surely the great majority of our possessions should be considered among our values. (I can just see one of Rokeach's students itemizing his values when someone drives off in his new Camaro. Then we'd see what his real values are!) As William James wrote:

It is clear that between what a man calls "me," and what he simply calls "mine," the line is difficult to draw. We feel and act about certain things that are ours very much as we feel and act about ourselves. Our fame, our children, the work of our hands, may be as dear to us as our bodies are, and arouse the same acts of reprisal if attacked. . . In its widest possible sense, however, a man's Self is the sum total of all that he can call his, [!] not only his body, and his psychic powers, but his clothes and his house, his wife and children, his ancestors and friends, his reputation and his works, his land and horses and yacht and bank account. All these things give him the same emotions. If they wax or prosper, he feels triumphant, if they dwindle and die away, he feels cast down—not in the same degree for each thing, but in much the same way for all.[1] [PP:291]

Certainly most people have at least 50 to 100 self-adopted values.

Turning now to our needs, in addition to the basic animal needs for food, oxygen, etc., children have bio-sociological needs for affection, protection, nurture, and to play and imitate others; and, as they mature, to fall in love, care for their young, and to seek acceptance (and dominance?) in their society. These are the SA-Needs we share with all social animals.

But again, the "I" gives us both the ability and the propensity to adopt many other "Needs." The average American needs his own home, three meals a day plus snacks, two or three television sets, stereo, a cell phone, two cars (and a two-car garage), a washer and dryer, a savings account, an air conditioner, modern clothes, good friends, respect, interesting work, vacations, entertainment, etc. I think it's safe to say that there must be at least fifty or more significant self-adopted needs in the Love/Belief Systems of most civilized people.

As noted earlier, each self-adopted Value and Need can be considered as a possessive Love (or Belief), and therefore generates a desire for the object, an envy of those who have it, a temporary joy when it is attained, a permanent fear of its loss, and a fear/hatred of those who threaten its loss.

Thomas Merton poignantly describes the state of a person with all these temporal Loves, Values, and Needs:

---

[1]   James has here given us an excellent description of the "inordinate attachments" of which we must dispossess ourselves if we are to Know God's love and His Peace in this life.

[Modern man] *lives not only below the level of grace, but below the level of nature—below his own humanity. No longer in contact with the created world or with himself, out of touch with reality of nature, he lives in the world of collective obsessions, the world of systems and fictions with which modern man has surrounded himself. In such a world, man's life is no longer even a seasonal cycle. It's a linear flight into nothingness, a flight from reality and from God, without purpose and without objective, except to keep moving, to keep from having to face reality.* [SC:51]

Next let's look at some typical beliefs. Most people seem to have a ready-made conscious or subconscious set of beliefs about: God, nature, men, women, children, wives, husbands, mothers-in-law, animals, nature, politicians, lawyers, doctors, policemen, movie-TV stars, Irish, English, Italians, Blacks, Whites, Orientals, Protestants, Catholics, Muslims, etc.

According to Rokeach, our total beliefs, conscious and subconscious, number in the tens—or perhaps hundreds—of thousands; but most are inconsequential beliefs. Among our most significant beliefs, according to Maltz, are those which constitute the self-image; beliefs about ourselves, our abilities, intelligence, worth, character, personality, physical prowess, appearance, etc. Our self-image can thus be seen to consist primarily of what we perceive to be our rating, or comparison with others, on the sublimated orders of values discussed above. But, as indicated earlier, perhaps the most significant and most deleterious of our self-image beliefs, the belief which most everyone takes for granted, the belief which could very well represent the fall of man, is our most basic self-image belief: "'I' am my mind/body."

In *Psycho-Cybernetics*, Maltz provides compelling evidence that our behavior and our performance are always governed and limited by our self-image, and that the self-image is much more powerful than our operant will or Desires. Where does it get this power? Not by its identification with the "I", but by its identification *as* the "I". More than anything else we confuse our "I" with our self-image, our roles: "I am a father; I am an American; I am an actor; I am a Republican; I am an Elk!" Hindus call these identifications *asmita*, and recognize them as detrimental to our spiritual development. As Assagioli says, "We are dominated by everything with which our self becomes identified." The reason, we see now, is that each of these self-identifications is an act of "I"-Love; it represents a strong affective attachment, since it represents our self-identity, it is related to our acceptance in society, and also represents how we will be remembered, therefore is intimately related to our "immortality."

And if "I" believe that I am a responsible person, then each of these self-identifications saddles me with the responsibility of fulfilling all my other beliefs about how fathers, Americans, actors, Republicans, and Elks *should* act and live. "I" come to believe that certain responses are required of me.[2] Thus our self-image becomes one of the most beloved, and therefore, powerful, factors in the Love/Belief System, second only to preservation of life, the lives of our Loved ones, and, perhaps, some other Loves.

As noted earlier, other significant beliefs are those related to our major Loves, Values, and Needs, beliefs which constitute our world-view, beliefs about significant others, people in general, God, the SA-Needs, life and death, and the future. All in all, there must be hundreds, perhaps thousands, of significant conscious and subconscious beliefs in the Love/Belief Systems of most mature people.

Turning now to our Desires and Fears, we see that these are the major outputs or products of the operations of the Love/Belief System. Desires and Fears represent a state of imbalance in the Love/Belief System; they signal a discrepancy between our perceived state or condition and one or more of our SA-Needs or Loves and Beliefs, and cause a state of tension or anxiety to permeate the Center of Consciousness.

Now since the "I"-Needs to Love and to Know do not manifest themselves in specific desires, neither do they give rise to fears. Only the "I"-Need to exist causes the aberrant fear of death.

But we have yet to distinguish between the desires and fears which are engendered by the SA-Needs and those which arise from our self-adopted Loves and Beliefs. Hunger causes a desire for food, fatigue a desire for rest, sexual urges a desire for intercourse, loneliness a desire for belongingness, etc. However, it seems that the only fears which could arise from the SA-Needs are: a fear of pain; in the child, a fear of abandonment; in the adult, a fear of rejection; and in the mother, a fear of harm to her offspring. These are the only fears the animal knows, and therefore the only ones we cannot avoid. All our other fears are the result of our possessive, self-chosen Loves and Beliefs, and ultimately, therefore, must be seen to be under our control.

As noted earlier, desires and fears which arise from the SA-Needs manifest themselves specifically in the Center of Consciousness, and subside when they are gratified/assuaged. But desires and fears which arise from our possessive Loves/Values/Needs for temporal things are, because they are objects of

---

[2]   See Karen Horney's "tyranny of the should," page 116.

possessive "I"-Love (albeit spurious objects), virtually impossible to gratify/ assuage; they become addictions, leading the individual ever further along the path to obsessive-compulsiveness in the gratification of his desires or the assuagement of his fears, i.e., hedonism or paranoia or both. The only desires and fears which arise from our unpossessive Loves and Values are for the welfare of those we Love. (See ¶ 7, p. 64)

Desires and fears fall into two categories:

> Constant, long-standing desires and fears, often arising from subconscious Love/Belief System Elements: e.g., the desire for immortality; the fear of failure; and,

> Immediate, impulsive, temporary desires and fears, arising from the operant SA-Needs or Love/Belief System Elements: e.g., the desire for food; the fear of lightning.

Now it is our operant conscious and subconscious desires and fears which determine our psychological set, what we are looking for in the world, and therefore, what we see. The Love/Belief System does not just evaluate— re-cognize—our perceptions; it also evaluates, and therefore selects, which of our perceptions are to be cognized in the first place. Except for overpowering stimuli, e.g., lightning and thunder, the only stimuli which reach the C.C are those our operant conscious and subconscious desires and fears have instructed them to look for. Our senses are always attuned to seek out only those portions of the world's stimuli which relate to our operant Desires and Fears. "It is now known that nerve signals produced by extraneous stimuli do not merely *seem* to be lessened when we concentrate, they *are* lessened." [Wooldridge: 140].

This is why the Sufis say, "We are all asleep in a nightmare of desires." We aren't seeing or experiencing the real (whole) world at all; only those few selective portions of it which relate to our operant desires and fears.

With the sheer genius which characterizes her work, the greatest of hagiographers slowly, kindly brings us to a shocking realization of our spiritual poverty with one of the most poignant questions ever penned:

> *You are enslaved by the verb "to have": all your reactions to life consist in corporate or individual demands, appetites, wants. That "love of life" of which we sometimes speak is mostly cupboard-love. We are quick to snap at her ankles when she locks the larder door: . . . The*

mystic knows not this attitude of demand. He tells us again and again, that he is "rid of all his asking;" that "henceforth the heat of having shall never scorch him more." Compare this to your normal attitude to the world, practical man: your quiet certitude that you are well within your rights in pushing the claim of "the I, the Me, the Mine;" your habit, if you be religious, of asking for the weather and the government that you want, of persuading the supernal powers to take a special interest in your national or personal health and prosperity. How often in each day do you deliberately revert to an attitude of disinterested adoration? Yet this is the only attitude in which true communion with the universe is possible. [PM:68]
—EVELYN UNDERHILL

And Desires and Fears, except those few which arise from the SA-Needs, are always the result of a discrepancy between our consciously or sub-consciously perceived condition or state, and one or more of our self-adopted, conscious or subconscious, Loves, Beliefs, Values, or Needs.

Therefore, we can change our perceptions, our emotions or feelings, and our behavior, all of which are determined almost entirely by our Desires and Fears, in two ways: either by a change in our state or condition; or by a change in the basic Loves and Beliefs which engender the great majority of our perceptions/Desires/Fears, and thereby determine our emotions and behavior. While the latter is the most difficult, it has the distinct advantage of being permanent. Of course, we can't eliminate the SA-Needs, but we can exercise the "I" in testing their minimums, and refuse to magnify them as most of us do by making them possessive Loves.

But most of us live our entire lives in anxiety, with the bovine conviction that all of our desires and fears are legitimate and appropriate, and that if only there were some changes in our external condition or state, we would be happy. But the least amount of introspection shows that desires and fears are "habits of the heart," and that whenever any of them are gratified/assuaged, others promptly arise to take their place. Peace is only attained when we are "rid of all our asking." "Nothing need change but our hearts."

Again, desires and fears come in an infinite variety. Some of the most common are fear of death, pain, disease, or injury, to ourselves or our Loved ones, and Fear of rejection, want, and failure; but most of us also have at least a dozen or so other significant personal fears, and of course, scores of desires. Obviously, then, our permanent, deep-seated desires and fears, both conscious and subconscious, exercise a constant and domineering influence over every aspect of our lives; and just one momentary, compelling desire or fear, can, in a single, thoughtless moment, bring all of our fondest aims to ruin.

On the subject of the power of our desires, I have found no more telling argument than that of William Law:

> *We are apt to think that our imagination and desires may be played with, that they rise and fall away as nothing because they do not always bring forth outward and visible effects. But indeed they are the greatest reality that we have, and are the true formers and raisers of all that is real and solid in us. All outward power that we exercise in the things about us is but as a shadow in comparison of that inward power that resides in our will, imagination, and desires. These communicate with eternity and kindle a life which always reaches either heaven or hell.* [Appeal:40]

And *The Cloud of Unknowing* teaches:

> *For heaven ghostly is as nigh down as up, and up as down; behind as before, before as behind; on one side as other. Inasmuch, that whoso had a true desire for to be at heaven, then that same time he were in heaven ghostly. For the high and the next way thither is run by desires, and not by paces of feet.* [CU:172] Beautiful?

With regard to our fears, 1 John says perfect love casts out all fear. (It also casts out most desires.) Now perfect love is unpossessive Love. It's alright to Love things, so long as we don't think of them as *ours*. Every possessive Love generates a desire for the Love-object when we have it not, an envy of those who have it, a fear of its loss when we attain it, and a fear/hatred of those who threaten it or our possession of it. And desires and fears are the elements which dominate our outlook on life. For example, the person who fears illness recognizes in himself the symptoms of every illness he hears about; and as Karen Horney has noted, the person desiring prestige evaluates everyone almost exclusively according to the prestige they enjoy.

We are all seeing and experiencing God,
the world, our neighbor, and ourselves,
through our Love/Belief Systems,
particularly through our Desires and Fears.

But "the truth waits for eyes unclouded by longing"—and fear.

So here we have the Love/Belief System—even in us average, normal, nice people, a real can of worms. It just sort of grew in us, like a garden growing wild, and now it is filled with weeds and vines and brush, all fighting with one another for a place in the sun. But this haphazardly developed Love/Belief System is the shaper of our lives, and the maker of our destinies. Everything we want from life, and everything we try to do, is largely determined by, and subject to, the Elements in our Love/Belief Systems. The "I", which started out as the Governor of our lives, has given up almost all its powers to its Deputy-Governors, its almost randomly selected Loves and Beliefs and their concomitant Desires and Fears; and in so doing has sacrificed both its power and its freedom.

In his classic Gold Record, *The Strangest Secret*, Earl Nightingale states unequivocally that, "Each of us is where he is because that is exactly where he really wants to be, whether he'll admit that or not."

Of course he's referring only to free adults, but most people disagree, saying, "I'm not where I want to be; I'd like to make more money, have more free time, travel more, have more friends, etc., etc., etc." But then ask them, in addition to these Desires, about their Fears. Honest people will admit they're afraid of death, poverty, pain, sickness, disease, failure, rejection, losing their jobs or reputations, etc. Then ask them to list some of their other Loves and Beliefs, and Nightingale's statement begins to make a lot of sense.

What he's saying is that our Love/Belief Systems are *averaging out* all of our conscious and subconscious Loves and Beliefs, Desires and Fears, and inexorably guiding us to the optimum positions in life, in society, in our professions, our income levels, our popularity, our power over others, etc., positions which will best satisfy all those Elements. And those optimum positions are right where we are! Free adults are where they are in each aspect of their lives because those positions represent the best possible average, or compromise, of all of their Loves and Beliefs.

The Love/Belief System, or RAS, the system which continuously monitors and regulates our respiration, heart rate, adrenalin levels, digestion, awareness, emotions, (even our tastes—nutritionally deprived people eat salt like candy), what we perceive and how we interpret our percepts, etc., *is the same system which regulates every aspect of our environmental, vocational, family, social, economic, and spiritual lives!*

Until we learn to live in the Present, guided by Love, we are not living—we are *being lived* **by our haphazardly acquired Loves and Beliefs and their concomitant Desires and Fears.**

Obviously then, in order to significantly and permanently improve or change our lives, we must first change the basic Loves and Beliefs which are determining every aspect of our existence.

To the extent that the theses of this book are valid, we are now learning how we have all surrendered control of our lives, and, knowing that, can now seek effective methods of improving our lives by changing our basic Loves and Beliefs, and restoring the sovereignty of the immortal "I".

Where "it" [id] was, there should become "I".
                        —SIGMUND FREUD

10
A New Paradigm of Mind

I have proposed that "mind" be redefined as a human brain, functionally, in its "input" capacity, consisting of a Memory, a Love/Belief System, or RAS, and a Center of Consciousness. We looked briefly at the C.C. in Chapter 8, and it would seem that the Memory, in both its conscious and subconscious aspects, can be considered simply the mind's "database," containing all the information the subject has ever experienced, seen, felt, known, imagined, etc.[1] Both Memory and C.C. can be seen to thus function somewhat passively in the operations of the mind. As indicated earlier (p. 93), the RAS, subject only to the "I"-Faculties, runs the brain, and through it, operates the body.

Now let's look in more detail at the machinations of the Love/Belief System as it processes data.[2]

The Love/Belief System processes information going through it in both directions, stimuli from the world, from the body and from the Love/Belief System itself, going to the Center of Consciousness, and action instructions from the Center of Consciousness to the mind/body. In processing information, the Love/Belief System can be seen to perform five functions: it 1) *Selects*, 2) *Identifies*, 3) *Evaluates*, 4) *Manipulates*, and 5) *Resolves* that data. As noted earlier, the Love/Belief System uses the amazing powers of the mind to perform these functions at speeds comparable to our best computers, at a rate of 10 trillion to 1,000 trillion bits of information per second, enabling the Love/Belief System to perform all of these functions before any external, physiological, or Love/Belief System stimuli fully penetrate the Center of Consciousness, or action instructions from the Center of Consciousness reach the muscles which will carry them out.

---

[1]   A recent book, *Memory, Brain & Belief* by Schacter and Scarry, maintains that memories can also be classified as beliefs.

[2]   For some of the current neurological evidence regarding the functions of the RAS described in this chapter, see Appendix A, and www.HowOurBrainsWork.com.

Now in the Love/Belief System's processing of stimuli from the environment, from the body, or from the Love/Belief System itself, to the Center of Consciousmess, we can discern two laws, or "If-then" computer programs which govern the process.

The Love/Belief System:

> Acts to suppress irrelevant stimuli ("Unimportant" Stimulus/Evaluation), and suppress and manipulate relevant stimuli which are incompatible with any of its conscious or subconscious Elements or their objects, but not threatening to either. ("Important/Bad/Benign" Stimulus/Evaluation)

> Acts as an accelerator, or clear channel, to stimuli which are compatible with any of its conscious or subconscious Elements or their objects, or which offer either a threat or enhancement possibility to any Element or its object. ("Important/ Good," or "Important/Bad/ Malignant," Stimulus/Evaluation)

With these two laws or programs in mind, let's look at each of the five functions of the Love/Belief System as it operates on incoming Stimuli.

Selection. Based on only the barest of subconscious identifications, the first function of the Love/Belief System is to *select* from the millions of sensory impressions reaching it only those relevant to its operant Desires and Fears, or to any major Love, Belief, Value, or Need, i.e., any stimuli which it has been programmed to consider Important. And instantly, it expands the processes of Identification and Evaluation, and suppresses all other "extraneous" signals. (See p. 188, & Wooldridge, MB:140)

Identification. The second function of the Love/Belief System is to identify each Important incoming Stimulus by comparing it with every relevant memory. And already, in this process, the Manipulations of the percept begin as the Love/Belief System tries to force it into one of its pigeonholes. Maslow cogently describes the way most "normal" people perceive the world:

> *Stereotyping is a concept that can apply not only to the social psychology of prejudice, but also to the basic process of perceiving. Perceiving may be something other than the absorption or registration*

of the intrinsic nature of the real event. It is more often a classifying, ticketing, or labeling of the experience rather than an examination of it, and ought therefore to be called by a name other than true perceiving.

For instance, it is possible in being introduced to [a person] to react to him freshly, to try to understand or to perceive this individual as a unique individual, not quite like anybody else living. More often what we do, however, is to ticket or label or place the man. We place him in a category. For instance he is a Chinaman, rather than Lum Wang who has dreams and ambitions and fears that are quite different from those of his brother. Or he is labeled as a millionaire or a member of society or a dame or a child or a Jew or a something. In other words, the person engaged in stereotyped perceiving ought to be compared. . . to a file clerk rather than a camera. The file clerk has a drawer full of folders, and her task is to put every letter on the desk into its appropriate folder under the A's or the B's or whatever. [M&P:20] (See also Orientals, etc., p. 119, and Wilson, p. 145)

So parts of the percept are pared away, and others filled in, to make it fit our pigeonholes. And this rubricizing of the identification of the percept continues the process of Evaluation of the percept.

Evaluation. As indicated, Evaluation is a continuous process. But now, since the stimuli has been evaluated as Important, begins a very sophisticated routing process, a veritable flood of signals between the conscious and subconscious sections of the Memory and the conscious and subconscious sections of the Love/Belief System to more thoroughly Evaluate the Stimulus. This is a completely free flow of information between the Memory and the Love/Belief System; millions of signals flowing back and forth in milliseconds (this shows up clearly on the new brain scan equipment) to further Evaluate the Stimulus as to whether it is Good or Bad; and, if Bad, whether it is Malignant or Benign. (Obviously, all of these Evaluations depend largely on the person's current psychological set based on the operant Desires and Fears.)

Manipulation. Next, depending on the Evaluation, the Love/Belief System begins some very significant Manipulations of the Stimulus. We'll look at these in detail after examining the fifth function of the Love/Belief System: Resolution.

Resolution. And now, if the Manipulations have not resulted in suppression of the Stimulus, the Love/Belief System refers the Manipulated/Stimulus/Evaluation simultaneously to both the Center of Consciousness (only now do "I" begin to become aware of—Know, re-cognize—the Stimulus), and back to the Memory in a search for precedents, i.e., previous successful or acceptable Responses to similar Stimulus/Evaluations.

When the Memory provides a relevant Response, the Manipulated/Stimulus/Evaluation/Response Impulse is then forwarded to the Center of Consciousness for action, following the Manipulated/Stimulus/Evaluation into the Center of Consciousness by only a fraction of a second—long before the "I" has fully cognized the Stimulus. If the Response Impulse enters the Center of Consciousness with enough force, it bursts through the Enact Level, and the person acts, involuntarily carrying out the indicated Response. If it is not that strong, or does not require immediate implementation, "I" can review the Response before allowing it to cross the Enact Level. In this way the Love/Belief System *Resolves* the Stimulus.

Now let's look in detail at the fourth function of the Love/Belief System: *Manipulation*.

In accordance with the If-then programs built into the Love/Belief System, a Stimulus/Evaluation of Unimportant—which obviously includes 99+% of our percepts—is immediately suppressed and forgotten. But a Stimulus which is evaluated as Important and Good, e.g., "I like your looks," is immediately forwarded to the Center of Consciousness without Manipulation, and to the Memory for appropriate Responses. These are the Love/Belief System Resolutions of Unimportant and Important/Good Stimuli. (Needless to say, most Good Stimuli always tend to also be evaluated as Important.)

But if an Important Stimulus is evaluated as Bad, i.e., detrimental to an operant SA-Need, Love/Belief System Element, or their objects, then the Love/Belief System must determine whether the Stimulus is Malignant or Benign, i.e., whether or not the Stimulus offers any threat to the Need, Element, or their objects on which it impinges. "I don't like your looks," is Bad/Benign; "I'm going to change your looks," is Bad/Malignant.

If the Stimulus is evaluated as Malignant, the Love/Belief System Resolution is to refer the Stimulus/Evaluation to the Center of Consciousness and to the Memory for the best precedent, the best earlier Response to the same or a similar threat, and now the combined signal, Stimulus/Evaluation/Response is then speeded to the Center of Consciousness for action.

But if the Stimulus is determined to be Bad/Benign, then, in accordance with the above laws, we begin to see the Love/Belief System performing some very fancy prestidigitation, i.e., Manipulations.

Suppression. The first Manipulation the Love/Belief System tries on a Bad/Benign Stimulus is to suppress it, prevent it from reaching the Center of Consciousness at all. It tries to reclassify the Stimulus as Unimportant, and bury it in the subconscious. When it succeeds in this endeavor, it is called *repression,* or *denial.* (See Blum, p. 144.)

Miscognition. The next thing the Love/Belief System tries to do with Bad/Benign Stimulus is distort it into something less bad. It continues the rubricizing functions; i.e., it tries to ignore certain aspects, and fill in, fabricate, other aspects in the Stimulus, more favorable to the Elements or their objects on which the Stimulus is impinging negatively.

Distraction. The Love/Belief System is aided in suppressing a Bad/Benign Stimulus by its trick of distraction; i.e., it finds other, more favorable stimuli in the environment, and rushes that into the Center of Consciousness instead!

Rationalization. This is the fourth tool the Love/Belief System uses to handle Bad/Benign news. The Love/Belief System draws out mitigating information from the Memory or from the environment, and attaches this information to the Stimulus/Evaluation (which then become Stimulus/Evaluation/Mitigating Circumstances) signals, before they are forwarded to the Center of Consciousness. "The grapes are probably sour anyway."

Isolation. Failing in the above, or even concurrently with some rationalization and miscognition, the Love/Belief System may find it necessary to allow the Stimulus/Evaluation to reach the Center of Consciousness, but be able to *isolate* its memory from the Element on which it impacted negatively.

Reaction-Formation. Failing in the above techniques, the Love/Belief System may resort to reaction-formation, forwarding a response, "It's not true, but it is awfully close to a very bad truth, and 'we' must prove it's not true, and prevent it from becoming true!"

Amnesia. The Love/Belief System can cause selective or total amnesia, forgetting the Stimulus/Evaluation, or, in extreme cases, forgetting everything.

Fainting. If the bad news is of vital importance, and often whether the bad news is Malignant or Benign, the Love/Belief System can cut off the supply of blood to the brain, causing the subject to faint, before the bad news fully registers in his Center of Consciousness.

Hysterical Blindness/Deafness. Again, with bad news of vital importance, the Love/Belief System may resort to one of the heaviest defenses in its arsenal, it can actually cause the person to stop all seeing or hearing.

These are some of the perceptual defense mechanisms in the Love/Belief System's arsenal for handling a Bad/Benign Stimulus, actually delaying and modifying the signal before it reaches the Center of Consciousness. In this respect, the Love/Belief System acts as a "shock-absorber." There is almost no limit to which the Love/Belief System will go to protect our beloved Loves and Beliefs from any derogation of either themselves or their objects. As Arieti writes in *The Will to Be Human:*

> *Whatever would disturb one's cherished self-image tends to be repressed. Whatever might make the individual appear to himself unworthy, guilty, inadequate, sadistic, inconsistent with his ideas or ideals* [Beliefs or Values], *escapist, or not living up to one's ideals, tends to be removed from consciousness.* [45]

And now we arrive at one of the most important points of this theory:

**The healthy Love/Belief System is always completely
logical and rational in its processing of information.**

Subject only to the person's mental state or psychological set, the healthy Love/Belief System is always providing the best Resolution of all the factors in 1) the environment, 2) any operant SA-Needs, relevant conscious and subconscious Memories and Love/Belief System Elements, and, 3) their relative weights or significances. Obviously, the big variable in all of these illations is the subject's mental state. We all tend to perceive our environment differently and respond much differently when we are anxious, or fearful, or angry, etc., than we do when we are at peace, joyful, or content. But our mental states are always the result of previous *logical* Stimuli processing by the Love/ Belief System.

(Note that we are referring to the healthy Love/Belief System. As we shall see, p. 121, an impaired Love/Belief System can yield schizophrenia.)

Adler correctly hypothesized that human actions were always logical, given the purposes of the individual. But then he erroneously concluded that the one general purpose of humankind is dominance or superiority. Carrying Adler's initial hypothesis one step further, we can now conclude that all human actions are logical, given the subject's mental state, environment, and the contents of her Memory and Love/Belief System.

The person who kills herself when she learns she has cancer, is doing the only logical thing she can do, given this knowledge, and the Elements in her Love/Belief System which relate to life and death and cancer.

Repression is the only logical way to process sexual needs when they are met with the conflicting beliefs, "Sex is dirty, (or immoral)," and, "I am a decent person."

The girl who hates her mother, but was brought up to believe one must love one's parents, is compelled to do the only logical thing she can do, given those two Elements, to knock herself out, to prove to her mother, the world, and herself, that she is a completely devoted daughter.

The obsessive-compulsive who washes her hands twenty times a day started out performing a completely logical action, given the contents of her Love/Belief System: she is assuaging an inordinate fear of germs, which, like all phobias, is a reflection of her denial of death. But just as the Response Impulses generated by Desires only grow stronger when they are enacted, the Response Impulses generated by root subconscious Fears also increase when they are assuaged. The root fear of death or disease has generated the Response Impulse to wash her hands so many times, that the neurological-physiological links have become wired; the Enact Level has been breached, and the Impulse now becomes the act. As Arieti writes:

> *The obsessive-compulsive is not insane. In almost all cases, the patient knows the compulsions are absurd, but a power stronger than reason compels him to carry them out. What is the nature of this bizarre power?* [WTBH:208]

I submit that it is nothing other than overpowering conditioned Response Impulses originally arising from conscious or subconscious inordinate, perhaps obsolete Desires or Fears in the indefatigable, completely rational, but unthinking, therefore often misguided, Love/Belief System.

Maslow wrote:

I have found it helpful in understanding psychopaths to assume that they have no love identifications with other human beings and can therefore hurt them or even kill them casually, without hate, and without pleasure, precisely as they kill animals who have come to be pests. [M&P:123]

Now if you will just assume one basic conscious or subconscious belief on the homicidal psychopath's part, "We're all animals; those who smile at me would just as soon kill me," her behavior becomes completely logical. Serial killer Ted Bundy, after years of fantasizing—*imagining*—finally came to believe that his victims weren't people—they were just bodies walking around waiting to be used. (See again, Law, p. 106.)

The neurotic described in such profound detail by Karen Horney in *Neurosis and Human Growth*, is simply one who has developed a self-image impossible of attainment, therefore always in conflict with the real world: the beliefs that she should be perfect, that everyone like her, etc. So Horney discovered what she called "the tyranny of the 'should'." But think. Isn't it obvious that what she is really talking about is a "tyranny of the *belief* that she 'should'"? She's right in calling it tyranny though; our beliefs are indeed, tyrants, and the subconscious beliefs of what one *should* be literally dominate the neurotic's life, and make that life unbearable.[3]

Paranoia is simply the belief that I am superior to others, coupled with the assumption (belief) that they naturally feel the way I would feel when confronted—if that were possible—with someone superior to me: jealous and vindictive. Or it can be a real hatred of others with the assumption that they must have the same feelings towards me.[4]

Now, with the exceptions noted earlier—chemical, genetic, etc.—most psychotics, neurotics, and the character-disordered, are only suffering an

---

[3]   Unfortunately, many psychologists inferred that if the "shoulds" were causing neurosis, then mental health would result from elimination of the shoulds, concluding that one's "feelings" are the only valid criteria of appropriate behavior; see p. 160.

[4]   This assumption, the belief that others share our feelings, has erroneously been called "projection." We do not project our feelings onto others with the ulterior motive of disowning them, as many psychologists suggest. We simply assume— *believe*—that everyone has the same feelings we do. These beliefs, like all our beliefs, become self-fulfilling prophecies; see, e.g., *Self-Fulfilling Stereotypes*, by Mark Snyder in Psychology Today, July '82.

extreme form of the same problems which beset all of humankind; an estrangement from our Selves, and an estrangement from Reality, a fractioning of our lives, a denial of death, ignorance of who and what we are, bewilderment at forces which seem to make our decisions for us, an inability to find any lasting satisfactions or even meaning in life, a forced graft of the mind/body to the "I" which never takes.

The erroneous root beliefs of neurotics/psychotics are simply a great deal more pernicious than the erroneous beliefs which the saints and sages tell us plague all humankind. Their beliefs, "I'm no good," "I should be perfect," "People are all animals (or haters)," are just more deleterious than those of us "normal" people who believe "I am my mind/body," "I am a decent person," (see page 132), "I am an accountant," etc. Psychologists find psychotics/ neurotics to be cognitively *wrong*; and of course they are; their Love/Belief Systems are distorting their perceptions of the world. But the saints and sages say we are *all* cognitively wrong; that until we can look at the world and our neighbor through the eyes of Love, i.e., through a Love/Belief System characterized by Love of God and our neighbor, we never see the world or our neighbor aright, and of course, we never see God.

So here, in Figure 8, we have the functional "mind," or human brain, which, to perform all mental processing of incoming stimuli, need only consist of a Memory, a Love/Belief System, or RAS, and a Center of Consciousness.

To my knowledge, this diagram is the first schematic representation of the internal mechanism of the "black box" (RAS) which determines all human Response Impulses; the black box behaviorists and determinists would have us believe is, if not inherent and immutable, at least unfathomable, and therefore unworthy of our attention.

The diagram is, of course, a highly simplified representation of the complexities of the machinations of the Love/Belief System. The eye can distinguish millions of colors, the ear, thousands of tones, and the Love/Belief System can distinguish thousands of combinations and gradations of Important/Unimportant, Good/Bad, Benign/Malignant.

The point of this diagram is to show that our senses' first report is always to the Love/Belief System, or RAS; that unless we are attending to our current circumstances and environment with Love, i.e., with attentive care and concern, our senses are programmed to select from the multiplicity of the world's stimuli only those which relate to our operant Desires and Fears, and, secondarily, to our major Loves and Beliefs; that the Love/Belief System then identifies, evaluates, manipulates, and resolves those stimuli signals *before* they fully penetrate the Center of Consciousness; and therefore that the Love/Belief

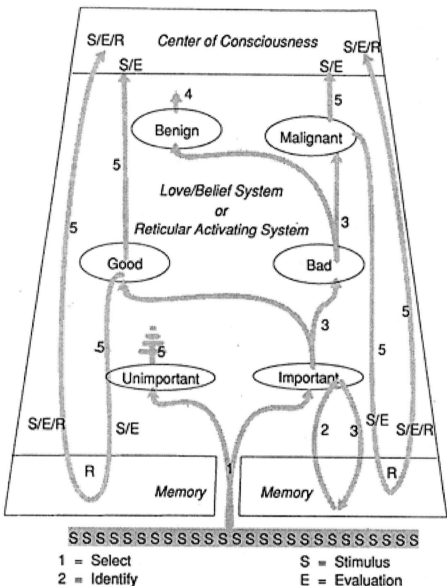

Figure 8 - The Love/Belief System Perception/Cognition/Response Process

System colors everything we see and hear in accordance with all of its conscious and subconscious programs.[5] The diagram illustrates the "central processing" in the "perceptual-cognitive sequence" referred to by Gerald S. Blum in his book, *Psychodynamics* (see pps. 144-45), and Arieti's observation on page 114. It also illustrates T. S. Eliot's criticism, "You are nothing but a set of obsolete responses."

The diagram shows why, in a recent research study, Americans did no better than chance in recognizing the pictures of Oriental faces they had seen before. It also explains why most poor people don't see rich people, they see lucky/selfish/dishonest people; rich people don't see poor people; they see people who are stupid, or lazy, or "just temporarily down on their luck." Many whites don't see blacks, and vice versa; Protestants don't see Catholics, straight people don't see gays, etc. We are like the Queen who ordered the North Gate of her capital city closed at night to prevent thieves from entering, only to find that her beloved sick sister was then denied admittance, and so perished. So we all, to the extent that we are acting in accordance with Response Impulses initiated by inordinate, irrational, deleterious, or obsolete Elements in our Love/Belief Systems, are, to that extent, living our lives subconsciously, exactly as the animals live.

Therefore, with all due respect to Rokeach's excellent analyses of the belief system, I must of course take exception to his theory that:

> *On the one hand [belief systems] represent Everyman's theory for understanding the world he lives in. On the other hand, they represent [his] defense network through which information is filtered, in order to render harmless that which threatens the ego. The beautiful thing about a belief system is that it seems to be constructed to serve both masters at once: to understand the world insofar as possible, and to defend against it insofar as necessary.* [OCM:400]

---

[5]   As indicated earlier, the "I"-Needs to Love and to Know do not manifest themselves in specific Desires or Fears, and the vague anxiety they continually generate is usually suppressed by keeping the mind occupied with the continual adoption of new Loves and Beliefs, i.e., by a continual expansion of the Love/Belief System, and by gratification/assuagement of the Desires and Fears which arise from the resulting Elements, i.e., by Wilber's "flight from death" (p.52), or Merton's "linear flight from reality and from God" (p. 102). So the pure "I"-Needs to Love and to Know do not normally figure in the Love/Belief System machinations; only the "I"-Need to Exist is manifested in the Love/Belief System, but indirectly, in the form of Love of our physical lives, Fear of death, etc.

Now I agree with the latter, the (Love/) Belief System's defensive function. But the idea that it helps us to understand the world is a gross glorification of its functions. Instead, as our diagrams and analysis have made clear:

> **Until we have learned to see the world through the eyes of**
> **unpossessive, unconditional Love, the cognitive function**
> **of the Love/Belief System is to interpret the world**
> **to us in accordance with its programs—**
> **its primary purpose is to *validate itself.***

This is why older people tend to become "set in their ways." Through hundreds of repetitions, the neurological links formed by our Loves and Beliefs become wired, while the Love/Belief System perpetually selects and collects "facts" from the environment which corroborate them, and rejects those which do not. As we age, our Love/Belief Systems *automate* our lives.

> *Thus the materials for the creative process lie all about us, equally*
> *accessible to everyone. What keeps us from being more creative is a*
> *frame of mind that persists in seeing only the commonplace in the*
> *familiar; we become frozen in the ice of our conservatism, and the world*
> *congeals about us.*
> —EARL NIGHTINGALE

Isn't that appalling?—the world *congeals* about us? We have all allowed an innumerable number of "boxes" to be created in our brains, boxes into which our Deputy-Governors, like good little bureaucrats, continually sort all our percepts and concepts of God, ourselves, our neighbor, and the world.

Obviously then, the most intelligent people have the most boxes into which to fit their experiences. But the *happiest* people have an infinite number of boxes; which, being interpreted, is *no* boxes. They see everything "through the eyes of Love;" every percept is a new percept, every day a new day, every person a new person. They live in the eternal Now, under the aspect of eternity, and "every morning they awake in heaven;" their world is Traherne's "House of God, and the Gate of Heaven."

But what if, because of chemical, neurological, etc., causes, the Love/Belief System breaks down, the computer is not able to hold its programs, and incorrectly processes the signals going through it? Obviously, we'd have *schizophrenia.* It now seems obvious that many of the wide variety of mental disorders which have been labeled "schizophrenia," *are entirely due to mal-*

functions of the Love/Belief System, or RAS. The RAS of schizophrenics seems to be largely inoperative, to have somehow "shorted out," and its programs keep sliding into the bit bucket. This could be due to nutritional, neurological, bacterial, chemical, genetic, or even traumatic sociological factors; but they always cause the subject to misinterpret her experiences—she suffers many sensory illusions and hallucinations—and to confuse her speech and actions. And these are the primary functions of the RAS: to interpret our sensory signals, and to execute our acts of will.[6] Moreover, as Becker says, schizophrenics do not identify with their mind/bodies—or a self-image. Having no personhood, they manufacture their personae. But these are creatures of their Imagination, and they cannot identify themSelves—their "I"'s—with "them." One schizophrenic described herself as "an 'I' trying to find a 'me'." With our new understanding of the person, could she have said it any plainer than that?

Schizophrenics exist primarily within their "I"'s, as do the mystics/ saints/sages (see Wapnick, 1980). But the saints have given up, set aside, their personhood in deference to their souls, but never entirely lose contact with their bodies and their self-image. The body and personhood of the schizophrenic however, seems to be "disappearing." She is losing her very *kinesthesia*, the constant flood of sensory reports that tell her she *has* a body, which is why she Knows "she" is not her mind/body, and also why she is so often impassible and incontinent. This fading sense of a physical self, and her inability to register the beliefs which would constitute a self-image, together with the nebulosity of the "I", causes her to live her life in Becker's "extraordinary state of terror," the terror of impending "engulfment," or "implosion," the thing humans dread most, the feeling that they are slipping into *oblivion* (see Laing DS:43,83,92); terror, incidentally, which is just another reflection of the "I"'s immutable Need to Exist. Losing contact with her mind/body, she seems always to be on the verge of extinction. Living exclusively in the "I" is like living in a dark, empty closet, with nothing to hold onto (see Laing PE: 86-87&105). Living in terror, she continually multiplies her perceptual defenses; and as her RF deteriorates and her perceptions more distorted, she becomes psychotic, "insane." Progressively,

---

[6]   The idea of a malfunctioning RAS as the cause of schizophrenia is an obvious derivation of our thesis; but to the best of my knowledge, an original one. It was gratifying to learn that recent studies at the University of Arkansas have found that *"autopsies of a small population of chronic, intractable schizophrenic patients . . [showed] an increase in cell number in an area of the brainstem which is part of the Reticular Activating System (RAS). . .suggesting a developmental etiology for schizophrenia as well as new directions for research and several new avenues for treating the disease."*

she becomes first catatonic, then comatose, brain-dead. When the deterioration of the RF reaches the root section which controls physiological functions—respiration, blood pressure, heart rate, etc.,— she dies.

So far, we have been discussing the RF in its input capacity, how it receives and interprets data. But of course the RF also processes both its own Response Impulses when they are enacted, and the "I"'s vision/belief/commitment decisions from the CC/RF to the motor neurons and back to the body. This explains why we fail to achieve so many of the things we set out to do; why, as Dr. Maltz proves, we find it impossible to perform outside the parameters of our self-image. All of our visions/beliefs/commitments must first pass through the RF before they are implemented. The conscious and sub-conscious Elements in the Love/Belief System identify, evaluate, manipulate, distort, and resolve those signals to make them conform to their objects and themselves; and in so doing, they debilitate our will. They suppress and distort our Responses. This is known as "displacement." If the Love/Belief System interprets a given action signal as being Bad/Malignant, that signal is suppressed until its energy can be directed to a more benign avenue. So the Response Impulse of the person who's mad at her boss, but Values her job, is suppressed, bottled up, until her husband says the wrong thing, and she then unloads on him. And it is exactly this same process by which most of our grand ambitions are "displaced."

As someone wrote, "We die with our best words unsaid, our best songs unsung, our best poems unwritten."

11
A New Paradigm of Person

Here then is "our" proposal for the new person paradigm, a schematic diagram which illustrates all human motivation, personality, and behavior: physical, emotional, sociological, and spiritual:

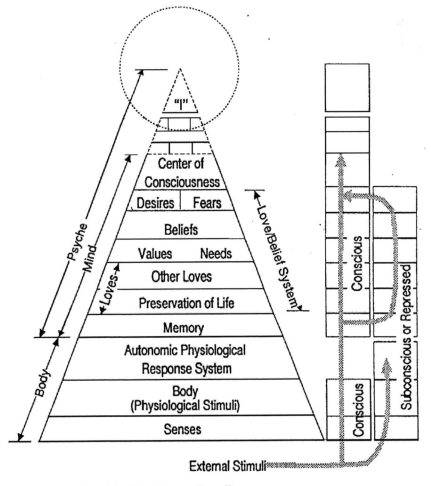

Figure 9 - Schematic of the New Person Paradigm

This diagram illustrates, and, with the preceding diagram and theorems, explains, all human motivation and behavior: physical, emotional, sociological, and spiritual. In particular, it explains and/or illustrates all of the following phenomena:

Freud's ego, id, libido, superego, subconscious, repressed desires, etc.;

Adler's logicality of human behavior, and superiority motif;

Jung's complexes, personal and collective unconscious, self, persona, and shadow;

Horney's neurotic trends, tyranny of the "should," and idealized self-image;

Maltz's self-image, consistency need, and creative imagination;

Assagioli's conscious self, higher self, dominance of self-identification entities, and "psychosynthesis;"

Laing's "inner" self, unembodied self, and ontological insecurity;

Kelly's personal constructs and roles;

Allport's proprium;

The behaviorist's stimulus/response transactions;

Gestalt interruptions, completions, and awareness exercises;

Maslow's prerequisite, basic and metaneeds, value system, self-actualization, rubricizing, and peak-and plateau-experiences;

Ellis' belief system and irrational "ideas;"

Cognitive psychology: social learning theory, and information processing;

Rokeach's belief-disbelief system, values, and open and closed mind;

Glasser's "Stations of the Mind" and "Behavior: Control of Perception Psychology;"

Theologian's heart, soul, and animal nature;

The needs, functions, and faculties we share with social animals;

The conscious and subconscious aspects of the human psyche.

Psychoses, neuroses, schizophrenia, repression, reaction-formation, sublimation, distraction, introjection, isolation, displacement, cognitive dissonance, the powers of suggestion and hypnosis, perceptual defense, split personality, hysterical blindness and deafness, amnesia, fainting, profound personality changes, phobias, dramatic religious conversions, regression, obsessive compulsions, etc.;

The autonomic nervous system.

Although I am painting with a broad brush, and much work remains to be done, I believe this diagram, together with the preceding diagrams and theorems, offers the outline of a complete explanation and illustration of *all* human motivation and behavior.

(The diagram clearly displays what I believe is the only accurate representation of the human as a *trinity,* consisting of soul, mind, and body, created in the image and likeness of a Triune God. I will leave it to others much more knowledgable than I to show the parallels—not identity—between these constituents and the Father, Son, and Holy Spirit of the Trinity. But I have already suggested that the "I", like God, is both Spirit and Love. Might it not be reasoned that the Son is the "mind" of God, and the Holy Spirit the "body" through which God acts in the world?)

The diagram is, of course, a schematic; the triangular shape is purely arbitrary, the mind is not made up of little boxes, and we can't draw sharp lines of distinction between Loves, Beliefs, memories, etc. But the spiritual "I" is at the top of the diagram, indicating its supreme position in the human being. The boxes under the "I" represent the "I"-Needs and Faculties.

The diagram clearly illustrates our major thesis:

A person is a social animal with a spiritual "I"
The exercise of the "I"-Faculties creates a Love/Belief System
in the brain, between the senses and consciousness, a system
which autonomically monitors, conditions, and initiates
response impulses to, all our perceptions and our acts of will.

Our perceptions of the world are obscured, distorted, and often erroneous, because we are looking at it through our Love/Belief Systems. By "purifying" the Love/Belief System, by learning to see things and people with unpossessive, unconditional Love, we can see them as they are: infinite, sacred; can learn to "see" God in the world.

If the doors of perception were cleansed,
 everything would appear to man as it is, infinite.
For man has closed himself up,
 till he sees all things thro' narrow chinks of his cavern.
 —WILLIAM BLAKE

Blake's doors of perception = the Love/Belief System, or Reticular Activating System. All stimuli from the world, or from our bodies and minds, are first screened for importance, or relevance, then processed through both the conscious and subconscious Elements of the Love/Belief System before they fully register in our Centers of Consciousness.

Also, as the diagram indicates, we can only act through our Love/Belief Systems. Signals emanating from the CC, which represent our will to do something must first pass through both the conscious and subconscious channels of our Love/Belief Systems, where they are screened, processed, and modified, before reaching the muscles which will enact that will. This explains the inexorable internal forces for fulfillment, i.e., actualization and realization in the world, of all of our significant Loves and Beliefs—why they all, to the extent that they do not conflict with other Elements, become "self-fulfilling prophecies;" and why our acts of will are so often "displaced" in their accomplishment.

To the right of the triangle is a "side-view" of the person, indicating the two levels, conscious and subconscious, of the mind and body functions. In other words, the diagram should be considered three-dimensional, with conscious Elements and functions on the surface of the triangle, but subconscious and repressed Elements and functions below the surface of the triangle, i.e., towards the right in the diagram on the right. As the arrows illustrate, all incoming stimuli signals (and outgoing action signals) go through both conscious and subconscious channels for processing. This explains why our subconscious Loves and Beliefs, Desires, and Fears are every bit as important in processing stimuli and determining our Response Impulses as are the conscious Elements, and, depending on their weight or significance, can be even more important than the conscious Elements.

The dotted circle represents that unbounded area of extra-sensory perceptions, the ethereal phenomena of which the "I" realizes an absolute Loving/Knowing, a communion, not through the senses. In the secular sense, it is Jung's collective unconscious; in the spiritual sense, it is God. But God is not sensible; only by "I"-Love/Knowledge may He be "gotten and holden."

The reader will note the *psyche* as a new element in the diagram. I have defined mind as a *human brain*, differing only from the animal brain in its conversion of the RAS to a Love/Belief System. But since *psyche* has been defined as "spirit, soul, mind," or as "a person's conscious and unconscious mental components," or as that which "governs the total organism in its interactions with the environment," it is difficult to retain all these meanings in the new paradigm. The "I" cannot be subsumed in the psyche, but it certainly participates in the actions of the mind. Therefore, in order to retain as much as possible of its former meanings, I suggest we now define psyche as:

the governing element of the human,
consisting of the *mind,* which acts in conjunction with,
and under the ultimate management of, the *soul.*

So this paradigm can explain all human capabilities, motivation and behavior. Except for a few instincts, all the differences between human capabilities and those of the chimpanzee can be explained by the existence, needs, and faculties of the "I", the soul, the Governor of the human being.

Looking at a modern metropolis and a jungle colony of chimpanzees, it can be readily reasoned that everything that exists and occurs in the city that doesn't exist or occur in the jungle, can be fully explained and accounted for by our "I"-Needs to Exist, to Love, and to Know, and our "I"-Faculties of Visualizing, Knowing, Deciding, and Loving (committing ourselves).

This paradigm resolves the "brain/mind knot" which has puzzled us since Plato: "What is the relationship of mind to brain?" Mind is now seen to be the human brain—a brain with a heart—and can now be defined as consisting of a Memory, a Love/Belief System, or RAS, and a Center of Consciousness. The "knot" arose because we have been defining mind as "that which thinks, perceives, feels, wills, etc.;" so "mind" had to account for all our capabilities. But now we can see mind as an animal brain modified by the faculties of the "I". It is the "I" which thinks (creatively), perceives, feels, wills, etc. Given the brain/body of a social animal, the "I" is both necessary and sufficient to account for all human motivation and behavior.

The diagram illustrates how, unless we are attending to our current circumstances with Love, our Love/Belief Systems exercise a vice-like control over our perceptions, our interpretations (re-cognitions), and our responses. It shows how the subconscious arises as RAS repressions of Love/Belief System Elements which conflict with other, contrary Elements.

It shows how Response Impulses reach our Consciousness without identification of the memories, Elements, or SA-Needs from which they sprang, and therefore that we don't really know *why* we do half the things we do, and why we must spend so much time searching our memories and Love/Belief Systems to rationalize—find more credible, more logical reasons for—Response Impulses generated by memories and Elements of whose existence we are not even aware. As has been aptly observed, we always have two reasons for everything we do: a good reason, and the real reason. In this insidious way we all *deceive ourselves* as to our true motives and purposes in life. As Underhill pointedly explains:

> *Likely enough if you really knew yourself—saw your own dim character, perpetually at the mercy of its environment; your true motives, stripped for inspection and measured against eternal values; your unacknowledged self-indulgences; your irrational loves and hates—you would be compelled to remodel your whole existence, . . .* [PM:57]

Ours has been called the age of anxiety, and the paradigm explains our primary anxieties as a "denial of death" and ungratified "I"-Needs, or the discrepancies between our perceived state and a Love/Belief System Element, or simply a conflict between two or more Love/Belief System Elements—conflicts which Festinger has aptly named cognitive dissonance.

These theorems also explain the powers of suggestion and hypnosis. These are beliefs introjected into the Love/Belief System which must then become realized in the person's life. Thus a hypnotized person can't move his arm if he's told he can't; and laughs after coming out of hypnosis if he's told that he will. Why? Because the belief was planted in his Love/Belief System. Is this any different than the actions of the obsessive-compulsive? Under hypnosis, even self-induced hypnosis, the Love/Belief System can even stop pain signals from reaching the Center of Consciousness; and hypnotized subjects who are led to believe they have been burned when touched with a piece of ice, develop blisters! Do we need any more proof of the *power* of our beliefs?

This paradigm also explains the "power of positive thinking," or a "positive mental attitude." In our theory, success in any endeavor results from positive belief and Self-commitment to the result. But if one acts or thinks positively, this can engender positive beliefs, which will yield positive results. The problem arises when we try to paste positive beliefs over basic, conscious or subconscious, negative beliefs. They can't possibly take effect. The positive thinkers are saying, "All things are possible to those who think (or act) positively." But Christ said, "All things are possible to those who *believe*."

The diagrams also show why we can't remember certain things. Information from our memories must first traverse the Love/Belief System before it reaches our Centers of Consciousness. Therefore we can't recall unpleasant things. And, as recent research has shown, we tend to *invent* memories which fit our beliefs. (*Journal of Personality & Social Psychology*, Vol.36, No.9). Consulting one's memory can be likened to a Governor sending a messenger to another town for information. The messenger knows which answer will most please the Governor, so he wanders through the town until he finds someone who will give him that answer, then returns with it to the Governor, and often it is a complete fabrication! Is it any wonder that enlightened people tell us we're all living in a world of shadows, like the people in Plato's cave?

The paradigm also explains multiple personality disorders, e.g., *The Three Faces of Eve*, or *Sybil*. The Love/Belief System's powers of suppression and isolation enable it to both compartmentalize (isolate), and temporarily at least, close off—"forget"—whole sections of both the Memory and the Love/Belief System itself. Since, as we have seen, behavior is determined primarily by the self-image, the split personality is simply a person with two or more, more or less complete, but isolated, self-images, who either chooses, or is forced, by conscious or subconscious Elements in the Love/Belief System, or by circumstances, to switch from one self-image to the other, losing all cognizance of the "other person's" existence.

What is known as "transpersonal" psychology, is now seen to be not at all *trans*-personal. Human experiences formerly considered transpersonal are now seen to be normal aspects of the human potential. Transpersonal should be changed to transcendental, since these experiences usually occur only when one transcends the ego with all of the (inordinate) attachments described by Huxley (pps. 98-97), and James (p. 101).

The popular "altered states of consciousness" are now seen to be the result of altered states of the Love/Belief System. Whenever one is overcome with hate or fear or desire or peace or joy or Love, he has entered an altered state of consciousness. Particularly when one's spiritual practices have enabled him to still the raucous Desires and Fears which usually dominate his consciousness, that consciousness is (beneficially and more lastingly) *altered*.

With regard to hallucinogens, Professor Grossman (see fn. p. 94) tells me that all the mood-altering drugs from marijuana to crack act primarily on what are known as the *monoaminergic neurons*; and guess where all the monoaminergic neurons are located. Right. They're all in a few discrete nuclei in the reticular formation. The drugs must have the effect of *unfocusing* the RF, and the subject begins to get some glimpses of the world and his neighbor as they are, as he saw them at four (p. 46-7)—without the Desires and Fears which dominate his outlook. The doors of perception are, to some degree, cleansed, and everything begins to appear as it is: infinite.[1]

This is the way the saints say they always see the world. But imagine the drug users' disappointment when they come down from the effects of the drug and must again view the world through their muddy Love/Belief Systems, see the world as they *believe* it is! They call this "coming back to reality." But exactly the reverse is true. Reality is only experienced when the Desires and Fears in the Love/Belief System are stilled, and we see the world through the eyes of unpossessive, unconditional Love. Then, they say, it is awesome, it is beautiful,

---

[1]   W. H. Auden writes, *"I have myself taken mescaline once and LSD once. Aside from a slight schizophrenic dissociation of the I from the Not-I including my body, nothing happened at all."*   The drug "dissociated" his "I" from his body, but he labeled it schizophrenic. If only he had known!   See Huxley's *The Doors of Perception* and Huston Smith's new book, *Cleansing the Doors of Perception*.

it is rife with miracles, it is *sacred.*

Of course, bad drug trips can occur, when the drug yields a sudden insight into some unpleasant, repressed memories or Elements, so shameful or painful that the Love/Belief System, when operating "normally," keeps them from consciousness. Stanislav Grof has made good use of this "psychedelic repression surfacing" phenomenon in his psychiatric practice.

Additional proofs of the existence and immortality of the "I" are coming to us through the thousands of reports of "near-death experiences," as described for example, by Carol Zaleski in *Otherworld Journeys.* These phenomenally similar experiences coming in from people of all ages from every part of the world are explained by the common element in all these accounts: the subject's surrender of his physical life, removing his denial of death—this rock of anxiety at the heart of his Love/Belief System—and opening him immediately to the ineffable realization of his true self, his "I", as immortal, spiritual Being: Lover, and Knower, in the image and likeness of God (see OJ:120). Many state that they didn't *want* to return to life.

These are the insights the saints enjoy regularly and often by virtue of their lengthy and arduous spiritual exercises of giving up their lives and their attachment to *things.* These are now seen to be exercises of the "I" which enable one to realize the "I", and restore its powers and its sovereignty in his life: to bring the SA-Needs under control, and eliminate the subconscious and deleterious, irrational, conflicting, obsolete, or inordinate Elements of the Love/Belief System, in order that he might regain control of his life, still the willful Desires and Fears which continually dominate his outlook, and free his "I" for communion with God. The "self-denial" which Christ commended is now seen as *Self- affirmation,* exercises of the "I", which represent a manifestation of the "I", and a restoration of its power. Conversely, every self-indulgence is a debilitation and a derogation of the "I". As Underhill explains:

> *We hear much of the mystical temperament, the mystical vision. The mystical character is far more important: and its chief ingredients are courage, singleness of heart, and self-control. It is towards the perfecting of these military virtues, not to the production of a pious softness, that the discipline of asceticism is largely directed; and the ascetic foundation, in one form or another, is the only enduring foundation of a sane contemplative life.* [PM:66]

Only in the practice of self-denial and unconditional, unpossessive Love can the "I" evince itself and restore its sovereignty in one's life - become at last, in St. Teresa's discerning phrase, a *royal* soul.

The seven deadly "sins" are not sins against God, they are sins of the "I" against itSelf; each a malfeasance of the "I" and a derogation and debilitation of its God-like faculties; "sins" only because they are inimical to the realization of its glorious heritage; but sins which can be eliminated through the unique "I"-exercises of self-denial and unpossessive, unconditional Love.

Lao Tse captures the way to spiritual enlightenment in just three lines:

Through return to simple living, comes control of desire.
In control of desire, stillness is attained.
In stillness, divinity is restored.

From Thomas à Kempis' *The Imitation of Christ*:

Son, thou oughtest diligently to attend to this; that in every place, every action or outward occupation, thou be inwardly free and mighty in thyself, and all things be under thee, and thou not under them; that thou be lord and governor of thy deeds, not servant.

And from *The Spiritual Exercises of St. Ignatius*,

By the term "Spiritual Exercises" is meant every method of examination of conscience, of meditation, of contemplation, of vocal and mental prayer, and of other spiritual activities. For just as taking a walk, journeying on foot, and running are bodily exercises, so we call Spiritual Exercises every way of preparing and disposing the soul [the "I"] *to rid itself of all inordinate attachments, and, after their removal, of seeking and finding the will of God in the disposition of our life for the salvation* [and enlightenment] *of our soul.*

These theorems and diagrams also explain and/or illustrate why and how people experience:

1. Profound religious conversions (e.g., see James, *The Varieties of Religious Experience)*;
2. Dramatic personality changes (e.g., see *Psycho-Cybernetics*);
3. Nervous breakdowns;
4. Insanity.

There are two ways to tear down a structure: either brick by brick starting at the top, or by pulling out a few major supports at the bottom. When a key or root or basic Love, Belief, Value, or Need which supports other Elements is invalidated, the Elements it supports, unless they have other supports, also fall. Depending on the type and severity of the damage to the Love/Belief System, any of the above circumstances can result: profound religious conversions, dramatic personality changes, nervous breakdowns, or even insanity.

You see, the insane person has suffered such severe damage to his Love/Belief System that he has *decided* to never again Love, Believe, Value, or Need anything in the real world which can be taken away from him. The shocks were so great that he doesn't dare risk another by becoming attached to anything real again. He has lost the "basic trust" which Erikson found essential to healthy human development. Therefore he won't accept anything anyone tells him; most often he doesn't even hear them. His perceptual defense is 100%. And this makes him "insane." Through his imagination, he has created a safer, fictional world in which to live out his days, a world impenetrable by anything or anyone in the outside world. In this sense he is doing the only, and the most logical, thing he can do, to prevent a recurrence of the pain he suffered when a major Element or structure in his Love/Belief System was destroyed.[1]

The religious conversion is often said to result in a "shift in values." But now we see that this is the *cause* as well as the effect of conversion. A change or elimination of any significant Love, Belief, Value, or Need, always causes changes throughout the entire structure of Elements to which it was connected. In the religious conversion, for example, when the Love of life and mammon has been replaced by the Love of God, all the Elements with which the former were associated are also changed, and many of the subject's motivations, behavior, personality, and Values are automatically and dramatically changed.

All of the above transformations are then seen as the result of a radical change of a major structure in the Love/Belief System. Is it any wonder we are so protective of our Loves and Beliefs?—that in the great majority of people, normal and abnormal, the maintenance of our Loves and Beliefs is compulsive? And all the saints say it is the content and compulsive maintenance of our Love/Belief Systems—only they call it the "hardness of our hearts"—that is keeping us from realizing the Kingdom of God.

For example, even the seemingly harmless belief, "I am a pretty decent person," while it may cause me to usually act in a socially acceptable way,

---

[1]   In *Decision Therapy,* Harold Greenwald reports asking psychotic patients when they *decided* to go bonkers. Many tell him the date and time. R. D. Laing was sure many "cures" occurred when psychotics *decided* to play at being sane. [DS:148]

absolutely prohibits me from attaining that abysmal self-Knowledge which the saints say is the only way to Peace. (See page 181.)

With regard to the list on page 124, I have in my own mind reconciled (and I believe any serious reader can also reconcile), all of these phenomena with the theses of this book. Perhaps the most significant parallels are with Maslow, Assagioli, and Freud. The interested reader will find scores of intimations of a Love/Belief System and its effects in the works of Maslow (see Appendix E), and it is obvious that these theses closely parallel the work of Assagioli,—the "I" is his "higher self" (but adds its needs and faculties), the Center of Consciousness his "conscious self," and his "identification and disidentification exercises" are efforts to free the "I" from its association with the mind, body, emotions, roles, etc. As Assagioli indicates, there are not really two selves (we only lost sight of our higher selves, or "I"'s, when as children, we identified them with our minds/bodies).

And, of course, this theory agrees perfectly with Assagioli's thesis, "We are dominated by everything with which our self becomes identified." But this does not mean that the self should be free of all identifications; we can make this law work to our advantage by learning to believe "'I' am spirit, Lover and Knower," thereby causing our lives to be dominated by Love, and fulfilling our heritage as children of God. The reader is urged to read Assagioli's *Psychosynthesis*, and *The Act of Will,* as well as the excellent more recent work, *What We May Be,* by one of his protégés, Piero Ferrucci.

Turning to Freud, I have already noted his identification of the "I" (which we call the ego) as the "Executive of Personality," with the functions of perception, conscious thought, memory, learning, choice, judgment, and action; an "I" which functions as a "mediator" between the forces of the id, the super-ego, and the demands of the world. What I am proposing is that Freud's "I" be redefined as the *spiritual* "I", with the functions of Loving, Knowing, Imagining, and Deciding, to which all of Freud's "I"-functions can be seen to be either equivalent or derivatives, and which enable it to act as the (usually harried and ineffectual) *mediator* between the demands of the SA-Needs, the "I"-Needs, the Love/Belief System Elements, and his social, economic, and physical environment.

Freud's "id" and "libido" are seen to be normal human physiological and bio-sociological needs,[2] needs which can of course become pathological if they become objects of "I"-Love, and/or are continually repressed; the "super-ego" has already been explained in our terms on page 57.

---

[2]   In *New Ways in Psychoanalysis*, Karen Horney says, ". . . the libido theory, in all its contentions, is unsubstantiated." [68]

Freud too, although he found nothing divine or spiritual in the "I", wanted to restore its sovereignty in the person's life.

Freud never believed that the most important aspects of our behavior are determined by our instincts and are therefore beyond the reach of our influence. . . As he wrote, . . the purpose of psychoanalysis is "to strengthen the I, to make it more independent of the above-I (the superego), to widen its field of perception and to extend its organization so that it can appropriate to itself new portions of the it (id)," and he added, "Where it was, there should become I." . . .

Psychoanalysis attempts to demonstrate that our most basic motives are subject to conscious recognition and deliberate alteration. If "I" am driven by fear or ambition or greed, "I" can do something about it. People, unlike animals, can change themselves in significant ways.[3]
[FMS:106]

—BRUNO BETTELHEIM

Repression and the subconscious represent Freud's greatest discoveries, and repression is now seen as the very logical way in which the Love/Belief System handles painful or embarrassing, external, SA-Need, or Love/Belief System stimuli—stimuli which conflict with its other Elements. And it is repression which gives rise to the subconscious.

Freud's reaction-formation is another very logical reaction to a Response Impulse which the individual's powers of imagination enable him to see would, if enacted, result in a conflict with other Elements in his Love/ Belief System. See "the girl who hates her mother" on page 115. "Freudian slips" can be seen simply as strong RAS initiated Response Impulses which cross the Enact Level without mediation by the "I", while it is otherwise occupied.

As for Freud's (and Jung's) "complexes," an inferiority complex is the belief that one is inferior; an Oedipus complex is an inordinate possessive Love, or love/need, for one's mother; a castration complex is a fear which could be the result of a threat (made in jest) by an older female suffering from penis envy,

---

[3] Bettelheim's book is an effort to establish Freud's "humanistic" orientation. He quotes a Freud letter to Jung: *"Psychoanalysis is in essence, a cure through love."* (Portents of Carl Rogers! See p. 206.) But he doesn't mention Freud's very perceptive confession, in a letter to Ludwig Binswanger, *"I have always confined myself to the ground floor and basement of the edifice called man."* Joseph Schwartz's new book, *Cassandra's Daughter - A History of Psychoanalysis,* makes one wonder if any of Freud's successors realize that there *are* upper floors.

which in turn is a possessive Love or Value, perhaps resulting from being made painfully aware that her parents wanted a boy. In short, complexes are simply deleterious, inordinate, irrational, obsolete, or conflicting, Loves and Beliefs, Desires or Fears.

When the neglect of the child's "I" is compounded by sexual abuse of the child (usually female), she is not only brought to believe she is her body, but that the most important thing about her is her genitalia. This is the ultimate, consummating degradation and nullification of what the child Knows is "I", and one from which most people never recover. Unfortunately, Freud found it hard to believe that so many of his patients had been sexually abused as children, and peer pressure induced him to disregard this degradation, this traumatic reduction to their genitalia, from which they still suffered, and invent "childish sexual fantasies" to explain their stories.

So everything that enters my Center of Consciousness is first filtered through my Love/Belief System, and altered to make the best fit with all of its conscious and subconscious Elements and operant SA-Needs. And everything "I" visualize/believe/commit to do, is also screened by the Love/Belief System, and modified to make it conform to all of its conscious and subconscious Elements and SA-Needs. No matter how much "I" may try to achieve a goal, my Love/Belief System will cause me to fail in its attainment if it conflicts with any Element which "I" have allowed to even become associated with a more important conscious or subconscious Love, Belief, Desire, or Fear, regardless of the rationality of the association.

When "I" present a problem to my mind for resolution, the mind cannot communicate the best solution to my "I" if it conflicts with an Element which is even associated with a more important conscious or subconscious Element, regardless of the rationality of the association.

It is not our experiences which shape our lives; it is how we interpret those experiences—the beliefs we derive from our experiences, based on what Martin Seligman calls our "explanatory style." A child who is punished severely may decide that the parent is a tyrant; another comes to believe, "The world is cruel," or "I'm no good;" still another adopts the more benign belief, "I'd better not get caught doing that again." But of course our explanatory style depends entirely on our basic Loves and Beliefs.

For example, when the Lindbergh baby was kidnapped and murdered, the newspapers and radio were full of the tragedy for weeks. One day I said, "We're just right, aren't we, Mom?" "What do you mean, 'just right?'," she asked. "Well," I said, "we have enough money to live on, but not so much that anyone would want to kidnap and kill Vince or me, would they?"

At that moment a belief locked itself in place in my Love/Belief System, one I've been able to corroborate many times since—every time I hear about a wealthy person who is attacked for their money—therefore a belief I still carry around with me: "Wealth is dangerous to your life." To this day, I still get nervous when my bank account starts to grow; therefore it seldom does! And I don't remember making that statement and reaching that conclusion, even after my Mother related the story to me.

In this insidious manner we have all lost control of our lives; lost the ability to receive undistorted messages from the world, and lost the ability to act and react rationally, to forward rational and appropriate action instructions to our minds and bodies—all because of the inexorable power of the indefatigable, hard-wired, Love/Belief System.

The Love/Belief System can thus be seen to grow in influence, appropriating the will, confounding the reason, suppressing and distorting the memory and senses, and frustrating the creative imagination.

But the message of hope which this book is meant to convey is that these forces which dominate our lives are not the boiling cauldron of dark satanic urges of Freud's id or libido, Jung's mythological primordial archetypes in the collective unconscious,[4] Adler's animal urges to dominance, or Horney's neurotic trends, the "psychic elements" which all except Horney imply we acquired at birth, if not at conception, and are therefore immutable, like our genes.

They are simply the logical responses required by the Loves and Beliefs which we have haphazardly adopted since childhood, and of which we can dispossess ourselves if we so will, i.e., visualize/believe/devote ourselves to adopting

---

[4]   I do not deny the existence of Jung's "primordial archetypes" in the psyche (if you believe in archetypes, you'll find archetypes); but maintain that their effects on our lives are insignificant in relationship to the effects of our self-adopted, conscious and subconscious, Loves and Beliefs, Desires, and Fears. As Linda Riebel writes in *Theory as Self-Portrait & the Ideal of Objectivity* in J.H.P., Vol.22, No.2: *"Part of the appeal of psychoanalysis is its implicit tribute to the depth, passion, and mystery lurking below the surface of even the most ordinary mortal. Jerome Frank . . . commented on 'the highly dramatic quality (in the theories of Freud and Jung). The patient is no longer an insignificant creature, but becomes the battleground of titanic forces or a store-house of the accumulated myths and wisdom of the ages.' . . . The fascinating inner drama **supposed** to go on in every patient confers heroic status on the genius able to figure it out."*
For an incisive critique of Freud's and Jung's spiritual myopia, see Appendix B.

a different set of Loves and Beliefs which determine our habits, our character, our personality. We must learn to use our God-like creative powers to bring about a reorganization of our Love/Belief Systems; learn to use the tremendous creative power of the "I" to change our Loves and Beliefs, and thereby, automatically change our lives.

We must learn to see all things through the eyes of unpossessive, unconditional Love, in order to "purify" the Love/Belief System, and see things and people as they are: infinite. From all the evidence of human nature which has been accumulated over the centuries, it now appears that:

**The basic self-image belief, "'I' am immortal Spirit:
Lover and Knower," could represent the psychological,
sociological, and spiritual panacea of our age.**

As we have seen, at the very heart of our Love/Belief Systems is Love of our physical lives, Fear of death, Desire for immortality, and the Beliefs which constitute our self-image, the "'I' am" beliefs. Knowing that we are immortal spirit tends to remove the neuroses we all suffer from our denial of death; and the belief, "'I' am Lover and Knower; 'I' am an exerciser of care and concern, responsiveness, respect, and knowledge," gives us a gracious, generous, creative: Loving approach to all of life's circumstances, and a freedom from the constricting roles we've all adopted, roles which dominate our lives. It gives us the "integrated outlook and attitude," the lack of which, John Dewey says, is the basic cause of the "despair [representing] the chief intellectual characteristic of the present age." It gives us a "knowledge of the right direction—of orientation,"—which William Sheldon says is "the most universal craving in the human makeup." It gives us, finally, the method by which we can lead whole, fulfilling, Self-actualizing, and *rational* lives.

In more general terms, we must also conclude that:

**In other than genetic, physical, or chemical dysfunctions,
and autonomic physiological responses, every human action
and reaction can be traced directly to the SA-Needs,
the "I"-Needs, and/or something the person consciously
or subconsciously Loves, Believes, Values, or Needs.**

Summing up, together with the SA-Needs we share with all social animals, and the "I"-Needs which are unique to the human, our self-adopted conscious and subconscious Loves and Beliefs give rise to Desires and Fears. These

"Elements" provide all of the motivations in our lives, and determine all of our behavioral tendencies. They determine our psychological set, what we are looking for, and therefore, what we see. They also interpret all of our experiences, thereby determining our Response Impulses. So we all see and experience the world *through* our Love/Belief Systems, and each and every significant Element in that System—whether conscious or subconscious—becomes a self-fulfilling prophecy.

Therefore, as every saint and psychologist knows, each of us literally creates his own world in which he lives. But for 99% of us it is a fictional world, a "dream" world, representing not only an infinitesimal segment of the real world, but a very *selective* segment; consisting only of those perceptions related to the operant Desires and Fears or major Elements in our Love/Belief Systems; a segment which makes our whole world simply a *mirror* of our Love/Belief Systems, our own almost randomly chosen, conscious and subconscious, Loves and Beliefs, and their resultant Desires and Fears.

All the mystics/saints/sages say, "We behold that which we are." When one's heart is filled with the Love of God and his neighbor, the world becomes, in Traherne's phrase, "a mirror of infinite Beauty." But to the "normal" person —whom Underhill so profoundly characterized as suffering "the ridiculous megalomania which makes each person the center of his universe"— the person whose Love/Belief System is filled with Love of self, or what he calls "life," or mammon, it is a world filled with danger and pain and ugliness.

> *It is not easy for man so to change himself. As we have seen, it is one of the most tragic facts about ourselves that we have always imagined that it was easy, but of no great profit, to change one's own nature, and hard, but immensely valuable, to change outer nature. Detailed examination of the problem is now showing the reverse to be the truth. Our construction of fact (what we call the outer universe) and ourselves we see as tied together in an intense interlock. We can change the world we see, but only in proportion as we have the self control and courage to let go of the present current construction. . .*

> *We must remember how even the best of us cling to the present picture of things. This world made by greed and fear suits most people so well that to suggest that it is brutal and in the end will prove disastrous is to awake even more fear and resentment. They will endure agonies rather than leave it. However much they complain, in all who are ruled by fear and greed there is no real wish for any other sort of world.*

The third ethic can therefore have one aim and one only: to set men free of fear and greed. And, because of the reciprocity of ethics and cosmology, vision and action, the consequence of living up to this ethic can be nothing less than the emergence into our sight of an objective world in which greed and fear are steadily diminishing elements.

This is the fundamental discovery of the third cosmology and its fundamental difference from the only other two cosmologies which have preceded it. Here is a cosmological-ethical revolution: man makes the universe; he has made its nightmare, arbitrary quality (of polytheism), its inaccessible righteousness (of monotheism), its blind, inhuman necessitarianism (of mechanism). Each of these cosmologies has been a part picture of an aspect of his nature. He has only been able to see in outer nature what confirms and answers to his inner nature. The invisible replies and materializes in the form in which it is summoned and imagined. But man can only remake the present crumbling picture of the universe into one which will not be a pure chaos, but an answer to his higher emergent, superindividual nature, if he will behave continually in such a superindividual way. The growth of the cosmology waits on the growth in the ethic; enlarging insight depends on the expansion due to exercise; vision on action, on acting up to the limit of what has been glimpsed.

Therefore man does not and cannot wait on an external God so that God may remake the universe in order that, when this has been safely accomplished, man may get on with his noble behavior, his idealistic activity, his saintly conduct. Man is more than God's vice-regent. He is the creative power's vice-creator, for he may make any universe up to the standard of which he is prepared to live. Absolute freedom from the individual self approaches absolute creative power. For as man dares act (this is the fact of creative faith), his apprehension-construction grows and he sees not subjectively but objectively a new reality. For he brings into being that which he has so dared to desire, . . . creates out of that same energy-radiation another world, a nobler world, but a world as firm as the world of common sense, because constructed and cemented by a desire as strong. The one fundamental objective fact is that the energy-radiation will sustain and substantiate any construction creative desire calls upon it to support and fulfill.

The Kingdom of God is not imminent but immanent; it is not "among you," about to break like a thunderstorm, but "within you," ready to be expressed the moment you understand your latent, common nature and how you must and can transcend your individuality, your egotism, which makes the world the obstacle it proves today to be to you. [TM:209]
—GERALD HEARD

All the mysteries of human behavior disappear when we realize:

1. That a person is a social animal with a spiritual "I", an "I" with needs to Exist, to Love, and to Know, and with the powers to Ideate, to Know or Believe, to Love, and freedom to Choose the objects of our Ideations, Beliefs, and Loves;

2. That the exercise of the "I"-Faculties results in the adoption of thousands of Loves and Beliefs which combine with the SA-Needs to form a computer-like Love/Belief System in the brain, a system which selects, then screens and processes all our perceptions of the world (as well as all our acts of will), and determines our Response Impulses to those perceptions, before they reach our consciousness; and,

3. That the "I" has the power to review and change those Response Impulses, and, long-range, to change our Loves and Beliefs, and therefore, most of our Desires and Fears; and thereby make *our* world into a heaven or a hell or anything in between.

The soul lives where it loves.
—ST. JOHN OF THE CROSS

12
The "Little Man" Inside Our Heads

Now, if in the above, I seem to have personified the Love/Belief System or RAS in its manipulations of our perceptions, cognitions, responses, and acts of will, it is because personification represents the only logical construction we can put on these Love/Belief System machinations. Each of our Love/Belief System Elements must be seen to have modified the reticular formation, and therefore has a life of its own, and a will of its own, and must be considered as a Deputy-Governor, with both the power and the authority to act for the Governor, the "I".

As we have seen, our Love/Belief System Elements: 1) generate Response Impulses and can implement those Impulses independently of the "I"; 2) grow in power; and, 3) procreate; i.e., each major Love, Belief, Value, and Need spawns other Loves and Beliefs which support it.

One of the major reasons for the growth in the power of our Loves and Beliefs is that each time one of them engenders a response, the neural/physiological links in our brains and nervous systems are strengthened, making it more conditioned or autonomic.

The procreative capacities of our beliefs is apparent in the fact that each belief automatically engenders disbeliefs which oppose it. It is also obvious that each of us tends to swallow whole any Beliefs, Values, or Needs which are compatible with, or supportive of, any other significant Love/Belief System Elements.

Karen Horney gives us an excellent description of the multiplying, propagating power of our beliefs: (Notice how many different words she uses for Loves, Beliefs, Values, and Needs.)

If "A" has built up a protective belief in reason and foresight, he will not only overrate (1) *what can be accomplished by reason in general, but also take a special pride* (2) *in his power of reasoning, his judgement, his predictions. His notions of* (3) *his superiority over others will then derive primarily from a conviction* (4) *that his is a superior intelligence. And if "B" feels* (5) *he cannot possibly stand on his own, but must have* (6) *a "partner" who gives content and direction to his life, he is bound to overrate* (7) *not only the power of love but also his own ability to love. He will mistake his need to hang on to another person for a particularly great ability to love, and take a special pride* (8) *in this illusory capacity. Finally, if "C"'s neurotic trend* (9) *is to master any situation by his own efforts, to be self-sufficient at any price, he will take an excessive pride* (10) *in being capable and self-reliant and in never needing anybody.*

The maintenance of these beliefs [now we have it !]— *"A"'s belief in his superior power of reasoning, "B"'s in his loving nature, "C"'s in competence to handle his affairs quite by himself—become as compulsive as the neurotic trends* [irrational Loves and Beliefs] *that produced them.* [SA:59]

Here we have perhaps the clearest statement possible of the self-propagating and self-perpetuating nature of our Loves and Beliefs. The neurotic, by definition, is more concerned with what others think of her, and more aware that her personality is nothing but a house of cards she has constructed to try to win their approval. Therefore she is naturally more defensive than others when she sees a chink in her armor. But it is one of the major points of this book that in all of us, neurotic or "normal," the maintenance of our Loves and Beliefs is compulsive. This is because, as indicated earlier, the Love/Belief System is made up of a series of structures of Elements built up around each of the major Loves and Beliefs. Derogation or abrogation of any significant Element threatens the entire structure to which it is connected. Most of us would much rather change our jobs, our houses, our cities, or our spouses, than subject ourselves to a major change in our Loves and Beliefs.

In view of all the above, we are inescapably, I think, led to the conclusion that the functions of the spiritual "I" must actually modify the reticular formation, and so bestow on each of our Loves and Beliefs and their concomitant Desires and Fears, a life and a will of its own.

Now let's look at a few examples of the semantic artifices and literary circumlocutions to which psychologists (and some wannabe psychologists) have had to resort in their denial of a self, and their failure to identify and/or appreciate the powers of the Love/Belief System.

I have already mentioned Gordon Allport's refusal to acknowledge a self, fearing that such an assumption would be "unscientific." And yet he felt he must hypothesize a function of knowing. He writes,

> *Do we not have in addition, a cognizing self—a knower, that transcends all other functions of the proprium and holds them in view? . . . We not only know things, but we know (i.e., are acquainted with) the empirical features of our own proprium. It is I [!] who have bodily sensation, I who recognize my self-identity from day to day; I who note and reflect upon my self-assertion, self-extension, my own rationalizations, as well as upon my interests and strivings. . . Since such knowing is beyond any doubt, a state that is particularly ours, we admit it as the eighth clear function of the "proprium". . . All eight functions of the proprium, must be admitted and included. . . In particular the unifying act of perceiving and knowing (of comprehending propriate states as belonging together and belonging to me) must be fully admitted.* [B:51,ff]

So he (reluctantly?) accepts the function of knowing, but, in spite of his acknowledgment that it is "I" who knows, refuses to grant a knower—a knowing entity, or a decider—in the person. (see pps. 26-7)

I have also mentioned Jung's recognition of a self, about which he said, "intellectually the self is no more than a psychological concept." Still, he said "it might equally well be called the God within us;" but then explained,

> *When . . . we make use of the concept of a God we are simply formulating a definite psychological fact, namely the independence and sovereignty of certain psychic contents which express themselves by their power to thwart our will, to obsess our consciousness, and to influence our moods and actions. We may be outraged at the idea of an inexplicable mood, a nervous disorder, or an uncontrollable vice being, so to speak a mani- festation of God. But it would be an irreparable loss for religious exper- ience if such things, perhaps even evil things, were artificially segregated from the sum of autonomous psychic contents.* [TEAP:238]

Jung's self, or God within us, can "thwart *our* will," manifest itself in "an uncontrollable vice, . . even evil things" etc. ! Omitting such "*manifesta- tions of God . .* would be an irreparable loss for religious experience. . ." No comment. See Appendix B.

Jung attributed the "characteristic disturbances" he observed in word association tests to "complexes," which he had great difficulty defining, but which he, too, found it necessary to personify:

> *A complex is an agglomeration of associations—a sort of picture of a more or less complicated psychological nature, sometimes of traumatic character, sometimes simply of a painful and highly toned character. . . Whenever there is a high tonus it is just as if that particular complex had a body of its own, . . . a complex with its given tension or energy has the tendency to form a little personality of itself. It has a sort of body, a certain amount of its own physiology. It can upset the stomach. It upsets the breathing, it disturbs the heart, in short, it behaves like a partial personality.* [AP:79]

Jung rendered a potentially great service to humanity when he refined Freud's word association tests to help identify the complexes; then set psychoanalysis back fifty years when he arbitrarily decided that:

> *I do not want to know the complexes of my patients. That is uninteresting to me.* [!] *I want to know what the DREAMS have to say about complexes, not what the complexes are, . . .* [AP:91]

and began a lifelong effort to relate dreams to the illusory "collective unconscious" and "primordial archetypes." Like Freud, he "knew no longing other than for philosophical insight," and couldn't believe that something as simple as the complexes might help him win the competition for a full understanding of human behavior. (see again, fn. p. 134)

In *Psychodynamics - The Science of Unconscious Mental Forces*, Dr. G. S. Blum makes some very cogent comments; e.g., he describes "denial" as:

> *a contradiction of something known or perceived. In a sense the individual "blinds" himself to the unpleasant aspects of reality. . .* [34] (see pps. 50-51)

He also writes,

> *Unconscious mental forces play a vital role in shaping these processes* [perceiving, thinking, acting, but concludes:] *A willingness to grant the*

existence of perceptual defense, . . . still leaves unanswered the intriguing
question concerning the mechanism by which it is carried out. Obvious-
ly, the "little man inside the head" [which he described earlier as one
"who decides in advance what should or should not be seen"] *notion is*
absurd. But if we conceive of the subject's response as the culmination
of a perceptual-cognitive sequence—beginning with sensory registration
of the stimulus, followed by central processing, which leads to the verbal
report—the possibility of interference and disruption along the way no
longer seems so far-fetched. [48,52]

You bet it doesn't, Dr. Blum. Sensory stimuli are processed through the
Love/Belief System before the Center of Consciousness receives a verbal report!
How else can we explain the classic movie, *Rashomon,* in which three witnesses
each describe a crime differently? Each of them was trying to be honest, but
each saw the event through her own peculiar Love/Belief System.

But in the Pulitzer Prize book, *On Human Nature*, socio-biologist Edward
O. Wilson ventures into psychologic theory with a discussion of

what cognitive psychologists call schemata or plans, . . . a schema is a
configuration within the brain, either inborn or learned, against which
the input of the nerve cells is compared. . . The schema can contribute
to a person's mental "set," the screening out of certain details in favor
of others, so that the conscious mind perceives a certain part of the
environment more vividly than others, and is likely to favor one kind of
decision over another. It can fill in details that are missing from the
actual sensory input and create a pattern in the mind that is not entirely
present in reality. . . Most significantly of all, schemata within the brain
could serve as the physical basis of will. [!] *An organism can be guided*
in its action by a feedback loop: a sequence of messages from the sense
organs to the brain schemata back to the sense organs and on around
again until the schemata "satisfy" themselves [themselves?] *that the*
correct action has been completed. The mind could be a republic of such
schemata, programmed to compete among themselves [?] *for control of*
the decision centers, individually waxing and waning in power in
response to the relative urgency of the physiological needs of the body
being signalled to the conscious mind through the brain stem and the
midbrain. Will might be the outcome of the competition, requiring the
action of neither a "little man" [what then are the "themselves" above?],

nor any other external agent. There is no proof that the mind works in just this way. . . suffice it to note that the basic mechanisms do exist; feedback loops, for example, control most of our automatic behavior. [75,ff]

Now if you will just substitute our Deputy-Governors in the Love/Belief System for Dr. Wilson's undefined *schemata*, you have an excellent description of the selecting, identifying, evaluating, manipulating, resolving functions of the Love/Belief System. Unknowingly and unintentionally, Wilson has given us a beautiful description of our army of Deputy-Governors in the Love/Belief System. He has replaced the "little man inside the head" with a veritable city of little men: "a *republic* of schemata contributing to a person's mental 'set' filling in details in the mind that are not actually present in reality; and competing for control of the decision centers—until satisfying *themselves* that the correct action has been taken."

Notice however, that he—almost surreptitiously—confines his hypothesis to responses to "the physiological needs of the body," omitting about 90% of human motivation. And when he suggests that his schemata could serve as a "physical basis of will," of the human decision-making power, he is endorsing biological determinism, the animalistic (Allportian) portrait of the person, without an "I", or Decider.

So too, does William James. In Chapter 10 of *Principles of Psychology*, James arbitrarily concludes that the I which knows, need not be considered to be an unchanging metaphysical entity like the Soul, and that speculations about the existence of a "knower" (other than the "passing thought") is a metaphysical problem, "on a par with our own psychological one," but one that "carries us beyond the psychological or naturalistic point of view." Thus he truncates psychology to a study of the "naturalistic," and helps to impede, for the next 100 years, its recognition and appreciation of the only thing which makes us human, and which therefore represents psychologists' only means of achieving their main purpose: understanding human behavior.

And in the very next chapter, on *Attention*, James describes "active or voluntary attention," wherein we "keep our mind occupied with some object, . . . we strive to sharpen and make distinct an idea which we but vaguely seem to have;" or, we *"resolutely hold fast to a thought."* But since, according to James, we *are* the passing thought, what he is now saying is that the passing thought is resolutely holding fast to itself!

Francis Crick, co-discoverer of the DNA helix, and one of the world's foremost scientists *in his field*, proposed in *The Astonishing Hypothesis,* that all human behavior is the result of purely neuronal activity, and the hypothesis of a soul is unnecessary. But then he says, *"What you see is not what is really there; it is what your brain 'believes' is there. . . but in some cases your 'beliefs' may turn out to be wrong."* How can a brain *believe?* And if there is no soul, what is the "your" whose beliefs may turn out to be wrong? Can anyone miss the irrationality of this figment? It's not astonishing, it's *incredible.*

Crick does admit that *"the probability of life originating at random is so utterly minuscule as to make it absurd."* So while he balks at hypothesizing a God, he has no compunctions about proposing a "panspermia" hypothesis that life was perhaps sent to earth in the form of seeds [!] from a faraway civilization. No comment.

One more example: in Appendix A, you'll read an excerpt from a "science" book which says, *"The brain then makes up its mind."* !

I could list hundreds more, but these few examples should serve to illustrate all the semantic artifices, the virtual humbuggery, to which scientismists have had to resort to try to explain human behavior without an "I", or self, and without recognition of the independent, decision-making power we bestow on our Loves and Beliefs. As Blum says, "the idea of a 'little man inside our heads' [who decides what should and should not be seen] is absurd." But *something* we do have in our heads which decides what we see and don't see, and we now have overwhelming neurologic and psychologic evidence that this "something" is best represented as a veritable *army* of little men, the thousands of hard-wired neuronal connections representing our SA-Needs, and our self-adopted, conscious and subconscious, Loves and Beliefs, Desires and Fears.

Perhaps you can best develop an accurate representation of yourself by picturing the "I" as a tiny replica of what you have always thought of as yourself, a little man or woman, in your image, residing in your head (although the spiritual "I" is certainly *non-local*; e.g., see Dossey) as the Governor of a province, your mind and body. Adjoining the "I"'s private office—to which You can retire in meditation—is a "Command and Control Center," representing the Center of Consciousness. In the Center is a large Conference Table, with a slot down the middle representing the Enact Level. Picture yourself sitting on one side of the table and facing a dozen fax machines on the other side.

Now all of your self-adopted Loves and Beliefs represent Deputy-Governors who, along with the SA-Needs (needs which are often repressed or compounded, exaggerated by the Deputy-Governors), are continually sending pictures of actions they recommend over the fax machines and trying to enact these pictures by pushing them into the Enact Level slot. Of course you never see the Deputy-Governors, only the pictures of their recommended actions. The force with which the pictures are pushed toward the Enact Slot represent the magnitude of the Desires and/or Fears the Deputy-Governors are able to generate in the Province.

Bear in mind that you became Governor of this Province before you were born, and many of the Deputy-Governors were appointed without your full cognizance of their powers, sometimes without the knowledge that an entity with their particular powers was ever appointed at all!

Bear in mind too, that your only contact with the outside world is through the pictures which come through the machines, pictures which represent less than one percent of your total possible perceptions, and that every one of these pictures, while it may have emanated from the real world, has since been modified, colored, and altered with additions and deletions, by your known and unknown Deputy-Governors, before it reached the Command Center.

This analogy became very valid to me when I interviewed the rather proud president of a large company. He said his major problem was trying to find out what was going on in the company. No one wanted to give him any bad news. (Obviously, he never thanked the messenger.) He could have complete havoc going on right next door, and never hear of it, but the minute something good happened, even a hundred miles away, a dozen people trooped into his office to tell him about it.

And this is precisely what our Deputy-Governors are doing to each of us, suppressing many of our pictures of the world, so they never reach our consciousness, and coloring all the rest to make them acceptable to us—to make them conform to our Loves and Beliefs.

Realize fully that your only functions are to visualize, believe, and devote yourself. You are an artist, and can create your own pictures and fax them back to your Deputy-Governors. Although each of them has a will of its own, they are *your* Deputies, and if you repeatedly fax back to them a clear picture of a result, with the determination that you want it done, and that you will accept any reasonable way of getting it done, your Deputy-Governors will go to work for you, and begin presenting you with pictures of the means by which you can realize your goal. If you do it right, they'll do the job.

Once you have this new picture of yourself firmly in mind, then you can start tracing the pictures you're getting through your machines back to the Deputy-Governors who originated or altered them, and begin firing some of them, taking over their responsibilities yourSelf, and replacing them with better Deputy-Governors. You can begin to live rationally, the way you were designed and ordained to live, can begin to recover the powers you have delegated to these bureaucratic, unthinking Deputy-Governors, and become, for the first time since you were a child, the Governor of your life.

If you wish to change yourself, remember, except for the "I", there is no "real" you, simply the person you have allowed yourself to become. "Your mind/body is God's gift (loan) to you; what you make of them is your gift to God."

> *Good people spiritualize their* [mind/] *bodies;*
> *bad people incarnate their souls.*
> —BENJAMIN WHICHCOTE

We will either subordinate the SA-Needs and the materialistic, egocentric Loves and Beliefs which characterize our society to the needs of the "I", or the powers and needs of the "I" will be subordinated to them. We cannot serve God and mammon.

You can become what you will (visualize/believe/commit) to become. To do this, you must go through Underhill's "costly ordering of your disordered Loves;" must reprioritize your Loves and change some basic Beliefs. Your reticular formation has been haphazardly hard-wired and is erroneously interpreting the world to you, and you must now re-wire it with new Loves, Beliefs, Values, and Needs.

In *The Strangest Secret*, Earl Nightingale says, "We become what we think about." This is also the thrust of Assagioli's *Psychosynthesis*. In our terms this means that if we can clearly Visualize and Love, i.e. identify ourselves with, a person (even an historical or imaginary person) who Loves and Believes certain things, then our Love/Belief Systems tend to be reorganized to conform to the picture. The Love/Vision eventually becomes a Belief, and the Belief a commitment. Instead, most of us grew up trying to mimic just the actions or attitudes of people we considered happy and/or successful, and became poor imitations of others (many of whom were not as successful or happy as we thought they were), instead of trying to adopt healthy Loves and Beliefs, and becoming our own unique persons. It is not our actions or attitudes that make us happy or successful; it is our Loves and Beliefs.

Can you visualize a self-confident person (who believes in herself) without being arrogant? Then you can become that person. Can you visualize a person who has no self-image? (see pps. 155-56) Then you can become that person. Can you visualize a person who believes, "'I' am spirit; 'I' am Lover/ Knower"? Then you can become that person. And if you can visualize a person who loves God with all her heart, soul, mind and strength, and her neighbor as herself, then you are not far from the Kingdom of God.[1] Through the grace of God, you will Know the truth—about God, and about your *Self*—and the truth will set You free.

---

[1]   You cannot manufacture a Love for God. Love for God, the key to the Kingdom of God, is a gift of God (see the Lozowick book, *The Only Grace is Loving God);* but it is only given to those who desire it (see again William Law and *The Cloud of Unknowing,* p. 106). Therefore you cannot work your way to heaven; you never *earn* this gift. However, "the knowledge of God cannot be attained by seeking, but only those who seek it find it" (Bayazid); and in the spiritual world, "everything is a gift, but nothing is free" (Huston Smith).

13
Conclusions

The Basic Human Needs

We must now simplify and restructure Maslow's "final" hierarchy of human needs consisting of about 25 items (see page 208), as follows:

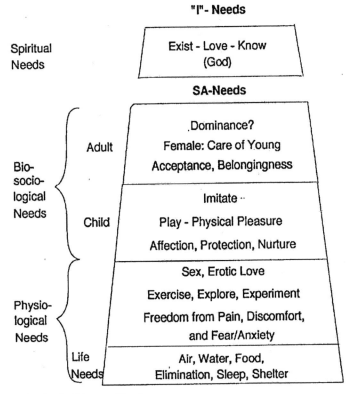

Figure 10 - The Basic Human Needs

In this chart we can trace the typical development of the human as he exercises his "I"-Faculties in identifying with (Loving/Knowing), then disidentifying from, one after another of the basic human needs—first as a body with all of its physiological needs, simply a pain/discomfort/fear avoider; then as a play/pleasure seeker and a loved, protected, nurtured child; then as a mind/ body, an imitator, explorer, experimenter; then with his sexuality and his ego: his self-image, reputation, character, personality, possessions, all the roles and paraphernalia which will serve as a semblance of a self-identity, symbolic of his place in society, and assure his acceptance, belongingness, position in the pecking order: father, mother, American, accountant, etc.; and finally, if he does not fixate at one or more of these levels (which 99.9% of us *do*), he identifies with his spirit, his immortal "I". Then, as Wilber describes the progressive, trans-egoic identifications of the "I", (self):

> *. . . as the center of the self was shown to be Archetype; and as the center of the Archetype was shown to be final-God; and as the center of final-God was shown to be Formlessness—so the center of Formlessness is shown to be not other than the entire world of Form. "Form is not other than Void, Void is not other than Form," says the most famous Buddhist Sutra. At that point the ordinary and the extraordinary, the supernatural and mundane, are precisely one and the same.*

Both the infant and the fully mature individual are in union with the world; but, rather than being "a regression in the service of the ego," as Freud believed, it is a *transcendence in the service of the soul*; and there is a profound difference between the two states. Again, from Wilber:

> *. . . the infantile fusion state . . . is pretemporal, prespatial, preverbal and prepersonal. The true mystic union, on the other hand, is transtemporal, transspatial, transverbal and transpersonal. Because both pre-x and trans-x are (in their own ways) non-x, they appear similar at first glance, . . . But two glances ought to be enough to convince any sane person of the actual and profound differences involved.* [AP:74]

Healthy human development can now be seen to consist of successive identifications and disidentifications (transcendences) of the "I" with each of the social animal needs, a process not to be completed (consummated) in this life, but of which the final temporal stage consists of a transcendence of all these needs, and a progressively more profound "I"-realization of its true nature: creative spirit, akin to God and all people. The driving forces of this process are the SA-Needs and the "I"-Needs; the latter—because of their non-specific manifestation, and society's resultant failure to recognize their existence and significance—usually frustrated in a compulsive, but fruitless effort to find fulfillment in gratification of the ever-increasing SA-Needs and the common human values, and fixation at a level in which one Loves an ever-changing combination of the world's infinite variety of *things*: love, sex, socializing, football, progeny, play, power, recognition, possessions, etc., etc. (see again, Huxley, p. 98-99, and Underhill, p. 104-5).

Healthy psychological development consists of progressive identifications and transcendences of the "I", culminating in its realization of itself as creative spirit, akin to God, sibling to all.

The Wilber quotes above are from his classic description of the outward and inward arcs of spiritual development, entitled *The Atman Project*, in which he delineates the successive identifications and differentiations as one develops from the womb to mystic union. My only differences with Wilber—and they are minor ones—are, 1) although he often mentions the self, he does not define it, calling it by such various names as self, Self, true Self, over-self, ego, subtle-self, consciousness, subtle regions, soul, (Maharshi's) I-I, etc.; 2) he describes human development almost exclusively from the standpoint of classical psycho-analysis, coupled with what he calls "Atman telos," the urge for unity (which I call the "I"-Need to Love and Know God), and does not, in my opinion, attribute sufficient significance to the common SA-Needs in human development; and 3) like Maslow, he sees human needs as homogeneous, all of "one cloth" (see Maslow, FRHN., pps. 327,331). But whereas Maslow sees our spiritual needs as a culminating aspect of our biological needs, Wilber tries to extend our spiritual need (for unity) backward into what I consider the physiological and bio-sociological (SA-) needs of the infant.[1]

As I said, these are minor differences—all in all, *The Atman Project* is a classic and deserves to be read by all who hope for enlightenment.

This diagram should now be self-explanatory. Unless they become objects of "I"-Love, fixating the person, the needs to exercise, explore, experiment, imitate, and play diminish as the child matures, as do the needs for affection, protection, and nurture, which are translated into the need for acceptance, belongingness, and sex, erotic love. The question mark after dominance

---

[1]   As noted earlier, 99+% of our genetic material is identical to that of the chimpanzee, whose infantile behavior patterns are identical to those of the child. It strains human credulity to suggest that our infantile motivations/needs differ, or that the animal's SA-Needs are (also) for "unity."

indicates its questionable innateness in the human (p.20). In the fully mature individual, these needs are then transcended in favor of the needs of the "I" to Exist, to Love, and to Know; needs which most of us only allay by the hundreds of distractions of an "active life;" but which can only be continuously, fully gratified in an Existence centered on an ever-increasing Love and Knowledge of God.

Repeating,

**The single most important objective for the human race,
individually and collectively, is the realization and
appreciation of our essentially spiritual nature,
our immortal "I"'s.**

The way to realize the "I" is through prayer, meditation, asceticism, reading, introspection, and good works. These are all seen to be exercises of the "I", by which it stills the heart's Desires and Fears, and by tracing the "I"-Functions back to their source, gradually comes to realize itself as Free Spiritual Being/Lover/Knower. Of course prayer is the primary exercise; but meditation and introspection are useful in identifying the conscious and subconscious Elements of the Love/Belief System, many of the latter disappearing as soon as they emerge into consciousness, so irrational they are unable to survive the light of day. "Meditation is a mirror which shows us our virtues and our vices," and has been described as a "window to the heart." Ascetic practices strengthen the "I"-Faculties, and divorce it from its roles, emotions, artificial Values and Needs, etc. Through these spiritual exercises comes the gradual "ordering of our disordered loves," and eventually, a realization of the "I" and the restoration of its sovereignty in the person's life. And these can be completely secular transformations, without religious considerations.

> *How shall I grasp it? Do not grasp it. That which
> remains when there is no more grasping is the Self.*
> —PANCHADASI

I believe the definitive exposition of the practices which lead to a realization of the "I" is found in the four Gospels in the words of Christ; next best are *Practical Mysticism* by Evelyn Underhill, *The Perennial Philosophy* by Aldous Huxley, *Awareness,* by Anthony de Mello, S.J., and *The Power of Now* by Eckhart Tolle. Also see Wilber's *No Boundary*, Alan Watts' *The Supreme Identity*, and Appendix C.

Mental Health/Illness

With our new paradigm of person, we can now identify three kinds or levels of mental "illness." The first or lower level is represented by those depressions and anxieties which are the result of a failure to satisfy the SA-Needs, for avoidance of pain, discomfort, fear, or anxiety, for food, vitamins, sleep, etc., or for sex, erotic love, acceptance/belongingness, (or dominance?).

On the second level of mental illness are the well-classified (if not well-understood) psychoses, neuroses, and character disorders with which most psychologists and psychiatrists are concerned. With only the exceptions noted earlier (chemical, genetic, etc.), these states are now seen to be the result of deleterious, irrational, inordinate, obsolete, or conflicting, conscious or subconscious Loves and Beliefs, Desires and Fears.

One of the most common characteristics of this level of psychopathology is a belief in one's inferiority and unworthiness. Simply put, neurotics believe "I'm not good enough;" psychotics believe "I'm not good enough, but neither is anyone else." But to assume, as most psychologists do, that the antidote for feelings of inferiority is to learn to think well of oneself, to have a positive self-image, improved self-esteem, or, as so many people are fond of saying, "You've got to love yourself first," is simply to err on the other side of the same coin.

Certainly it is beneficial to help psychotics and neurotics to think less ill of themselves. But to think less ill of oneself does not require that one think well of oneself. This just moves the person toward an even more common character disorder: pride, egoism, or narcissism, toward what Underhill describes as "the ridiculous megalomania which makes each person the center of their universe." The saints tell us there is a middle ground which leads to mental health, and that is one in which the person does not think of himself at all; a state in which the person has no qualitative—*or even a negative*—self-image. Their self-image is a matter of no-issue or no-concern; they have achieved the "transcendence of self," (of selfhood and self-concern, i.e., the *humility*), which Maslow observed in self-actualizing people. Their self-image has been reduced to one of, "'I' am immortal spirit, Lover and Knower."

The isolated, inwardly regarding self stands at the heart of our spiritual life: in the strained elevation of the mystic, in the "grace" of the courtly lover, in the insistent reasoning of the philosopher. Yet there is a curious lack . . . Among all these glorified selves we have yet to encounter a

unique recognizable individual. As with the self of Descartes' Medita-
tions, their singularity casts no shadow. Dean Inge once remarked, of
the many mystical treatises he had read, that they might all have been
written by a single person, so much did the unity of their language and
experience give a sense of impersonality to their ecstasies. When Eckhart
or Plotinus wrote "I," nothing remained of their singleness. They leapt
abruptly, and with no emotional residue, from the particular into the
universal.

—PAUL ZWEIG

Not only have they lost all concern for self-respect, and—though they are anxious not to offend—their concern for the respect of others, to the extent that they think of themselves at all, it is most often with a healthy *disrespect* for their physical and mental capabilities. They have come to Know with Jeremiah that "the heart of man is infinitely deceitful, and who can know it?"—have developed a perpetual mistrust of their own motives and competence. In short, they have been graced with the world's greatest anxiety/neurosis/psychosis dispeller, the essential prerequisite of Wisdom: *Humility.*

As regards self-image then, the continuum of mental health ranges from, "I'm no good," (neurotic-psychotic); to "I'm as good as anyone else," or, "I'm OK, you're OK," (normal?); to, "'I' am spirit, the spirit of Free Being/Loving/ Knowing, associated with the brain/body of a social animal; 'I' Exist in a perpetual state of Knowing, only to the extent that I act with Love in all my affairs: with care and concern, responsiveness, respect, and knowledge," (enlightened, liberated).

This latter self-image results in a Love/Belief System—and, therefore, a life—characterized by Love, tends to remove all rigidity or conditioned response tendencies from our lives, and to allow the greatest possible freedom of action, sovereignty of the "I", and the fullest possible gratification of the "I"-Needs to Exist, to Love, and to Know. The highest form of self-actualization is now seen as "I"-actualization, the ever-growing realization of the powers and satisfactions of the "I", exercised most gratifyingly in the Love of God and one's neighbor.

And now we can see a higher or third level of mental illness, from which most of the human race suffers. On this level we find what we now call "burnout"—the "depression, anomie, anhedonia, rootlessness, meaninglessness, existential boredom, spiritual starvation," of Maslow, the "restriction to the normal [which] signifies the bed of Procrustes, unbearable boredom, infernal sterility and hopelessness," of Jung, or the "existential vacuum" of Frankl.

These higher mental illnesses are now seen to result from a failure to gratify the "I"-Needs to Exist (forever), and to Love and to Know (a worthy object). Frankl's existential vacuum is only apparently due to a "lack of meaning" in the person's life; actually it is caused by our always unsuccessful denial of death, and our lack of suitable objects of "I"-Love/Knowledge. People in Love, completely fascinated by, and devoted to learning to Know, a subject or a person or God, never even think to *ask* about life's "meaning."

Earlier I said that our most debilitating fear is our fear of death: the common misery of life. It is now becoming obvious that a corollary and equally basic, equally demoralizing misery of humankind is the lack of worthy objects of "I"-Love/Knowledge. As Maslow says (¶4, p. 64), "The therapeutic and psychologic effects of experiencing B-Love are very profound and wide-spread." Sorokin agrees: "Unselfish love has enormous creative and therapeutic potentialities." This is because the exercise of "I"- (or B-) Love renders inoperative questions about our reason for being; it fulfills the greatest human need, after existence, the need to give ourselves to someone or something worthy of our total, unpossessive, unconditional "I"-Love.

Indeed, there is ample evidence that when one attains some fulfillment of the "I"-Needs to Love and to Know, many of the more common psychological aberrations from which he may have suffered tend to disappear. It's an old adage that "a homeless puppy is the best psychiatrist;" his adoption often substantially ameliorating many neuroses, psychoses, and character disorders.

Fulfillment of the "I"-Needs to Exist, to Love, and to Know *is* the human's reason for being, and renders meaningless the question of life's "meaning."

Mental health, then, should no longer be defined negatively, as simply the absence of psychoses, neuroses, and character disorders, but rather as:

Freedom from inordinate, self-induced fear, desire, and anxiety;
Ability to respond to any and all of life's circumstances with "I"-Love: care and concern, responsiveness, respect, and knowledge.

This state is seen to result from having a coherent Love/Belief System, at least a nominal satisfaction of the SA-Needs, and consistent gratification of the "I"-Needs. Conversely, mental illness results from an unhealthy Love/Belief System and/or failure to gratify the SA- or "I"-Needs. Therefore mental health/ illness constitutes a continuum from the unhealthiest to the healthiest Love/Belief

System, from the psychotics, neurotics, and character-disordered, through the great majority of people who are thought of as normal (most of whom lead "lives of quiet desperation"), up to the enlightened, liberated people who have learned to live with only a nominal satisfaction of the SA-Needs, and a maximum satisfaction of the "I"-Needs, to Exist, to Love, and to Know—either God, or (less enlightened), a god-substitute, such as one of John Lilly's *Simulations of God*.

As noted earlier, much of the subconscious is made up of memories and beliefs—facts—which have been repressed because they represented a threat to one of our major Loves, Beliefs, Values, or Needs, e.g., the Love of our lives, or to our self-image or possessions. And, to the extent that our Responses are emanating from subconscious Elements in the Love/Belief System, we must be seen to be living subconsciously—not living, but, as Arieti says, being lived, by our subconscious Desires and Fears. But since the saints have replaced the Love of life with the Love of God, and have no concern for their image or their possessions, they have eliminated the great majority of their subconscious, and are now able to live *consciously*. Saints and animals have no subconscious! And this accounts for the "animal-like naturalness and grace," which Maslow observed in "self-actualizing, saintly, sagacious, rational" people. The difference is that the animal never developed a subconscious, but the saints, through arduous and scrupulously honest self-examination of their Love/Belief Systems (hearts) have eliminated theirs, and established, as the major Elements in their Love/Belief Systems, the Love of God and their neighbor. Therefore they alone are able to respond rationally, i.e., graciously, generously, and creatively: *Lovingly*, to all the circumstances of life.

Instead of a perpetual concern with gratification of the SA-Needs and the common human values, these enlightened people have discovered the far greater fulfillment which results from gratification of the "I"-Needs, to Exist in the Love and Knowledge of God. Except for the most nominal satisfaction of the most essential SA-Needs, they have transcended these needs in favor of satisfaction of the "I"-Needs.

Summing up, both major and minor psychopathologies can result from a failure to satisfy the human's inherent "I"-Needs or SA-Needs, or a failure to gratify/assuage the self-adopted Loves and Beliefs, and their concomitant Desires and Fears, which constitute the preponderant constituents of the Love/Belief System.

Needless to say, the great majority of the human race suffers to some degree from all three, and most of us never find any true or consistent fulfillment of the "I"-Needs.

Education

People must be taught how their minds function, how the Love/Belief System, or RAS, shapes their responses to the circumstances of life. They must be made aware of the existence and the needs and faculties of the "I", and the constitution and powers of the Love/Belief System.

We should teach our children that they are not their mind/bodies, that they are spirit, and that death does not claim "them," minimizing their denial of death. This thesis implies that an elementary level course in "Alternatives of Behavior" would be helpful to the child, a course devoted to the study of alternative responses to common stimuli, and to acting out those responses: psychodrama directed to the study of rational responses to life experiences.

As always, an ounce of prevention is worth a pound of cure. If we could teach children early in life the significance of their Loves, Beliefs, Values, and Needs, we could perhaps help them to be more discriminating in the adoption of Loves and Beliefs, which they would know can be changed later in life only with great difficulty.[2]

We should now teach our children (and ourselves) how to use their creative powers of Visualization, Belief, and Love; in particular, teach them how to use the neglected right side of the brain to first visualize clearly the desired result of any task they undertake. As Stephen Covey says in *Seven Habits of Highly Effective People,* "Always start with the end in mind."

The Real Self

It is easy to infer from advice to seek our "true selves" that somewhere inside us is an effective, self-actualized person waiting to flower. But now it is obvious that there is no pre-ordained person we were "meant to become." The true self is spirit; the person is whatever his temperament, his environment, the creative powers of the "I", and the grace of God have made him.

(Nor does God have a *plan* for each of our lives. This is proven in the parable of the talents. God gave us free will and certain talents, and we will be judged by what we do with them. God seems to be saying, "Surprise Me."

(The fact that there is no "real," innate person I must "find" or "be true

---

[2]   However, we must not raise them as skeptics either. As we've seen, doubts too are beliefs, and as Carol Zaleski observes: *"Both* [Adam of Eynsham and Gregory the Great] *suggest that unbelief is not a 'tough-minded' or neutral position, in which the intellect demands hard evidence and reserves judgment until the facts are in; rather, it is a weakness, a disease or deformity of the will."* [OJ:88]

to," no pre-ordained plan for my life; but that "I" am daily—with the help of God—*fashioning* a person, *creating* a life, is one of the most challenging yet liberating ideas I've ever encountered. It gives full meaning to the "purpose-driven life.")

Personality

It seems that ultimately, personality can only be defined as a person's behavior; and his behavior, as we have seen, is almost entirely shaped by his temperament and the contents of his Love/Belief System, particularly by his self-image, and his other significant Loves and Beliefs.

Feelings/Emotions

Feelings and emotions are now seen to be *involuntary, autonomic,* Love/Belief System Response Impulses to the person's perceptions, and are only useful therapeutically in tracing them back to the Love, Belief, Value, or Need which caused them. Full expression of one's feelings is pure libertinism and hedonism, and in direct opposition to "I"-actualization. We must discontinue therapies which suggest that our feelings are the only valid criteria of appropriate behavior. Trusting one's feelings, when those feelings can be the result of completely irrational, deleterious, obsolete, inordinate, or erroneous Loves and Beliefs, is the worst possible advice. Only when one's Love/Belief System is characterized by Love of God and his neighbor can he trust his feelings. As St. Augustine said, "Love and do what you like."

Until then, we must heed the advice Assagioli gave his friend, Piero Ferrucci, when the latter suggested that we should "follow our feelings," as reported in *What We May Be*. Assagioli's reply was, "But you must *not* follow your feelings. Your feelings must follow you." Good advice. (See again the exhortation of à Kempis, p. 131.)

Research

We should determine both the characteristics: consistency, flexibility, permeability, etc., and the specific Elements, which constitute healthy and unhealthy Love/Belief Systems; i.e., determine which specific Loves and Beliefs are beneficial to the person's mental health, and which are detrimental. (I'll suggest some healthy secular beliefs at the conclusion of this chapter, and spiritual beliefs in Chapter 14.)

We should determine the best methods of realizing the "I" and learning to appreciate its powers and its needs. We need methods by which the individual can eliminate, and/or change, undesirable root Elements in his Love/Belief System.

There is ample evidence that failure to live through one stage of development through the SA-Needs and "I"-Needs before passing on to the next can result in a warping of one's personality, a fixation of certain elements of his character, and potentially, later in life, a crashing regression to even lower levels of development. This is usually the result of attempts to repress, rather than transcend the more elementary "I"-identifications.[3] We should develop criteria for determining conditions or benchmarks which will indicate attainment of the various stages of I"-identification/disidentification and readiness to proceed, without these deleterious side-effects or regressions.

We should try to determine the limits of the creative powers of the "I" in visualization/belief/devotion. Can we move mountains?

Behaviorism/Cognitivism

We must acknowledge that most of our actions and emotions are simply conditioned responses; that we have actually allowed a great many physiological/neural stimulus/response links to be created in our systems, and that these links can sometimes best be broken by positive or negative reinforcement, or by changing the way we cognize events.

However, pure behaviorists and cognitivists are now seen to be two steps and one step respectively removed from the *cause* of our behavior. We can, of course, change behavior temporarily by reinforcement or by changing the way we cognize events; but these changes will only be permanent when they result in changes in our Love/Belief Systems. And both cognition and behavior can be changed permanently by changing the basic Loves and Beliefs which determine our Desires and Fears, our perceptions, our cognitions, and our behavior.

Specious reinforcement of behavior in an effort to make it a conditioned response is now seen to be useless when the behavior results from Loves or Beliefs which remain unchanged by the exercise. Behavioral changes are only effective when they are directed to helping the client reach new conclusions (Beliefs) regarding his behavior.

---

[3]   The important distinction between repression and transcendence was drawn, *in those terms*, by Fr. Augustine Baker circa 1635 ! [HW:215]

Cognitive/behavioral, rational-emotive, psychosynthesis, and client-centered therapies are, of course, closest to the mark. Many of their practices are directed toward belief changes, and many use visual imagery to help implement those changes, and behavioral exercises to help the client test the validity of his beliefs and practice new behaviors, which, whether they know it or not, is a very effective exercise of the "I". But most do not include a consideration of Loves, Values, or Needs; and therefore confusedly call them thoughts, notions, ideas, expectations, themes, explanatory style, assumptions, "tapes," perceptions, schema, cognitions, etc., all of which are now seen to be Loves and Beliefs or functions of our Loves and Beliefs.

But the major weakness of all these therapies is their neglect of the "I" and its Needs and Faculties, with the implicit assumption that a simple rationalization of one's beliefs, without consideration of the "I"-Needs, can lead to fulfillment.

All the effective practices of cognitive/behavioral, rational-emotive, client-centered, and psychosynthesis therapies can and should now be subsumed in "Open-Heart Therapy," (See Appendix D).

Psychotherapy

All psychotherapies must now be seen to be effective to the extent that they help the client to 1) understand the existence, needs, and faculties of the "I", 2) understand that the SA-Needs and his self-adopted conscious and subconscious Loves and Belief, Desires and Fears are controlling his life, 3) learn how to map his own Love/Belief System by tracing his actions and emotions (feelings) back to the Loves and Beliefs that cause them, and 4) learn methods by which he can eliminate unhealthy and adopt healthy Loves and Beliefs, and 4), restore the sovereignty of the "I".

All psychotherapy should be "Open-Heart Therapy," therapy which enables the client, operating as an "I", to open his heart first to himself, then to the world, to his neighbor, and to God.

The most important objectives for psychologists/psychiatrists is to teach us "how we work"—how the Love/Belief System generates our thoughts, our emotions, and our behavior; and to develop methods by which we can identify and change the Elements in our Love/Belief Systems, and restore the sovereignty of the "I".

It seems obvious too, that psychiatrists might best help their clients by helping them select and adopt healthy root Loves and Beliefs, rather than digging into their pasts in an effort to find the causes of their problems. The causes of most mental and emotional problems are now seen to be deleterious, inordinate, irrational, obsolete, or conflicting conscious or subconscious Loves, Beliefs, Desires, and Fears. It would seem that these might be eliminated, without even bothering to identify them, by helping the client to replace them with healthy root Loves and Beliefs.

In the case of seriously disturbed neurotics and psychotics, and of course only with their complete approval and cooperation, we should immediately begin experiments using Rokeach's hypnotic belief changes [BAV:Ch.2], to try to inject—very gradually, of course—some healthy root Beliefs in their Love/Belief Systems. Can there be any doubt that to the extent to which they were able to accept healthier root beliefs, it would automatically change their lives for the better?

Definitions: Mind and Psyche

I have already proposed that "mind" be defined as a *human brain,* physiologically identical to that of the chimpanzee, and functionally consisting of the Reticular Activating System or Love/Belief System, the Memory, and the Center of Consciousness. The rest of the brain is the RF's "toolbox."

But in spite of the traditional definitions of psyche as "soul, mind, spirit," or "that which governs the organism," the soul ("I") cannot be considered as just a component of the psyche, on a par with "mind." Soul is distinct from mind, monitors and manages the mind, and shapes and changes the mind. Therefore in order to retain as much as possible of its former meaning, I propose that we now define "psyche," as *the governing element of the human, consisting of the* **mind,** *which acts in conjunction with, and under the ultimate management of, the soul."* The components of psyche would then be soul (superior) and mind (inferior); the person, a trinity of soul, mind, and body.

Healthy Secular Beliefs

We are what we Love, Believe, Value, and Need. If we are able to develop healthy root Loves and Beliefs, we can literally program ourselves for whatever we wish to become, provided that we adopt root Loves and Beliefs, not just superficial, surface ones.

It would seem that some healthy secular root Beliefs would be:

"I" am spirit, the spirit of Free Being/Loving/Knowing; temporarily associated with the brain/body of a very proficient social animal, whose physiological, sociological, and psychological needs "I" must not allow to dominate my life.

Whatever "I" Visualize, Believe, and Love, devote myself to, will become real in my life and come into existence, provided only that it does not conflict with my other, or other people's, Visions, Beliefs, and Loves.

The world I see is not the real world, but simply a mirror of my own Love/Belief System, my own haphazardly acquired, conscious and subconscious Loves and Beliefs, and their concomitant Desires and Fears. "I" have allowed an obscuring, diffracting screen to come into being between me and the world, a screen which is invisible to me, but which appropriates my will, confounds my reason, suppresses and distorts my memory and senses, and renders my creative imagination ineffectual. Only unpossessive, unconditional Love will remove this screen.

"I" only truly see that which "I" look at with unpossessive, unconditional Love. "I" only come to really Know that which "I" first have Loved—devoted mySelf to, or identified mySelf with.

"I" am responsible for my own life; I am today where my Loves and Beliefs have brought me, and I will be tomorrow where they bring me. My life is what "I" make it; "I" create my own future with my Loves and Beliefs.

There is no "real" person that I am destined to be, or that I must "find," or "be true to,"—simply the person "I" have allowed myself to become. "I" am daily creating my personhood with my Loves and Beliefs.

Every moment of life, under almost any circumstances, is an exciting, precious, miraculous, event. "The world is full of beauty when the heart is full of Love."

"Life is difficult." This is the entire first paragraph in M. Scott Peck's excellent book, *The Road Less Traveled*. He continues, "This is a great truth, . . . because once we truly see this truth, we transcend it."

Life can be difficult, but I'll be happier if I learn to face life and deal with it, than if I try to run away from or ignore life's problems.

"Life does not need comfort, when it can be offered meaning, nor pleasure, when it can be shown purpose."

As a person, I am a unique individual with physical, mental and social assets and liabilities; there is no one in the world, nor has there ever been, nor will there ever be, someone exactly like me. Therefore I should not be compared favorably or unfavorably with anyone else, nor need I compete with anyone else. My only competition should be what I was yesterday.

Some people will like me; and some will not. I do not require people's approval to be happy. Since I do have faults, and since I can become what "I" will, the people who criticize me can be my best "helpers," enabling me to identify my faults, and use that information to create a better person.

"Most people are about as happy as they make up their minds to be." Most of my feelings are the results of my Loves and Beliefs; since "I" adopted them, "I" can also disown them, develop new Loves and Beliefs, and thereby change my feelings.

People are all different; all have some good in them, and some bad; some intelligence and some ignorance; some honesty, and some dishonesty; no one is perfect, no one irredeemable. Therefore I can find good and bad in everyone. I'll be happier if I look for the good. Since no one should judge me, I must not judge others.

Although I can help or hurt everyone I meet, I will be happier if I try to help them; however, I cannot take full responsibility for how any other adult lives.

It is only fair that I should treat people as I expect to be treated.

We cannot all be great, but we can be associated with something great.

I must accept death as the "price" of life; not dread it, nor dwell on it, but accept it when it comes to others, and when it comes to me.

These certainly represent much healthier beliefs than, for example, the Gestalt "prayer," "I am I and you are you. I'm not in this world to live up to your expectations, and you're not in this world to live up to mine."—an obvious effort to alter one's needs and beliefs to create a less caring attitude.

In the next chapter, I'll list some beliefs conducive to our spiritual development, and show how the theories of this book relate to the Perennial Philosophy, which I think is best represented by the words of Christ. Confirmed agnostics, atheists, or adherents of other faiths—even perhaps some Christians who don't agree with my existential, esoteric interpretation of the Gospels—may want to skip this final chapter which contains an outline of Christ's teaching.

For those people, if I could choose only one thought to leave with you, it would be that, with or without religion, none of us are seeing or experiencing the *real* world, but only a reflection of our Love/Belief Systems; our worlds are literally painted over with dozens of thick "coats" of our Loves and Beliefs, Desires and Fears.

For most of us, the world *has* congealed about us, our hearts are waxed gross, our ears are dull of hearing, and our eyes we have closed, solely because of the "hardness of our hearts," or Love/Belief Systems. We have all forgotten what the real world looks and feels like, the world we knew when we were four—the world the mystics/saints/sages keep trying to tell us about. Our haphazardly acquired Loves and Beliefs have created a screen between ourselves and the real world; we have become blinded to its awesome sacred miraculousness, numbed to the ineffable *wonder*, the exciting amazed admiration it once inspired in us, and the overwhelming *gratitude* we used to feel at just being alive with the capacity to enjoy it.

Worse still, not only are many of our Loves and Beliefs subconscious, and/or erroneous, inordinate, irrational, contradictory, obsolete, or negative, we all have a strong compulsion to maintain them, even though we must continually repair their poor semblance of "consistency." They represent to each of us the only safe interpretation of a confusing and frightening world; and so far, they have kept us alive, sane, and with some acceptance in our societies. The fulfillment enlightened people extol seems, perhaps, far too ephemeral a reward for the risk of disturbing the precarious balance in which most of us laboriously and irrationally try to maintain our haphazardly constructed Love/Belief Systems.

But as the old saying goes, if you haven't tried it, don't knock it—it's even more than they can say.

14
Soul-Actualization:
The Kingdom of God

All over the world, people are seeking self-actualization, self-fulfillment, enlightenment, salvation, nirvana, altered states of consciousness. Even where one might least expect to find it, among American business professionals, the American Management Association found that one of their major goals was a more perfected religious faith.

But those in the western world, the vast majority of them professing Christians, are ignoring the Kingdom of God, as preached and practiced by Christ according to the four Gospels, and which has provided to thousands of Christians throughout the ages, the total fulfillment of all these ambitions. They are traveling the world in search of gurus, ignoring the ultimate "Guru," Jesus of Nazareth, Christ, the Son of God, and His Holy Spirit, Whose guidance He has promised to those who accept Him and keep His commandments, and Which will guide us here on earth, while we live, into the Kingdom of God.

Christ said He came to preach the Kingdom of God which He said was "within us," "at hand;" a manifest indwelling of God, which we must seek first, as we would seek a treasure hidden in a field, or a pearl of great price, worth sacrificing anything else that we own or desire (even our hand or foot or eye, if necessary) to attain, see, enter, realize. If, as Christ said, God is our Father, then the Kingdom of God is surely our "home" here on earth.

The riches of Christ's words are inexhaustible; there is no bottom to them. Repeated study of Christ's words continually and perpetually reveals additional glorious insights into the nature of God, and no one's life is so long, nor his study of Christ's words so thorough, that he can fail to gain additional blessings from re-reading, re-studying, re-savoring them.

As our study of the power of our Loves and Beliefs in our lives has shown, it is obviously not enough to just hear or read the words of Christ. You must, as Christ said, "Let these sayings sink down into your ears," until you "understand with your *heart*." In the parable of the sower, we learn that the seed (Christ's words) must be planted deep, in good soil, kept free of thorns, and the seed will grow!

In *The Denial of Death,* Ernest Becker comes to the conclusion that, for our *psychological* well-being, we must be born again; and in its sequel, *Escape From Evil,* writes, "I think that today Christianity is in trouble, not because its myths are dead, but because it does not offer its ideal of heroic sainthood as an immediate personal one to be lived by all believers."

Meanwhile, unfortunately, most Christian clergy must preach to millions of potential saints, doctrines which contain only half the demands, and therefore, none of the this-world spiritual riches of the doctrine they espouse. As Christ said of the scribes and Pharisees, they stand at the gates of the Kingdom of God, and enter not in themselves, nor do they encourage others to enter.

The reason is not hard to find, and the fault is not entirely theirs. Christ's promises of the riches of the Kingdom of God on earth and eternal life hereafter, are counterbalanced by the great demands He makes on us to be converted, to reform our natural way-of-being in the world through a complete reorganization of our Love/Belief Systems. But because of the "hardness of our hearts," His words are no more palatable today than they were to His original audiences; Christ's words simply don't fill pews.

I heard about a clergyman in an affluent American suburb who gave a sermon on an unpopular social issue, and his collections fell 50%. Imagine what would have happened if he had commended Becker's "ideal of heroic sainthood as an immediate personal one to be lived by all believers"!

The fundamental truths [of this religion] are to be found in the esoteric teachings of all religions, among all races, and have been imparted to these religions by the original founders. . . through their favored disciples. These teachings become impaired with each generation of followers, until the original truths are almost entirely lost sight of. As an illustration of this fact, read the "Sermon on the Mount," the teachings of which are understood and venerated by occultists and mystics of all schools and countries. Then see how His followers maintain the outward form while stating boldly and unblushingly that Christ's teachings are "not practicable." Unbelievers may deny the truth of Christ's teachings, but it remains for professing Christians to pronounce them "foolish" and not fitted for the use of mankind.

These words were penned by Yogi Ramacharaka in explaining to his students "the fundamental ideas and teachings of the Gnani Yogis." It seems that truth comes not only out of the mouths of babes, but also out of the mouths of some whom many self-professed Christians call "heathens."

But, you will say, Do not all Christians desire to have Christ to be their Savior? Yes. But here is the deceit; all would have Christ to be their Savior in the next world, and to help them into heaven when they die, by His power, and merits with God. But this is not willing Christ to be thy Savior; for His salvation, if it is had, must be had in this world; if He saves thee, it must be done in this life, by changing and altering all that is within thee, by helping thee to a new heart as He helped the blind to see, the lame to walk, and the dumb to speak. For to have salvation from Christ, is nothing else but to be made like unto Him; it is to have His humility and meekness, His mortification and self-denial, His renun- iation of the spirit, wisdom, and honours of this world, His love of God, His desire of doing God's will, and seeking only His honour. To have these tempers formed and begotten in thy heart, is to have salvation from Christ. But if thou willest not to have these tempers brought forth in thee, if thy faith and desire does not seek, and cry to Christ for them, in the same reality as the lame asked to walk, and the blind to see, then thou must be said to be unwilling to have Christ to be thy Savior. [SP:41]
—WILLIAM LAW

And the same argument from the Eastern tradition:

O Friend, hope for Him whilst you live,
    know whilst you live, understand whilst you live;
    for in life deliverance abides.
If your bonds be not broken whilst living,
    what hope of deliverance in death?
It is but an empty dream that the soul shall have union
    with Him because it has passed from the body;
If He is found now, He is found then;
If not, we do but go to dwell in the City of Death.
—KABIR

It is in the literal teachings of Christ that we find a clarion call to the "ideal of heroic sainthood as an immediate personal one to be lived by all believers." On pps. 182-183 is an outline of Christ's words arranged in major categories, or principles, in the hope that in this form they might be more readily understood, remembered, and practiced.

Maslow found "self-actualizing" people to have achieved a "detachment," a "transcendence of self," and an "ability to love." It will be apparent that they also exhibit high degrees of faith and integrity. Now it is notable that, except for Christ's first commandment, to Love God with all our heart, soul, mind and strength, these characteristics are identical with Christ's teachings that to enter the Kingdom of God we must deny ourselves, detach ourselves from mammon, Love (God and) our neighbor, and develop, with God's help, the habits of faith, humility, and righteousness.

But it's interesting to see what Christ has to say about Maslow's "basic needs," the needs which occupy 99% of the time and attention of 99% of the world's people.

> With regard to preservation of life, Christ said, "Take no thought for your life;" and, "Fear not them which kill the body," and to those who woke him in fear of the storm, "Why are you fearful, oh you of little faith?" and, "He who loves his life loses it."

> Concerning security, He said, "Take no thought for the morrow." To the man who built bigger barns to store all his goods for future security, He said, "This night thy soul may be required of thee."

> Regarding recognition, He said, "You justify yourselves in the sight of men, but God knows your hearts; for that which is highly esteemed among men is detestable in the sight of God." God knows our Love/ Belief Systems, even though we do not, and most of us are seeking recognition, not the Kingdom of God. To those who prayed and gave alms in public, "that they might be seen of men," He said, "They have their reward."

> About self-esteem, Christ said a publican and a Pharisee prayed in a temple. The Pharisee thanked God that he was not as other men, and itemized his virtues; the publican "would not even lift his eyes to heaven, but beat upon his breast, saying, 'Lord, be merciful to me a sinner;'" and he was justified, rather than the other.

> Regarding self-actualization, He preached only the Kingdom of God as a "pearl of great price," or a "treasure hidden in a field," worth selling all that one had to obtain, and saying, "The Kingdom of God is within you: seek first the Kingdom of God; but whoever does not receive the Kingdom of God like a child, shall not enter it at all."

So Christ shows that the only way to self-actualization, or "I"-actualization, is by a transcendence of most of the other needs that Maslow correctly identified as the natural person's—and the social animal's—basic needs.

From the Christian standpoint then, the following beliefs would seem to be beneficial to our spiritual development:

"I" am immortal spirit, the spirit of Free Being/Loving/Knowing, in the image and likeness of God; associated with the brain/body of a social animal from which "I" will one day be separated; but whose physiological, sociological, and psychological needs "I" must not allow to dominate my life.

As spirit, in the image and likeness of God, my primary needs are to Exist, to Love, and to Know; my ultimate Self-actualization is in the Kingdom of God: eternal Existence in the ever-growing Love and Knowledge of God.

But, "I" am deceived. "I" have accepted dozens of fictions about God, my neighbor, the world, and my Self, in an effort to maintain some semblance of order and consistency in my Love/Belief System—my heart—and acceptance in my society; and now "I" cannot even trust my own perceptions.

Essentially, "I" am Lover/Knower; "I" am care and concern, responsiveness, respect, and knowledge. Through my own efforts (1%) and the grace of God (99%), "I" can be released to exercise Love in all my affairs, and thereby exist in a state of perpetual discovery, of ever-gratifying new Knowledge, Knowledge of people, Knowledge of the world, Knowledge of my Self, and Knowledge of God.

Only in the exercise of Love can I fulfill my true Self, and realize my purpose in life. So Self-fulfilling is the exercise of Love that I will learn even to Love my enemies, those who hate me, and who despitefully use me and persecute me, in order to fulfill my glorious potential as a child of God, "for He makes His sun rise on the evil and the good, and sends rain on the just and on the unjust."

Eternity is Now.

Existence in the Love and Knowledge of God *is* Heaven.

*The only sorrow is **not** to be a saint.*
—LEON BLOY

A study of the lives of the saints indicates that the spiritual search for the Kingdom of God can be likened to a trip to the moon. Initially, in earth orbit, earth gravity represents the attractions of material things, the things of the earth to which we are attached. And we are in a death spiral, each orbit bringing us closer to the point where our momentum will no longer sustain us, and we will burn up in the atmosphere.

It takes a sizeable and continuing effort to launch us on a path to the moon, and, as we travel, earth gravity, the attraction of temporal joys and pleasures, continually tries to pull us backward. But if we persist in work and prayer then, through the grace of God, we continue on our way, and the pull of the earth grows less and less. This is the detachment, mortification, or purgation stage of our journey, Underhill's "costly ordering of our disordered loves," where we identify and rid the soul of its "inordinate attachments." It is St. Augustine's purification of the "eye of the heart whereby God may be seen."

We may find it strange that the saints deny themselves even the simplest inclinations. But they know that God will only occupy a vacant heart, only unite with a sovereign "I". So they try to thwart every desire—good, bad or indifferent. Although responsive to the needs of family and friends, they tend to dissociate from them socially, realizing that most friendships are co-dependencies —that we choose as friends, not challengers, but enablers who help us maintain our egocentric Love/Belief Systems rather than purify them.

But these self-denials are not to earn indulgences or a place in a posthumous heaven, or to make us "good." Rather they are means of "purifying our hearts;" of breaking up our conditioned Love/Belief System responses—each of which is an "I"-debilitator, an erosion of the "I"'s authority. The practices of self-denial and unconditional, unpossessive Love, coupled with meditation and prayer are exercises of the "I" to restore its sovereignty in our lives. After all, how can one devote to God, or to anything else, a life he doesn't control?

Eventually we reach the point of zero gravity, the point at which we are balanced between two mighty forces, the attractions of the earth, and the pull of the moon (= God's Love), and as a result, we feel nothing. We have lost our desire for the things of the earth, but as yet do not feel the power of God's Love in our lives. We become like the bridesmaids who have collected their oil (Love) and hold it in readiness for the coming of their lord, and now can do nothing but wait. And it is excruciating. Nothing, it seems, is more painful than an empty heart—the heart, like nature, abhors a vacuum.

The saints call this the Purification of the Spirit, or the "dark night of the soul," between the "cloud of forgetting and the cloud of unknowing," where "there is no more that we can do of ourselves, but there is much that may and must be done to us." All we can do here is try to "pierce the cloud of unknowing with a sharp dart of longing Love." But this stage of the journey is essential, for it represents what Underhill so poignantly describes as *"that state of passive suffering which is to complete the decentralization of our character, test the purity of our love, and perfect our education in humility."* We are now in Hilton's "rich nothingness," or "essential nothingness."

But God, who invented Nature, also abhors a vacuum. He will not long fail to inhabit a heart empty of all but desire for Him. As Eckhart says, "God is bound to act, to pour into you as soon as He shall find thee ready."[1]

Eventually the pull of God's Love becomes stronger, and we recognize this as the still small Voice within, which has been drawing us on throughout our entire journey. We begin to enter the "unitive way," the beneficent circle (spiral) where our Love for God results in some Knowledge—not feelings or emotions or visions, but absolute Knowledge—of God. And each increment in our Knowledge of God increases our Love for God, and vice versa, and so on to the end of our days, and forever.

The saints have a name for this experience of Being/Loving/Knowing, the state of being where Knower, Known, and Knowledge become one. They call it "infused contemplation," and say that its gratifications, transcending all others, are ineffable. They do not feel joy, they *are* joy, and peace and wisdom and light and Love. Having found their True Selves, the universe, including the mind/body, is subsumed in the "I"—"that art thou"—and both are subsumed in God. Their "I"'s, having been stripped of selfhood and "inordinate attachments," are resumed in, abide in, God.

But to complete our analogy, they do not leave the world and its people. Instead they say, "For now, 'I' am my mind/body," and embrace all people as brothers and sisters in Christ.

I saw a mass of matter of a dull gloomy colour between the North and the East, and was informed that this mass was human beings, in as great a misery as they could be, and live; and that I was mixed up with them and henceforth I must not consider myself as a distinct or separate being.
—JOHN WOOLMAN

---

[1] I'm sure the great Meister would have accepted the alternative: "as soon as He, with thy acquiescence, shall *have made* thee ready."

Christ has told us God is Spirit. It's also been said "the only hands He has are ours." Although God certainly can, and has, acted independently of us, He seems to prefer to answer our prayers through others; either those whose will is compatible with ours, or those whose will is His. Like the man in Acts 9:10, who, when the Lord said, "Ananias," responded immediately with, "Here I am, Lord."

But people whose will is God's are few. As St. Teresa said, "For every soul which prays 'Speak, Lord, for Thy servant heareth,' there are ten who pray, 'Listen, Lord, for Thy servant speaketh,' and"—she adds emphatically—"there is no rest for these."

Yet, in the Lord's prayer, we learn that God's will is done in heaven. How can we expect to find any comfort there if we do not learn to Love and try to do God's will while we live? As Anatole France said, "We don't know what to do with this short life, and we want another which shall be eternal."

No Heaven can come to us unless our hearts find rest in it today. Take Heaven! No peace lies in the future which is not hidden in this present little instant. Take peace! The gloom of the world is but a shadow. Behind it, yet within our reach, is joy. There is radiance and glory in the darkness, could we but see; and to see, we have only to look . . . I beseech you to look.

Life is so generous a giver, but we, judging its gifts by their covering, cast them away as ugly or heavy or hard. Remove the covering, and you will find beneath it a living splendour, woven of love, by wisdom, with power. Welcome it, grasp it, and you touch the Angel's hand that brings it to you. Everything we call a trial, a sorrow, or a duty; believe me, that angel's hand is there; the gift is there, and the wonder of an over-shadowing Presence. Our joys, too: be not content with them as joys; they too conceal diviner gifts.

Life is so full of meaning and of purpose, so full of beauty - beneath its covering - that you will find that earth but cloaks your heaven. Courage, then, to claim it: this is all! But courage you have; and the knowledge that we are pilgrims together, wending through unknown country, home.
　　　　　　　　　　　　　　　　　　　　　　　—FRA GIOVANNI

People whose will is God's are few; and He keeps them so busy. Theoretically, however, if the human race does not destroy itself first, the world could attain a critical mass of people whose will was God's—enough for Him to be able to answer all the prayers of all the others—and at that very moment, the millennium would begin: God's will done on earth as it is in heaven. "Man may create any universe up to the standard of which he is willing to live." (See again Heard, pps.138-40).

> *In theistic terms, to be directly confronted by infinite goodness and love, infinite knowledge and power, infinite fullness of being and life, would deprive us of any independence. There would be no room for a free human response of faith and love, or of trust and obedience. Indeed, the disparity between our finite selves and the infinite divine reality would exclude our very existence as relatively autonomous centers of finite freedom. Therefore God has to be the hidden God, veiling Himself by creating us at an epistemic distance in order that He may then progressively reveal Himself to us in limited ways which respect and preserve our human freedom as persons. Again, in nontheistic terms, it is the finite individual's relative ignorance (avidya) of Brahman that constitutes his own finite individuality. As he rightly exercises his freedom through the long process of samsara, separate individuality is eventually transcended and he becomes the infinite Spirit. . .*

> *It has been suggested, for example by Bergson, that one function of the brain is to filter out the virtual infinity of information reaching us through our senses, so that what comes to consciousness is the relatively simple and manageable world which we perceive and can successfully inhabit. We also have a system for filtering out the Transcendent and reducing it to forms with which we can cope; for "human kind cannot bear very much reality." This system is religion, which is our resistance (in the electronic sense) to the infinite Transcendent. In the earliest stages of man's development, the Transcendent was reduced . . . to the dimensions of man's own image, so that the gods were, like human kings, often cruel and bloodthirsty; or to the dimensions of the tribe or nation, as the symbol of its unity and power; or again to the more ample dimensions of the forces of nature, such as the life-giving and yet burning radiance of the sun, or the destructive power of storm and earthquake, or the mysterious pervasive force of fertility. And the response that was required, the way of life which such awareness rendered appropriate, was a communal response. For the anthropologists have shown us how closely knit primitive societies have been, and how little scope they offered for individual thought, whether in religion or in other aspects of life.*

As Robertson Smith wrote long ago, "Religion in primitive times was not a system of belief and practical applications: it was a body of fixed traditional practices, to which every member of society conformed as a matter of course." It was with the gradual emergence of individuality, in what Jaspers has called the axial period, particularly during the second half of the first millennium B.C., that higher conceptions of the Transcendent developed in correlation with a deeper sense of moral claim on human life, and upon the individual as well as the collectivity.

For it was the emergence of the individual, and in particular of the religious individual, that made possible those great souls or mahatmas on whose consciousness the Transcendent impinged in new ways or with new intensity and power. The greatest of these became founders of religious traditions—Moses, Zoroaster, Confucious, Gautama, Jesus, and later Mohammed.

Others effected important developments within existing traditions—the Hebrew prophets, the writers of the Upanishads and Bhagavad Gita, Pythagoras, Socrates, Plato. Each of the great religious traditions has continued to develop in larger and smaller ways through the centuries.

. . . The broad hypothesis which I am suggesting, then, is that the infinite Spirit presses in all the time upon the multiplicity of finite human spirits, and yet always so that our finite awareness of this encompassing reality is filtered through a set of human religious concepts. When the developing human race produces a spirit who is able to respond to the Transcendent in a new and fuller way, his (or her) experience of the Transcendent overflows or breaks the system of religious concepts inherited from his culture, and he proclaims a new truth about God or about the meaning of the process of existence, bringing with it new demands for the living of human life. [M&S:50]
—JOHN HICK

How acute and profound this analysis of our inability to see God! Once said, it seems so obvious that God *must* remain the "hidden" God; for God to reveal Himself to us "in His infinite goodness and love, His infinite knowledge and power, His infinite fullness of being and life," would paralyze us with a shame-filled awe, and deprive us of our independence. Therefore, God will only reveal Himself in ways which preserve our free will.

Carrying Hick's insight one step further, it follows then, that the "spirits

who are able to respond to the Transcendent in a new and fuller way,"—"those
. . . on whose consciousness the Transcendent impinged in new ways or with
new intensity and power"—can only be those to whom God can reveal Himself
more fully because they have abandoned all self-will, *who have no inde-*
pendence of which to be deprived, and can therefore begin to withstand the
impact—the certain Knowledge—of God's "infinite goodness and love," His
"infinite knowledge and power," His "infinite fullness of being and life."

All this is contained in the simple expression, to which most of us give
only lip service every day, "Thy will be done." We have put on thick blindfolds,
made up entirely of self-will, and then we go stumbling blindly around with our
arms outstretched, crying, "Where is God? Where is God?"

If thou couldst empty all thyself of Self,
  Like to a shell dishabited,
Then might He find thee on the ocean shelf
  And say, "This is not dead;"
And fill thee with Himself instead.

But thou art all replete with very thou,
  And hast such shrewd activity,
That when He comes He says, "This is enow
  Unto itself— 'twere better let it be.
It is so small and full; there is no room for me."
  —T. E. Brown

Happy is the man who, by continually effacing all images and through
introversion and the lifting up of his mind to God, at last forgets and
leaves behind all such hindrances. For by such means only, he operates
inwardly, with his naked, pure, simple intellect and affections, about the
most pure and simple object, God. Therefore see that thy whole exercise
about God within thee may depend wholly and only on that naked
intellect, affection and will. For indeed, this exercise cannot be dis-
charged by any bodily organ, or by the external senses, but only by that
which constitutes the essence of man—understanding and love. If
therefore, thou desirest a safe stair and short path to arrive at the end
of true bliss, then, with an intent mind, earnestly desire and aspire after
continual cleanness of heart and purity of mind. Add to this a constant
calm and tranquillity of the senses, and a recollecting of the affections
of the heart, continually fixing them above. Work to simplify the heart,
that, being immovable and at peace from any invading vain phantasms,

thou mayest always stand fast in the Lord within thee, to that degree as if thy soul had already entered the always present now of eternity—that is, the state of the deity. To mount to God is to enter into oneself. For he who so mounts and enters and goest above and beyond himself, he truly mounts up to God. The mind must then raise itself above itself and say, "He who above all I need is above all I know." And so carried into the darkness of the mind, gathering itself into that all-sufficient good, it learns to stay at home and with its whole affection it cleaves and becomes habitually fixed in the supreme good within. Thus continue, until thou becomest immutable and dost arrive at that true life which is God Himself, perpetually, without any vicissitude of space and time, reposing in that inward quiet and secret mansion of the deity.
—ALBERTUS MAGNUS (?)

Look now forwards and let the backwards be. And see what thou lackest and not what thou hast; for that is the readiest getting and keeping of meekness. All thy life now must all ways stand in desire, if thou shalt advance in degree of perfection. This desire must all ways be wrought in thy will, by the hand of Almighty God and thy consent. But one thing I tell thee: He is a jealous lover and suffereth no fellowship, and He liketh not to work in thy will unless He be only with thee by Himself. He asketh no help but only thyself. He wills thou do but look upon Him and let Him alone. And keep thou the windows and the door from flies and enemies assailing. And if thou be willing to do this, thou needest but meekly to set upon Him with prayer, and soon He will help thee. Set on then: let me see how thou bearest thee. He is full ready, and doth but abide thee.
—THE CLOUD OF UNKNOWING

Reverend Edward Leen says in *In the Likeness of Christ*, "The personal effort to live the Gospel, gives one an understanding of the Gospel. Study, no matter how able or profound, unsupported by this effort, will leave Jesus Christ still an enigma for the student."

St. John of the Cross says, "The goods of God, which are beyond all measure, can only be contained in an empty and solitary heart."

Paraphrasing the Admirable (and brilliant) Jan of Ruysbroeck, through the grace of God, "you are as holy as you will to be."

It was G. K. Chesterton who observed, "The Christian ideal has not been tried and found wanting; it has been found difficult, and left untried."

And Mark Twain added, "It ain't those parts of the Bible that I don't understand that bother me; it is the parts that I do understand."

The greatest promise ever made was Christ's "If a man love me, he will keep my words: and my Father will love him, and we will come unto him, and make our abode with him."

But hear the frustration in Christ's voice as He cries, "And why do you call me, 'Lord, Lord,' and do not do what I say? If you love me, keep my commandments."

Finally, I am constrained, since we all have some Mark Twain in us, and in defense of the theological foundation of this book—i.e., the Perennial Philosophy as represented by the words of Christ—to quote once more the beloved and brilliant author of *The Ascent of Mount Carmel:*

> . . . *if some people still find difficulty in understanding this doctrine, it will be due to my deficient knowledge and awkward style, for the doctrine itself is good and very necessary. But I am inclined to believe that even if it were presented with greater accuracy and polish, only a few would find profit in it, because we are not writing on pleasing and delightful themes addressed to the kind of spiritual people who like to approach God along sweet and satisfying paths. We are presenting a substantial and solid doctrine for all those who desire to reach this nakedness of spirit.* [CW:72]
> —ST. JOHN OF THE CROSS

"The Kingdom of God is not imminent; it is immanent,—within you." But, "the gate is small, the way is narrow, and few are those who find it."

If you undertake this incredible journey, this heroic voyage to the bottom of your heart, where your magnificent, sacred, immortal "I" lies, cowering, beleaguered, squandering its faculties in the never-ending task of rebuilding its ever-crumbling defenses, subjugating its needs, burying its talents, atrophying— this conscientious, sustained effort to understand and practice Christ's teachings, to seek first the Kingdom of God and His righteousness—you can be sure that the prayers of all the angels in heaven go with you.

And one day you will *Know* that God is Spirit, God is Love.

And so are You.

The mature Christian, under the guidance of the Holy Spirit, and by self-denial and regular and scrupulously honest "examination of conscience," has eliminated most of the subconscious and repressed Elements in his/her Love/Belief System, represented by asterisks in the following diagram. As noted earlier, saints (and animals) have little or no subconscious. Having abjured their "selfhood," they have been relieved of the arduous perpetual exercise of Self-deceit which it required. Having been led through the purging eye of the needle into the Truth of Humility—the Truth which makes them free—they have come at last to Know the Peace which passes understanding.

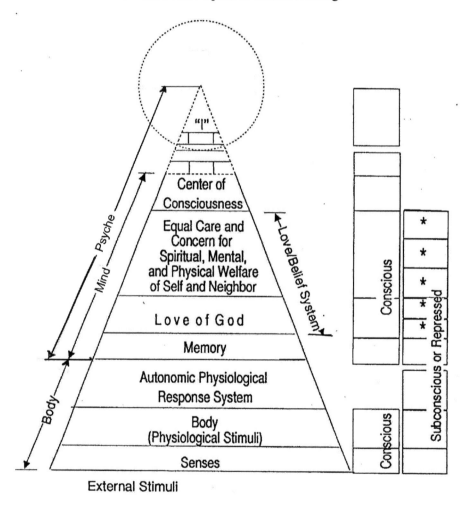

Figure 11 - The Mature Christian

THE CHRISTIAN QUEST

Breaking to the peak
   of the mountain of Self-Knowledge,
One finds only desolate cognizance
   of his obdurate, inviolable Ignorance
   of the profusion and profundity
   of his Prides, Idolatries, and Hypocrisies;
And there espies,
   Through the Valley of Repentance,
   a difficult slippery path,
   the narrow way of Humility;
   Leading to the hills of Faith,
   Gratitude, Righteousness, Service.
Farther still, higher still,
   the heaven-reaching, cloud-hidden spires
   of the mountain of Selfless Christian Love,
   the eternal haven,
The Kingdom of God.

—IAN BANTLOG

If You Love Me

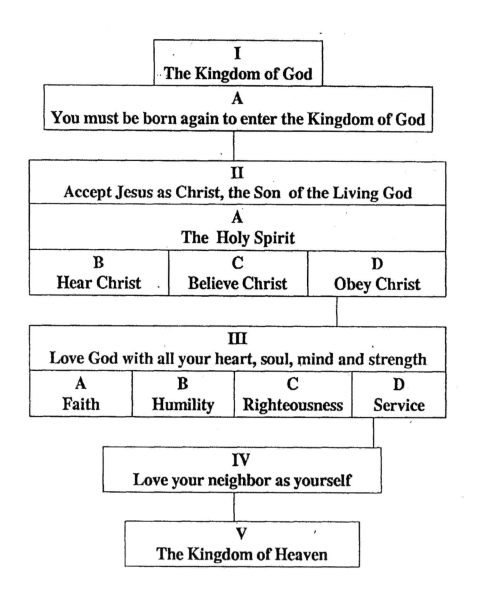

The Principles of Christianity

I. THE KINGDOM OF GOD
Mark 1:14-15
Luke 4:42-43
Luke 9:11
Luke 9:2
Luke 17:20-21
Mark 9:1
Luke 9:57-62
Matt 13:44-46
Mark 4:26-32
Luke 13:18-21
Mark 12:28-34
Mark 9:43-50
Luke 18:28-30
Matt 23:13
Matt 21:33-43

A. YOU MUST BE BORN AGAIN TO
ENTER THE KINGDOM OF GOD
John 3:1-8
Mark 1:14-15
Matt 11:20-22
John 12:23-25
Matt 10:37-39
Matt 18:1-4
Mark 10:13-16
Matt 21:28-32
Luke13:1-5
Luke 15:1-10
Luke 15:11-32

II. ACCEPT JESUS AS CHRIST,
THE SON OF THE LIVING GOD
Matt 16:13-17

A. THE HOLY SPIRIT
Mark 1:6-8
John 16:12-13
John 14:16-17, 26
Luke 11:9-13

B. HEAR CHRIST
Matt 17:1-5
Mark 4:24-25
Matt 13:1-23
Matt 4:1-4

C. BELIEVE CHRIST
John 3:13-21
John 14:1-14
John 15:1-8
John 3:25-36
John 1:17
John 1:32-34
John 1:11-14
Matt 11:27-30
John 6:25-29
John 3:12

C. BELIEVE CHRIST (cont.)
John 5:19-24
John 16:27-28
John 20:24-29
Matt 11:1-6
Matt 10:40
John 6:47-48
John 7:16-17
John 6:65-69

D. OBEY CHRIST
John 14:15
Luke 6:46-49
Matt 7:21
Luke 12:41-48
Matt 5:17-20
John 15:10
John 15:14
John 8:31-36
Matt 12:46-50
John 14:21-23
Matt 28:18-20

III. LOVE GOD WITH ALL YOUR HEART,
SOUL, MIND, AND STRENGTH
Matt 22:35-38

A. FAITH
Mark 11:22-25
Luke 17:5-6
John 14:12-14
Luke 17:12-19
Luke 11:9-13
Luke 18:1-8
Matt 21:18-22
Matt 18:18-20
Matt 17:14-21
Matt 15:21-28
Matt 14:22-33
Matt 10:28-31
Matt 9:27-30
Matt 9:20-22
Matt 8:23-27
Matt 8:5-13
Mark 2:1-12
Mark 10:46-52
Nark 5:21-24,35-43
Mark 6:1-6
Matt 4:5-7

B. HUMILITY
Matt 11:25-26
Matt 23:1-12
Luke 14:7-11
Matt 20:25-28
Luke 18:9-14
John 13:1-17
Luke 17:7-10

C: RIGHTEOUSNESS
John 4:21-24
Matt 5:43-48
Matt 5:1-12
Matt 5:19-20
John 8:1-11
Matt 7:13-14
Matt 23:23-24
Matt 5:21-24
Matt 5:27-28
Matt 5:38-42
Matt 5:13-16
Matt 13:33-37
Luke 12:35-40
Matt 15:10-11,15-20
Matt 12:34-37

D. SERVICE
Matt 4:8-11
Matt 6:24-34
(Luke 12:26)
Matt 16:24-27
Matt 6:19-21
Mark 10:17-27
Luke 16:1-12
Matt 22:15-22
Matt 15:8-9
Luke 14:12-14
Matt 6:16-18
Matt 6:5-6
Matt 6:1-4
Luke 12:15-21

IV. LOVE YOUR NEIGHBOR
AS YOURSELF
Matt 22:35-40
Matt 7:12
John 13:33-36
1 Cor 13:1-13
Matt 25:31-46
Matt 18:21-35
Luke 17:1-4
Matt 12:1-7
Mark 11:25
Matt 6:14-15
Luke 10:25-37
Luke 11:37-41
Matt 10:41-42
Matt 10:8
Matt 18:5-6

V. THE KINGDOM OF HEAVEN
Matt 13:47-50
Matt 25:14-30
Luke 21:1-4
Matt 20:1-16
Matt 13:24-43
Matt 25:1-13

Appendix A
The Reticular Activating System

In 1949 physiologists Moruzzi and Magoun at U.C.L.A. identified some functions of a centrally located segment of the brain known as the "reticular formation," (RF). Together with its communication pathways to and from the body and the brain, they called it the "Reticular Activating System" (RAS), because of its capacity to control waking and sleeping functions. Today we know that it does a great deal more than that. Recent research shows that the RAS includes functions of the limbic system and the cortex, i.e., practically the entire brain. In animals, the RAS acts as the "Organism Control Center;" in the person, it is also the "Love/Belief System," or human "heart."

The reticular formation is centrally located inside the brain stem, and has communication pathways to and from practically every other part of the brain, and with all of the sensory receptors and motor nerves, i.e., with every part of the body. A *single neuron in the RF* may connect with *millions* of other nerve cells. As one writer says, *"It is well placed to monitor all the nerves connecting brain and body. It 'knows' what is going on better than any other part of the brain."* But not only does it *monitor* all brain communications; it has also been found that the RF, working in conjunction with the limbic system and the cortex, can *adjudicate the relative importance* of incoming messages, by initiating its own "pay attention" signals to the relevant area of the cortex. And, as we have seen, it can generate Response Impulses "appropriate" to the sensory messages, and reduce the strength of "extraneous" signals (p. 104). The RAS determines what we see and hear and what our responses should be! All areas of the cortex also send signals to the RF, completing the "feedback loop." There is evidence that the RF also adjudicates all messages from the brain to the muscle motor nerves, thereby influencing our actions (try putting your finger in a candle flame!). Signals from the senses back to the RF complete that loop.

As the following quotes show, ongoing analysis of the Reticular Activating System has shown its functions to be identical to those which I have

ascribed to the Love/Belief System. The Love/Belief System is the exact
equivalent of the Reticular Activating System.

Reticular Activating System = Love/Belief System = mind's "heart" !

> *The pineal clock that establishes these day-night [waking-sleeping]
> rhythms do not abruptly switch the brain from one activity to another,
> but rather informs it that the appropriate moment for switching is at
> hand. The brain then makes up its mind.* (Sic? Sic. Sick! "The brain
> makes up its mind!" See how impossible it is to explain human behavior
> without a deciding "I"?) . . . *The actual change in consciousness is
> accomplished in a different part of the brain, by a network of nerve cells
> rooted in one small part of the brain stem. This master switch of
> awareness, no bigger than the little finger, is the reticular activating
> system, or RAS. It alerts the brain to incoming information from the
> senses, and from the centers of thought, memory and feeling. More than
> that, it adjudicates the relative importance of that information, permit-
> ting the mind to focus on a single stimulus. When a child searches for
> a four-leaf clover, the RAS focuses his mind on the object of the search.
> When an adult wants to read a book in a room full of children, the RAS
> filters out the din, yet allows him to hear his name spoken from across
> the room.*
>
> *In a way the RAS is like a vigilant secretary, sorting out the trivia from
> the incoming messages. Like a good secretary, it does not block any
> messages completely* [Oh yes it does!]; *rather, it seems to put a priority
> tag on some items. As the nerve fibers carrying information to the
> executive decision levels at the brain's cortex*[2] *pass through the RAS, the
> nerve cells within the RAS fire off their own messages, timing them to
> arrive simultaneously with the incoming message.* [! !] . . .
>
> *Clearly, the primary purpose of the RAS is self-preservation, for its
> unfailing trigger is danger or the threat of danger. Signals, for instance,
> from such internal functions as breathing and heartbeat pepper the brain
> cortex constantly, yet the brain pays little attention to them unless the
> RAS alerts it that something is wrong. Similarly, a mother will sleep*

---

[2]   Here again, we see the cortex identified as the "decision center," a figment dis-
credited in Chapter 7.

through heavy traffic noise but waken at the faintest cry from her baby, while a sleeping father may not hear a child crying but is likely to be immediately aroused by a whiff of smoke.
                    —THE ROLE OF THE BRAIN
                      Ronald H. Bailey and the
                      editors of Time-Life Books 1975

From a 1982 book:

Consciousness

People disagree about what consciousness implies.   Some equate consciousness with self-awareness. Many think of consciousness as the activity of the mind, something supposedly more than just a function of the brain. One scientist simply and precisely defines consciousness as the activity of all neurons not otherwise engaged, multiplied by their connections.

*Without consciousness the body functions little better than a cabbage. People sought the seat of consciousness for centuries.   The seventeenth-century philosopher René Descartes located consciousness in the pineal gland. Early this century neurologists placed it in the convoluted cerebrum, acclaimed then as the center of our highest faculties. From there, academic theory moved it to the limbic system. **Research suggests that consciousness resides in none of these, but in the reticular formation,** a group of cells inside the brainstem—oldest, "lowliest" region of the brain.*

Besides their main paths to the cerebral cortex, sensory nerves route branch lines through the reticular formation. Many of its cells supply the thalamus. From there, other cells fan out around the brain: to hypothalamus, corpus striatum, cerebellum, and different regions of the cerebral cortex. Various kinds of stimuli fed in to the brain start the reticular formation firing signals at targets all around the brain, measurably altering electrical impulses from the cerebral cortex and arousing this so-called higher center.

As one writer puts it, the cerebral cortex without the reticular formation to drive it is like a great computer without a power supply.
(emphasis added)

Hallucinogens

> *Hallucinogens have strong effects on the limbic system, influencing mood*
> *and emotions, and on the reticular formation, making the user acutely*
> *conscious of sensory input.* . . [165] (See page 127)
>   —THE BRAIN - A USER'S MANUAL
>   The Diagram Group - 1982

And from a 1963 (!) book:

The brain's response selector has been given the name reticular
activating system [3] by H. W. Magoun and his coworkers at U.C.L.A. The
reticular activating system consists of a mass of undifferentiated neurons
that extend from the top of the spinal cord through the brainstem on up
into the thalamus and hypothalamus. These two structures are at the
extreme top and forward part of the brainstem and are well inside, but
not a part of, the surrounding cerebral cortex. The hypothalamus, part
of which is included in the reticular activating system, appeared in our
earlier discussion as the seat of temperature control of the body. The
reticular formation gets its name from the fact that it looks like a more
or less homogeneous network of cells; it shows little evidence of
organization into anatomically distinct "nuclei", although it passes
through and around a number of nuclei in traversing the length of the
brainstem. Close examination of the reticular form-ation shows that it
consists of a mixture of large and small neurons, many, but not all,
having short axons.

Nature appears to have gone to great pains to cause essentially all the
incoming and outgoing communication channels of the brain to pass
through the reticular system. *This is done by means of "collaterals."*
For example, a main nerve coming from the spinal cord and carrying
sensory information to the cortex does not go directly through the
reticular formation, but as it passes by, its main fibers send off smaller
branches to terminate on reticular neurons. A collateral arrangement
is also found in the motor nerves as they pass by the reticular formation

---

[3]   As we have seen, the RAS is not only the "response selector", more, it is the
percept selector, selecting only "relevant" percepts, *and* it is the servomechanism
which implements its and the "I"'s decisions.

on their way from the higher centers of the brain to the main cable of the spinal cord. Similar branches are displayed by the nerves running to and from the cerebellum. But the reticular activating system does not content itself with wire taps on the communication lines that pass by it; it also has direct lines of command to the stations of interest to it. These receiving stations include half a dozen major areas of the cortex and probably all the nuclei of the brainstem. The recticular activating system also sends its fibers down the spinal cord, where it exercises its influences on the peripheral sensory and motor systems.

Electrical measurements made by means of fine probes placed within the reticular activating system reveal an interesting property: the response of its neurons is "unspecific." A single neuron in this region may respond to stimulation of a touch receptor in the foot, a sound receptor in the ear, a light receptor in the eye, or a chemical receptor in the stomach. The reticular neurons appear to perform some kind of summation of the over-all nervous activity of the organism. Such integration would be of limited usefulness if all reticular nerve cells were to perform it in the same way. Fortunately, this does not appear to be the case. Although many neurons in the RAS system may respond to the same set of nervous stimuli, their responses are not quantitatively alike. One neuron may be more sensitive to optical stimuli than to pain; another neuron may show the reverse emphasis. The resulting weighted averages would appear to be just what is needed to monitor the incoming stimuli for patterned relationships that might indicate the necessity for one or another type of response by the muscles and glands of the body.

There is also direct evidence that the RAS is able to produce the kinds of effects on the operation of the muscles and glands that would accompany the role of a response-selecting mechanism. It seems to be able to sensitize or "awaken" selected nervous circuits and desensitize others. This is sometimes accomplished by selective muscular activation: electric signals sent over reticular nerve fibers down the spinal cord to terminate on the relay nerve cells whose axons pass out to the muscles achieve a sort of "volume-control" action that increases or decreases the magnitude of the muscular response. Sometimes the reticular activating system works on the input side of the response mechanism; it turns down the volume control of certain input stimuli and lets others come through.

Concurrent with the selection by an organism of one of several alternate behavior patterns, there is often need for adjustment of some of the operating parameters. In our missile example, the shift from mid-course to terminal guidance usually must be accompanied by changes in the dynamic response characteristics of the steering mechanism. During the final approach to the target, a tighter kind of "muscular" control of the missile is required. . . .

The reticular activating system includes among its capabilities this kind of adjustment of the dynamic response characteristic of the body mechanism. In fact, an almost exact analog of our "servo-tightness" guided-missile example is provided by one of the prevalent theories of the so-called gamma-efferent mechanism of motor control. In this process, the muscular command emitted by the brain does not act directly on the muscle effector nerves, but instead appears to adjust the "zero point" of a stretch-sensitive receptor attached to the muscle so that its firing rate will be at a minimum when the muscle subsequently achieves the degree of stretch desired. The actual change in the stretch of the muscle is then believed to be accomplished through a spinal reflex circuit that connects the output of the stretch-receptor nerve back around to the muscle-effector nerve. This reflex circuit automatically causes the muscle to seek out just the degree of contraction that will minimize the firing frequency of the stretch receptor. In the language of the computer engineer, this is an effective position-control servo-mechanism, useful when the controlled organ needs to hold its position despite external deviating forces of a varying or unpredictable nature. Our brain seems to employ this control mechanism to maintain suitable postural interrelationships among the parts of the body in the presence of complex and disturbing effects such as those caused by walking or running. This gamma-efferent mechanism appears to be neatly analogous to the part of a missile guidance system that brings the missile heading back into alignment with the direction of a gyroscopic element if deviations are produced by gusts of wind or other extraneous influences. The "tightness" of this kind of control system—the magnitude of the force that is brought to bear to counter a deviation from the desired position—will be increased or decreased if the amount of the "error signal" produced by a given deviation is increased or decreased. In this context the chart below is most interesting, for it seems to display exactly this kind of tightness-control effect: the frequency of the signal sent out by a stretch receptor to indicate a given degree of extension of the attached muscle can be either increased or decreased by electric stimulation of the reticular activating system!

Fig. 4-3. Increase and decrease in stretch-receptor output frequency caused by stimulation of excitatory and inhibitory reticular-formation neurons. The amount of stretch of muscle spindle is shown to the left of the records. *(After E. Eldred, R. Granit, and P. A. Merton, Journal of Physiology, vol. 122 (1953), pp. 498–523. By permission of the publishers.)*

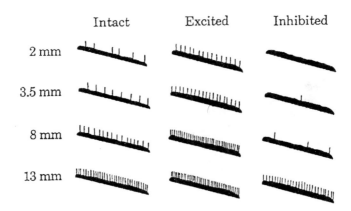

DEAN WOOLDRIDGE
The Machinery of the Brain - **1963** !

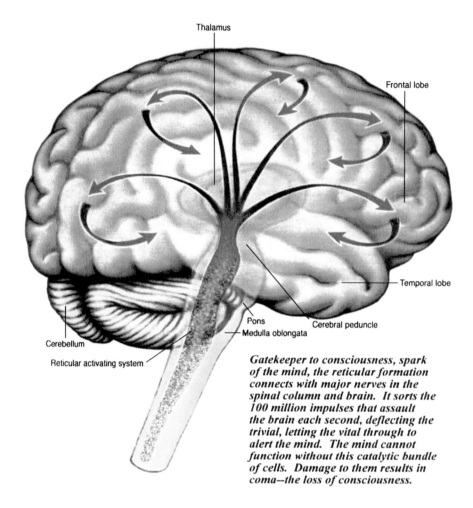

Thalamus

Frontal lobe

Temporal lobe

Pons
Cerebral peduncle
Medulla oblongata

Cerebellum

Reticular activating system

Gatekeeper to consciousness, spark of the mind, the reticular formation connects with major nerves in the spinal column and brain. It sorts the 100 million impulses that assault the brain each second, deflecting the trivial, letting the vital through to alert the mind. The mind cannot function without this catalytic bundle of cells. Damage to them results in coma—the loss of consciousness.

—THE BRAIN - MYSTERY OF MATTER AND MIND
U. S. News Books - 1981

There it is - the neurologic/theologic "heart !"   It was thrilling to find this beautiful rendering in the library eight years after I had inferred a "Love/ Belief System" in the human brain and written the first five or six versions of this book.

But "vital" and "trivial" are subjective terms. How does the RF *know* what is vital or trivial to the individual, if not in the way this book describes? I can find no serious literature which even addresses the question.

And of course the RAS is more than just "catalytic." It is better described as the "Chief Operating Officer;" the "I" is the "C.E.O."

Appendix B
The Experience of Nada

The experience of nothingness lies at the heart of the whole spiritual life. It is the beginning of the mystical journey.

Nada is the one mystery where all religious traditions of both East and West converge. . . . Nothingness may enliven or destroy those who face it, but those who ignore it are condemned to unreality. They cannot pretend to a real life, which, if it is full of real risk, it is also full of promise. . .

There is a big difference—and it's an important distinction—between being nothing and sensing my own nothingness. The first makes me less than mortal; the other places me among the immortals. . .

Only to the degree that I recognize and accept my nothingness am I something. On this nothingness of mine which is eternal and immutable, I can build a moral life that is impregnable and boundless.

There is something infinite about my nothingness. We all share it. We are surrounded by it. It permeates everything. . .

On the level of being, reality and nothingness are contraries. But on the level of love they are reciprocal and equal partners. . . Our perceptive appreciation of the All depends essentially on how deeply we recognize our own nothingness.

Nothingness is not only the exclusive entrance into the mystic way; it is the only door into mental health and moral freedom. It is therefore regrettable that neither Freud nor Jung opened this door. Freud was a good scientist but a poor philosopher. Thanks to his friend and disciple Ernest Jones, who wrote a three-volume biography about him, we now know that Freud was also emotionally disturbed. Empirically he made a monumental contribution to our fund of knowledge regarding human nature. He was the first to understand the mystery, power and depth of the subconscious, and the first to assign adequate importance to the sexual impulse. But his knowledge of human nature was so specialized and limited and his followers so numerous and naive that at this point in history it seems quite probable that Freud did more harm than good.

In "The Future of an Illusion" (1927), Freud dismissed religion as an illusion based upon man's desire for a father figure. Wise men of the time objected that their religion was founded upon a feeling which they called "the oceanic feeling," using a phrase of Whitman's. By this they obviously meant a broad, overwhelming sense of meaning. Freud's extremely limited philosophical approach meant he had no phenomenology for dealing with such a notion. Philosophically speaking, his feet were firmly cemented into the "natural standpoint," the "triviality of everydayness."

What precisely can these people mean by "oceanic feeling?" asks Freud. Adults have a sharp sense of their own limits which keeps them confined in a personal ego. Only babies—or the mentally ill—lack this clear dividing line. A baby is not consciously aware of where his own face ends and his mother's breast begins; it is all one warm, hazy cloud. Freud concludes triumphantly that we can explain this "oceanic feeling" as a throwback to early childhood, and see clearly that it has nothing to do with religion. Here one can see the essence of the reductionist method to solve a subtle problem by pretending it is, in fact, a crude and obvious one.

Freud's psychology is purely clinical, derived from the consulting room. It lacks what previous psychologies possessed; an account of the way we apprehend "meaning." Meaning is essentially what the Canadian theologian-philosopher Bernard Lonergan calls "insight." A Freudian psychology of mysticism is impossible because Freud's was an instinctual psychology. Instinct and spirit are incommensurable concepts. The question of whether or not a phenomenon is instinctual or spiritual is more important than whether it is conscious or unconscious. Why? Because, in contrast to the psychoanalytic concept, being human is not being driven but freely deciding what one is going to be. Being human is being existentially responsible for one's own existence.

Freud betrayed the self when he surrendered it to the id; and he denigrated the unconscious by limiting it to the instinctual. The person is spiritual and has a psychophysical overlay. Because he is spiritual at the core, a human being can become individualized and integrated.

It was the recognition of this fact that forced Carl Jung to part with his master, Sigmund Freud. Though Jung was not a God-centered man,—indeed he had no faith,—he did have a keen sense of "religion."

> "Among all my patients in the second half of life—that is to say, over thirty-five—there has not been one whose problem in the last resort was not that of finding a religious outlook on life. It is safe to say that every

one of them fell ill because he had lost that which the living religions of every age have given to their followers, and none of them has been really healed who did not regain his religious outlook."
—C. G. JUNG

But Jung did not achieve a genuine unifying synthesis. He should have relied on Aristotelian phenomenology. Jung can be criticized for many reasons, but underlying all complaints against him is one fundamental inconsistency: upon a realistic view of the subjective and objective worlds as two independent realities mutually influencing each other, he superimposes the Kantian belief that we are unable to know anything at all about the objective world. Jung escapes Freud's sexual reductionism and falls into Kant's theoretical agnosticism. Jung does not say that man invents God; but neither does God exist objectively in and by himself. He is the personification of psychic forces.

Jung's "God" is a convenient abstraction covering all the different ideas of deity that have ever occurred in mankind's checkered history. Jung is not interested in God as an ontological reality but only the repercussions of this archetype in the human psyche. And so he prefers to use the technical word "self" rather than the ambiguous word "God."

God is for Jung an archetype, i.e., a type in the psyche. The word "type" is derived from the Greek "typos" meaning "imprint." Although Jung says that an imprint presupposes an imprinter, as a psychologist he is concerned with typos, the imprint, a "symbol of an unknown and incomprehensible content." Jung assiduously avoided confrontation with the unknown and referred to it insularly as "the religious point of view," lumping metaphysics, theology and faith under the same peculiar category.

From 1935 on Jung grew more aware of the centrality of religion in Western culture and in the psychic development of the human person. But the recognition of the value of the "imprint" evoked no personal belief in or religious response to the imprinter. Jung's faithlessness could not have been due to lack of grace. This was an explanation to which he himself often resorted. But such a position is theologically untenable. Grace is indeed a gift, but one that is gratuitously and divinely bestowed on everyone.

A more likely reason for Jung's practical atheism—though he never denied God—was the unbending nature of his scientific mind, his single view which made any kind of faith whatever unacceptable. Carl Jung tried hard to escape from Freudian psychologism wherein religion is regarded as nothing more than a sublimation of an instinct. This was obviously a successful effort.

He was, it seems, less successful in escaping from his own far more subtle version of psychologism or psychoidolatry, wherein God is nothing more than a psychic reality even though, as Jung says, this reality is irreducible.

Strictly speaking, Jung was not an atheist, not even an agnostic. He was an empirical investigator and allowed or forced both himself and his work to suffer enormously from the narrow confines of a rigid empiricism. Despite his rapacious desire to understand everything and the brilliant mind with which to do just that, he failed. And he failed precisely because he did not believe. He did not embrace the All. He could not adore.

In a recent life of Jung (C. G. Jung: "The Haunted Prophet," 1976), Dr. Paul Stern points out how many psychological difficulties Jung had to cope with himself, how he was not always very successful, and how damaging the effects sometimes were. Despite this, his contribution was prodigious. But if I had to choose between Jung and Freud as a spiritual guide, I would choose Freud. I am not alone. According to Augustine Léonard, O.P., "In comparison and because his method is so strict, Freud is less dangerous (from the religious point of view). That which Jung calls religion, that which he honestly believes to be religion, is not religion at all; even from the empirical point of view. It appears to be only a very incidental manifestation."

Jung's inspired achievements suggest that, like Columbus, he discovered a continent without realizing what he had found. Columbus thought he had reached the Indies. Whenever Jung refers to the numinous archetype, which in "fear and trembling" discloses the mysterium tremendum in the depths of the soul, he always concludes with the somewhat embarrassed modesty of modern scientists who will tell us that only verifiable data are the objects of science. Jung can prove the "fear and trembling" which man exhibits when confronted with mystery. But fear and trembling of what? The answer, says Jung, does not concern science. Thus the most acute psychologist of our time is as helpless on the borders of the newly discovered continent as any other son of this scientific age.

Both Freud and Jung were bogged down by empiricism. From that limited standpoint there was no way they could enjoy insight into the meaning of nothingness. It seems to me that we have taken Freud and Jung too seriously. They were not the free men, nor were they the liberators we thought they were. If only we would take Christ, the psychologist par excellence, the perfect liberator, that seriously! He is the one who frees us from everything except love. Christ himself was the perfectly live man. He summoned every man to the same kind of freedom, the same perfection of love: "You must be made perfect as your heavenly Father is perfect" (Matt. 5:48). He points out in unmistakable terms the salient features of the individuation process, describing in detail both the dangers encountered and the means by which man and societies may become whole. The early Christian diagnosis of man makes comparable psychological attempts seem like a very weak cup of tea indeed. The discoveries of analytical psychology do little else than repeat, in modern phraseology, and with detailed empirical evidence, the principal injunctions of the Christian way.

Above all, Jesus preached the deep center, man's truest self, that something indestructible in the depths that never gives way, the kingdom of heaven within a man. It is the smallest of all seeds which will become the greatest of all herbs, a tree. It is the leaven that works upon and transforms the lump. It is the treasure hidden in a field, the pearl of great price, for which a man gives all. It is the bridegroom who comes when least expected, for whom unremitting watch must be kept. It is the narrow way which few discover, the straight gate by which a man finds his way to God. [CM:C h. 4]

—FR. WILLIAM MCNAMARA, O.C.D.

Appendix C
How a Man Shall Know His Own Soul

It is necessary for the soul who would come to know spiritual things first to have knowledge of itself. For it cannot come to know a nature beyond itself unless it first has knowledge of itself. That happens when the soul is so gathered within itself and separated from attention to all earthly things and from the use of the body's senses that it experiences itself as it is in its own nature without a body.

Then, if you desire to know and see what your soul is, you must not direct your thoughts inside your body in order to seek it and experience it there, as though it were hidden within your heart of flesh as your heart is hidden and held within your body. If you look for your soul in this way, you'll never find it as it is in itself. The more you seek to find it and experience it the way you would experience a physical thing, the farthest you are from it.

For your soul is not a body. It is an invisible life, not hidden inside a man but holding and bringing life to the body. It is much greater in power and virtue than your body is. Then, if you would find your soul, withdraw your thoughts from all physical, outward things, from attention to your own body as well, and from each of your five senses, as far as you can.

Then meditate on the nature of the spiritual soul which has the power of reason, just as you would meditate on a single virtue (like essential truth, or meekness, or any other virtue) in order to come to know it. In just this way, consider that the soul is an undying and invisible life which has power in itself to see and recognize the sovereign essential truth and to love the sovereign goodness that God is. When you see this, then you are experiencing something of yourself.

Seek yourself in no other place, but the more fully and the more clearly you can meditate on what the nature and the worthiness of the reasoning soul are, and what its natural way of working is, the better you are seeing yourself.

It is very hard for the crude soul which is deeply enfleshed to have the sight and knowledge of itself in this way, for when it wants to meditate on itself, or on an angel, or on God, it drops at once into imagining physical shapes. It imagines that this way it will see itself and, thereby, God and other spiritual things—but that's not possible. For all spiritual things are seen and known by the soul's understanding, not by imagination. Just as the soul sees by understanding that the virtue of justice demands that one yield to each being what it ought to have, so in the same way the soul can see itself through understanding.

Nevertheless, I'm not saying that your soul will rest peacefully in this knowledge, but that it must, by this route, seek knowledge above itself—that is, of the nature of God. For your soul is only a mirror in which you will see God spiritually. Therefore, you must first find your mirror and keep it bright and clean, free from fleshly filth and worldly vanity. Hold it well up from the earth, so that you may see it and also see our Lord in it.

For to this end all chosen souls labor in this life in their determination and intention, even though they do not specifically have this experience of it. And for this reason, what I have said before is true - that many souls who are beginning to grow in grace have many intense fervors and much sweetness in devotion and, as it seems, are completely immersed in love and yet do not have perfect love nor the spiritual knowing of God. For be well aware that no matter how much fervor a soul experiences, even if it is so intense that it seems to him that his body can't bear it, or that he will entirely melt into weeping, as long as his meditating and his contemplating of God is mostly or entirely in imagination and not in understanding, he has not yet come into perfect love nor to contemplation.

. . . One can say the same thing about other kinds of feelings that are similar to these bodily ones—for instance, the hearing of delightful music or the feeling of a comforting heat in the body, or the seeing of light or the sweetness of physical savors. These are not spiritual experiences, for spiritual experiences are felt in the powers of the soul, chiefly in the understanding and in love, and little in the imagination. But these experiences are in the imagination and, therefore, are not spiritual experiences. Even when they are best and most true, they are still only outward signs of the inward grace which is experienced in the powers of the soul. [SP:272]

—WALTER HILTON

Appendix D
Open-Heart Therapy

The principles of Open-Heart Therapy are three-fold:

1. Clients should be brought to understand the diagrams of human behavior; how we all respond, physically, mentally, and emotionally to the circumstances of life; to understand the needs and faculties of the "I"; and the constitution and operations of the Love/Belief System, or RAS, in both its conscious and subconscious aspects.

2. Clients should be helped to develop methods of identifying the significant conscious and subconscious Elements in their Love/Belief Systems.

3. Clients should be helped to develop methods of eliminating, changing, and adopting healthy new, root Love/Belief System Elements, and, most importantly, to find ways of gratifying the "I"-Needs.

The theoretical foundation of Open-Heart Therapy is that except for chemical, physical, or genetic deficiencies, all mental and emotional problems are the result of:

1. Unhealthy environmental conditions or personal relationships, and/or deleterious, irrational, inordinate, obsolete, or conflicting Elements in the Love/Belief System; always coupled with the fact that clients have allowed themselves to become identified with those life situations or Love/Belief System Elements; and/or,

2. A failure to gratify the "I"-Needs to Exist, to Love, and to Know.

By making clients aware of the "I" and its needs and faculties, and helping them to identify significant Love/Belief System Elements, they are enabled to disidentify from the latter, disown and replace negative and deleterious Elements, to seek fulfillment of the all-important "I"-Needs, and eventually, bring their lives under control of the "I".

There are five significant breakthroughs provided by Open-Heart Therapy:

1. Open-Heart Therapy starts with a pardigmatic shift in the client's self-image. By coming to an understanding of the diagrams of how we all work, clients are enabled to dissociate from their deleterious Loves and Beliefs—particularly their most pernicious belief: "I am my mind/body"—and become a partner to the therapist in the exploration of their Love/Belief Systems, rather than a "case" to be "cured." By demystifying the cause of errant behavior and emotions, both client and therapist are relieved of the awful burden of believing that there is something innately wrong with the client. The problem (to identify and change unhealthy Loves and Beliefs) becomes a mutual objective, not a client problem to be solved or resolved by the therapist.

2. Therapists should now be aware of the underlying psychopathologies in all their clients: a denial of death, and a failure to find adequate objects of "I"-Love/Knowledge; must realize that a simple rationalization of the client's Beliefs, Values, and Needs, and even an enhancement of the client's self-image or self-esteem, without some significant gratification of the "I"- Needs to Exist, to Love, and to Know, will not, of itself, enable him/her to lead a fulfilling or gratifying life. On the contrary, superficial successes in these areas may distract the client from the more important task of finding ways of gratifying the "I"-Needs, as therapist Frank Haronian points out.

3. For the first time in history, therapists now know what they are looking for. They are looking for 1) unfavorable environmental circumstances, 2) irrational, deleterious, inordinate, obsolete, or conflicting Loves and Beliefs, and/or 3)—the most important difference with other therapies—a failure to gratify the "I"-Needs to Exist, to Love, and to Know.

Their only interest in the client's past is to try to help the client identify conscious or subconscious Love/Belief System Elements which his/her experiences have generated, and to see how they are unwittingly and harmfully being lived out in the client's life. They are only interested in clients' "feelings" in order to trace them back to the Elements that cause them. Therapists are now aware that the client's illusive (and uncorrectable) archetypes, attitudes, trends, thoughts, feelings, ideas, etc., are all just symptoms of deleterious, obsolete, irrational, conflicting, or inordinate Elements in their Love/Belief Systems. Heretofore, therapists have not had this point of focus for their efforts.

Therapists must now realize that the way to mental health and self-fulfillment for people who think ill of themselves is not to try to think well of themselves, to develop more self-esteem, or to find areas in which they are superior to others; it is to eliminate all such comparisons and competition; and to concentrate on doing something (anything worthwhile) well; to quit thinking about themselves so much; to "lose themselves" in a cause.

4. The Love/Belief Therapist now knows what constitutes mental health, and human fulfillment. It lies in a nominal gratification of the SA-Needs, and the maximum gratification of the "I"-Needs, to Exist, to Love, and to Know. Therapists can now direct their efforts to helping clients change their root Beliefs, rather than superficial ones, and to seeking and finding gratification of the "I"-Needs.

5. Once clients have come to an understanding of the mechanics of human behavior, and have learned how to trace their actions and emotions back to the Elements that cause them, they become their own life-long therapists, and can practice the avocation of self-discovery and self-improvement: of ever-increasing mental health and "Soul-actualization."

With regard to specific methodology,[4] after the diagrams are explained, (using a spiritual "I" only with theists, Freud's "I" with atheists or adamant agnostics) the therapist's role should be that of a partner (not a teacher or authority figure) in the exploration of the client's life circumstances and the contents of his/her Love/Belief System. The therapist should act as an expert spelunker who is helping someone explore a cave on their property—as an invited guest, but one who can point out promising avenues of exploration and avoid dangers. Needless to say, the therapist must accept all revelations from the client in an attentive and non-judgmental way; asking pointed questions, but never probing sensitive areas, and always leaving the decisions to explore or not to explore certain areas, and to keep or reject specific Elements, up to the client.

The therapist must realize that clients have a sizeable vested interest in maintaining their Love/Belief Systems in their present form, and may be very

---

[4] I am deeply indebted to Frank Haronian, Ph.D., (1922-1994), who was a practicing psychotherapist in Lawrenceville, NJ., for his professional review and important contributions to the suggested methods and principles of "Open-Heart Therapy."

resistant to the idea of changing any significant Elements, since they form the fabric of their worlds, and their self-images—their very identities; that clients have expended, and are expending, tremendous amounts of energy in developing and holding together their Love/Belief Systems, and that any change may affect some of their most precious Elements.

Clients should be made aware that the unhealthy Elements in their Love/Belief Systems may once have served a very useful purpose in their lives, perhaps as children, weak, powerless, dependent, and unable to make rational judgements; but that now that they are grown, those Elements can and should now be replaced with healthier new Elements.

Clients should be assured that they will be making all the decisions regarding changes in their Love/Belief Systems, and helped to understand that in governing their lives, they have been acting almost exclusively in their Judicial capacity, simply enforcing the hodge-podge of "laws" of their lives, their haphazardly acquired Loves and Beliefs; that they must now resume the role of Legislator, identifying, re-evaluating, repealing, and rewriting some of those laws, and restoring their Executive powers; must undertake a thorough review of those old laws in relation to their new "Constitution:" as social animals with an "I"; i.e., in relation to their social animal needs, but also, and primarily, in relation to their "I"-Needs to Exist, to Love, and to Know.

It would appear that one effective method, following explanation of the diagrams, is to lay out a sheet of paper divided into six areas of Loves, Beliefs, Values, Needs, Desires, and Fears; then to begin a cooperative effort between therapist and client to "map the territory," i.e., to identify the specific significant Elements (regarding the client's self-image, cosmology, significant others, people in general, the SA-Needs, life and death, the future, and God) in each category.

After explaining the diagrams, there are several methods of identifying the client's life circumstances and the conscious and subconscious Love/Belief System Elements. All should be considered in each case, and, in most cases more than one should be used.

1. The first step consists of one or more unstructured interviews, aimed at establishing rapport, defining the client's "problems" and goals, and developing a mutual sense of trust and cooperation.

2. Next, a simple questionnaire and a personality assessment such as a sentence-completion form should be used; the instruments depending on the training and preferences of the therapist.

3. Because so many problems spring from the self-image, and since meditation

has been described as "the window to our innermost thoughts ," the client should be taught, e.g., Carrington's *Clinically Standardized Meditation*, and asked to complete, between each meeting, 10-15 new sentences beginning with "I am . . .", listing their beliefs regarding their physical, mental, psychological, and sociological characteristics. This practice will bring the client to a gradual and relatively painless (since the list is private) penetration of the "shadow," the negative, repressed aspects of the self-image. When the client has exhausted his list of characteristics, and the time is right, the therapist might suggest that he burn the list, forget about his self-image. (see p. 158)

4. Ongoing client exercises of keeping a daily diary or journal, and tracing significant events, feelings, conflicts, actions, and emotions back to the Love/Belief System Elements involved.

5. Client-centered counseling, reviewing the above, and directed toward the further identification of unfavorable life circumstances, and all significant conscious and subconscious Love/Belief System Elements.

6. Clients should be asked to prioritize their Loves, Values, and Needs, and, in cooperation with the therapist, to select and write down some healthy root Beliefs, for review several times a day, in order to impress them into their Love/Belief Systems.

7. The therapist should assign in vivo client exercises of imagining and gradually starting to act out the new beliefs, with the understanding that they will seem forced and artificial at first, but with practice, will become an integral part of their new "personhood."

8. Word-association tests, followed by 5., above.

9. Of course, in the case of deep-seated or debilitating psychosis, neurosis, or depression, the therapist should recognize the need for referral to a psychiatrist for evaluation of the need for medication.

Needless to say, all of the above assumes that the therapist is educated and experienced in modern client-centered, cognitive/behavioral, psycho-synthesis, or rational-emotive psychotherapeutic practices.

But, as is becoming well-known, proficiency in these practices is a poor second in importance to the necessity of approaching the client with sincere care and concern, responsiveness, respect, and knowledge, i.e., with unconditional, unpossessive Love. As Carl Rogers wrote to me shortly before his death, "I think caring, prizing, or love, is a very important ingredient in therapy, but it is a very special kind of sharpened, focused, non-possessive love."

In our terms, it is Fromm's care and concern, reponsiveness, respect, and knowledge: a mature, unconditional, unpossessive devotion to, or identification with, the client. **It is "I"-Love.**

Appendix E
The Farther Reaches of
Abraham H. Maslow

And now, I will try to acknowledge an unrepayable debt to the giant in the development of the Third Force, or Humanistic, school of psychology, Abraham H. Maslow, by showing how much his studies and findings have contributed to the theses of The Immortal "I". It was certainly Maslow, more than any other psychologist, who danced around the precipice of the concept of the "I" and the Love/Belief System in dozens of ways. He developed the "hierarchy of needs," which is compatible with, and contributed importantly to this theory; he studied "self-actualizing" people, i.e., healthy people, in great depth; he studied "peak" and "plateau" experiences in which "all things seem to come together in the person's world," secular "intimations of immortality" which have strong spiritual overtones; he studied the "rubricizing," cataloging perceptive practices of people, which I have ascribed to the machinations of the Love/Belief System or RAS; he studied and identified the "B- (being) Values," as opposed to the "D- (deficiency) Values," and "D-love" as opposed to "B-love" (see pps. 63-64), which I have distinguished as possessive vs. unpossessive, unconditional "I"-Love, etc.

In short, it was Maslow alone who has made the greatest contribution to date in reconciling the field of humanistic psychology with that of the Perennial Philosophy. Therefore a careful reading of Maslow's works should help immeasurably in validating many of the hypotheses I have propounded in this book.

But of course I must fault Maslow for his recommendation of unbridled self-gratification as the means to human fulfillment, which along with Rogers, contributed significantly to the excesses of the "me generation."

Most readers will be aware of Maslow's five levels of "hierarchy of needs." But later, Maslow found it necessary to include 16 "metaneeds" or "B-Values" to his self-actualization category, and add a new category of "prepotent" needs, even more basic than his original "basic" needs, as noted on the following diagram. I hope the reader will agree that ours is a simpler yet more comprehensive representation of human "needs."

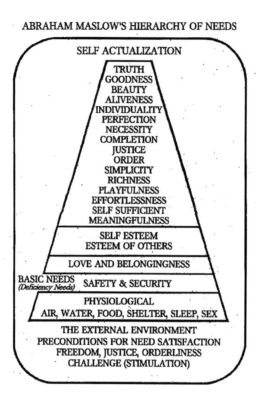

But I enjoyed another significant insight from my intensive study of Maslow, relating to his "B-Values" or metaneeds, which he described as:

1. Truth: honesty; reality; (nakedness; simplicity; richness; essentiality; oughtness; beauty; pure; clean and unadulterated completeness).

2. Goodness: (rightness; desirability; oughtness; justice; benevolence; honesty); (we love it, are attracted to it, approve of it).

3. Beauty: (rightness; form; aliveness; simplicity; richness; wholeness; perfection; completion; uniqueness; honesty).

4. Wholeness: (unity; integration; tendency to oneness; interconnectedness; simplicity; organization; structure; order; not dissociated; synergy; homonymous and integrative tendencies).

4a. Dichotomy-transcendence: (acceptance, resolution, integration, or transcendence of dichotomies, polarities, opposites, contradictions); synergy (i.e., transformation of oppositions into unities, of antagonists into collaborating or mutually enhancing partners).

5. Aliveness: (process; dynamic; eternal; flowing; self-perpetuating; spontaneous; self-moving energy; self-forming; self-regulation; full-functioning; changing and yet (changeless); expressing itself; never-ending).

6. Uniqueness: (idiosyncrasy; individuality; singularity; non-comparabilit y; its defining-characteristics; novelty; quale; suchness; nothing else like it).

7. Perfection: (nothing superfluous; nothing lacking; everything in its right place; unimprovable; just-rightness; just-so-ness; suitability; justice; completeness; nothing beyond; oughtness).

7a. Necessity: (inevitability; it must be JUST that way; not changed in any slightest way; and it is good that it IS that way.

8. Completion: (ending; finality; justice; it's finished; . . . fulfillment; finis and telos; nothing missing or lacking; totality; fulfillment of destiny; cessation; climax; consummation; closure; death before rebirth; cessation and completion of growth and development; total gratification with no more gratification possible; no striving; no movement toward any goal because already there; not pointing to anything beyond itself).

9. Justice: (fairness; oughtness; suitability; architectonic quality; necessity; inevitability; disinterestedness; non-partiality).

9a. Order: (lawfulness; rightness; rhythm; regularity; symmetry; structure; nothing superfluous; perfectly arranged).

10. Simplicity: (honesty; nakedness; purity; essentiality; succinctness; (mathematical) elegance; abstract; unmistakability; essential skeletal structure; the heart of the matter; bluntness; only that which is necessary; without ornament; nothing extra or superfluous).

11. Richness: (totality; differentiation; complexity; intricacy; nothing missing or hidden; all there; "non-importance," i.e., everything is equally important;

nothing is unimportant; everything left the way it is, without improving, simplifying, abstracting, rearranging; comprehensiveness).

12. Effortlessness: (ease; lack of strain, striving, or difficulty; grace; perfect and beautiful functioning).

13. Playfulness: (fun; joy; amusement; gaiety; humor; exuberance; effortlessness).

14. Self-sufficiency: (autonomy; independence; not needing anything other than itself in order to be itself; self-determining; environment-transcendence; separateness; living by its own laws; identity). [RVPE:92]

To most people the B-Values are just a group of very nice words; they cannot have the ineffable significance that they do to those fortunate few who have experienced their reality. Maslow gives us an excellent description of this experience, what I call "I"-Love:

> *The descriptive B-Values, seen as aspects of reality, should be distinguished from the attitudes or emotions of the B-cognizer toward this cognized reality and its attributes, e.g., awe, love, adoration, worship, humility, feeling of smallness plus godlikeness, reverence, approval of, agreement with, wonder, sense of mystery, gratitude, devotion, dedication, identification with, belonging to, fusion with, surprise and incredulousness, fear, joy, rapture, bliss, ecstasy, etc.* [RVPE:94]

And here I found a point of closure of Maslow's lifelong studies of Self-Actualization, B-Values, and Peak- and Plateau-Experiences, with the principles of The Immortal "I", the point I'm sure he would have reached except for his untimely death. Maslow himself gives us the clue:

> *If B-Values are as necessary as vitamins and love, and if their absence can make you sick, then what people have talked about for thousands of years as the religious or platonic or rational life seems to be a very basic part of human nature. Man is a hierarchy of needs, with the biological needs at the base of the hierarchy and the spiritual needs at the top. Unlike the biological needs, however, the B-Values are not hierarchical in and of themselves. One is as important as the next, and each one can be defined in terms of all the others. Truth, for example, must be*

complete, aesthetic, comprehensive, and strangely enough, it must be funny in an Olympian god-like sense. Beauty must be true, good, comprehensive, etc. Now if the B-Values are all definable in terms of each other, we know from factor-analysis that some general factor underlies them all - a G-factor, to use the statistical term. The B-Values are not separate piles of sticks, but rather the different facets of one jewel. Both the scientist who is devoted to truth and the lawyer who is devoted to justice are devoted to the same thing. . . [FRHN:186]

So Maslow tells us about a "G-Factor", something all the B-Values have in common. What is it? He gives us another clue:

An interesting aspect of the B-Values is that they transcend many traditional dichotomies, such as selfishness and unselfishness, flesh and spirit, religious and secular. Take the dichotomy of "religious" and "secular." The form of religion that was offered to me as a child seemed so ludicrous that I abandoned all interest in religion and experienced no desire to "find God."

Yet my religious friends, at least those who had gotten beyond the peasants' view of God as having a skin and beard, talk about God the way I talk about the B-Values. . . [FRHN:187]

What then, IS the G-Factor in Maslow's metaneeds?

Purely fortuitously, I found our answer provided ready-made by John Middleton Murry. Notice that the first of Maslow's B-Values is Truth, the third is Beauty. Mr. Murry shows us the common factor in these Values, and in so doing, shows us the common factor in them all.

"Beauty is Truth, Truth Beauty." The words to many are meaningless. And it is certain that by no poring over the words themselves can the vision which they express be attained. Nor, probably, if we turn them about, like a jewel of many facets, will they reflect a gleam. We may turn them in many ways. We may say that the Real is Beautiful. The answer straightway is that the Real is full of ugliness and pain. And this is true: who will deny it? But the Beauty of the Real is a Beauty which resides as surely in pain and ugliness as in beauty itself. There is the sorrow which makes:

"Sorrow more beautiful than Beauty's self."

But that sorrow may still be called, by our human standards, beautiful. The Beauty of the Real is beyond this. It lies in the perfection of uniqueness which belongs to every thing, or thought, simply because it IS. But this is not Beauty. And indeed it is not what men commonly call Beauty, any more than the Love with which all high religion invests its Deity is what is commonly called Love among men, any more than the Perfection which, Spinoza said, belonged to every existence is what men commonly call perfection. None the less, the great sayings that "God is Love," and that "Omnis existentia est perfectio," have their meaning for those who understand them. Keats uttered another saying worthy to stand with these simple and lucid finalities. "Beauty is Truth, Truth Beauty" belongs to the same order as they; nor can any one truly understand any one of these sayings without understanding the others.

For the only name for the faculty by which we can discern that element of Beauty which is present in every Fact, which we must discern in every Fact before it becomes Truth for us, is Love. Whether it is Love which discovers the Beauty in Fact, whereby it becomes Truth; or whether it is the Beauty of Fact which causes the motion of Love to arise in our souls, and so to discern its Truth—to such questions there is no answer, nor any need to answer them. The relation between these things is simple and inextricable. When we love a Fact, it becomes Truth; when we attain that detachment from our passions whereby it becomes possible for us to love all Facts, then we have reached our Peace. If a Truth cannot be loved, it is not Truth, but only Fact. But the Fact does not change, in order that it may become Truth; it is we who change. All Fact is beautiful; it is we who have to regain our innocence to see its Beauty.

But this is inhuman, it may be said. And if it is indeed inhuman to be detached for a moment from all human passion, to see for a moment all things that happen as sheer happenings, to cease for a moment to feel what men call love and hate in the peace of a Love that is distinct from, and beyond them both, then it is inhuman. But this ultimate disinterestedness begins at home. It is achieved only by disinterestedness towards the pain and ugliness of one's own experience; and it is achieved chiefly by those to whom the pain of others has been as their own pain. This detachment is reached not through insensibility, but through sensibility grown intolerable.

> *None can usurp this height*
> *But those to whom the miseries of this world*
> *Are misery and will not let them rest.*

Whether or not it is easily intelligible, there is a meaning in "Beauty is Truth, Truth Beauty". . . It is simple, but not easy; and it involves a great renunciation. . . To attain the vision which Keats describes as the knowledge that "Beauty is Truth, Truth Beauty," we are required to put away all our human desires and beliefs and anxieties. Our joys and sorrows must become remote as though they happened to others than ourselves, or to ourselves in some other mode of existence from which we have awakened as from a dream. All the infinite, the all but total activities of man, conscious or unconscious, which are directed toward the maintenance and assertion of the instinctive will to live, must be put away. Cease they cannot, nor can we make them cease; but we must cease to be identified with them. They are the substrate of our vision; without them we cannot see as we desire to see. But when we have become an Eye [an "I"?], the Eye cannot belong to them, nor they to it. It sees them with the same utter detachment with which it sees all things else. And this detachment is a real detaching. Than this no greater renunciation is possible. . . [K:222]
JOHN MIDDLETON MURRY

So the identity between Truth and Beauty is only understandable to those who have "put away all their human desires and beliefs and anxieties," who "have ceased to be identified with them," who have attained a "real detaching," to those "whose joys and sorrows are as remote as though they happened to . . . ourselves in some other mode of existence from which we have awakened as from a dream." Indeed, the saints tell us, they did happen to someone in another mode of existence, the persons they were prior to this spiritual rebirth into the Kingdom of God. ". . . the only name for the faculty by which we can discern that element of Beauty which is present in every Fact, which we must discern in every Fact before it becomes Truth for us, is Love. . ."

The common element in Beauty and Truth is Love, and so Love is the common element in all of Maslow's B-Values. And since God is Love, his

G-Factor is also seen to be God. Indeed, the student of Christian theology will recognize many of the B-Values as the "Names of God." Maslow's use of the letter "G" is prophetic. This is the universal human B-Value or metaneed, our need to Love and to Know God; this is the "I"'s and therefore the human's primary need: to Love, to find an object worthy of our total unpossessive, unconditional Love. Only by a complete and total dedication of ourselves and all we possess, to the most Love-worthy "Object," God, only in our wholehearted acceptance of everything He sends us, searching for the Truth which is Beauty in every Fact with which we are presented, do we fulfill ourselves. Only in this way do we perceive God, and life, and the world, and our neighbor, and our Selves, as true, and good, and beautiful, and holy, and meaningful, and significant, and honest, and unified, and whole, and alive, and unique, and simple, and orderly, and rich, and effortless, and playful, and self-sufficient, and completed, and perfected; only in this way do we realize our kinship—more, our sonship and daughtership of God. In this realization, the saints tell us, we will not feel joy; we will find that we *are* Joy—and Peace, and Light, and Wisdom, and Love.

Our indebtedness to Abraham H. Maslow is incalculable. May he rest in Peace.

Bibliography

Matthew, Mark, Luke, and John - The words of Christ

Allport, Gordon W., *Becoming.* Yale University Press 1976

Ames & Il, Gesell Institute, *Your Four Year Old.* Delta Book 1976

Anonymous, *A Course in Miracles.* Foundation for Inner Peace 1983

Anonymous, *Dionysius the Areopagite.* S.P.C.K. (London) 1971

Anonymous, *The Book of Enoch.* S.P.C.K. (London) 1974

Anonymous, *The Cloud of Unknowing.* John M. Watkins (London) 1946

Anonymous, *The Dhammapada.* Penguin 1977

Anonymous, *The Gospel According to Thomas.* Harper & Row 1959

Anonymous, *The Nag Hammadi Library.* Harper & Row 1977

Anonymous, *The Upanishads.* Mentor Book 1957

Anonymous, *Theologica Germanica.* Pantheon Books 1949

Arieti, Silvano, *The Will to be Human.* Quadrangle 1972

Assagioli, Roberto, *Psychosynthesis.* Esalen 1973
    The Act of Will. Viking Press 1973

Auden, W. H., *The Living Thoughts of Kierkegaard.* Midland 1963

Augustine, St., *The Confessions of St. Augustine.* Image Books 1960
    The City of God. Modern Library 1950

Becker, Ernest, *The Denial of Death.* Free Press 1973
    Escape From Evil. Free Press 1975

Benedict of Nursia, St., *The Rule of St. Benedict.* Image Books 1975

Bergson, Henri, *Creative Evolution.* Greenwood Press 1977
    Time and Free Will. Humanities Press 1971
    The Two Sources of Morality and Religion. Greenwood Press1977
    Introduction to Metaphysics. Liberal Arts Press 1955

Bernard of Clairvaux, St., *Selected Letters.* Henry Regnery 1953
    Treatises II. Consortium Press 1974

Berne, Eric, *Games People Play.* Ballantine 1973

Bettelheim, Bruno, *Freud and Man's Soul.* Alfred A. Knopf 1982

Bloom, Allan, *The Closing of the American Mind.* Simon & Schuster 1987

Blum, Gerald S., *Psychodynamics.* Wadsworth Publishing Co. - 1968

Boehme, Jacob, *Personal Christianity.* Constable & Co. (London)

Brown, Barbara B., *New Mind, New Body.* Harper & Row 1974

Buber, Martin, *I and Thou.* Scribner's 1970

Capra, Fritjof, *The Tao of Physics.* Bantam Books 1984

Carrel, Alexis, *Man the Unknown.* MacFadden 1961

Carrington, Patricia, *Clinically Standardized Meditation.* Pace 1979

Changeux, Jean-Pierre, *Neuronal Man.* Oxford 1985

Cheney, Sheldon, *Men Who Have Walked With God.* Delta Book 1974

Chesterton, G. K., *Saint Thomas Aquinas.* Image 1955

Colledge & Walsh, *Julian of Norwich.* Paulist Press 1978

Connolly, Terence L., S.J., *St. Bernard on the Love of God.* Spiritual Book
    Associates - 1937

Coward & Penelhum, Ed., *Mystics and Scholars.* Canadian Corporation for Studies
    in Religion 1977

Crick, Francis, *The Astonishing Hypothesis,* Scribner 1994

Curtayne, Alice, *St. Catherine of Siena.* Sheed & Ward (London) 1952

Damasio, Antonio R., *Decartes' Error.* G. P. Putnam 1994
    The Feeling of What Happens. Harcourt Brace 1999

D'Aygalliers, A. Wautier, *Ruysbroeck the Admirable.* Dent & Sons (London) 1925

De Caussade, Jean-Pierre, *Abandonment to Divine Providence.* Image 1975

de Mello, Anthony, S.J., *Awareness - The Perils and Opportunities of Reality.*
Image 1992

De Sales, Francis, St., *Introduction to the Devout Life.* Dent & Sons, (London) 1961

Deikman, Arthur J., *The Observing Self.* Beacon Press 1982

Dossey, Larry, M.D., *Recovering the Soul.* Bantam Book 1989

Eckhart, Meister, *Meister Eckhart - A Modern Translation.* Harper & Brothers 1957

Ellis & Harper, *A New Guide to Rational Living.* Melvin Powers - Wilshire 1975

Evans, Donald, *Struggle and Fulfillment.* Fortress Press 1981

Fenelon, Francois, *Christian Perfection.* Harper Brothers 1947
    Letters to Men and Women. Riband Books (London) 1965

Ferrucci, Piero, *What We May Be.* Tarcher 1982

Frankl, Viktor E., *Man's Search For Meaning.* Washington Square Press 1968
    The Will to Meaning. Plume Books 1975

Freud, Sigmund, *The Interpretation of Dreams.* Avon 1965
    The Basic Writings of Sigmund Freud. Modern Library 1965

Fromm, Erich, *The Art of Loving.* Harper & Row 1974
    Psychoanalysis and Religion. Bantam Book 1977

Frost, Bede, *The Art of Mental Prayer.* Compton Printing Works (London) 1960

Gesell, Ilg, & Ames, *The Child From Five to Ten.* Harper & Row 1977
    (See also, Ames & Ilg)

Glasser, William, M.D., *Reality Therapy.* Harper & Row 1975
    Stations of the Mind. Harper & Row 1981

Goble, Frank G., *The Third Force.* Pocket Books 1978

Goleman, Daniel, *The Meditative Mind.* Tarcher 1988

Grof, Stanislav, *Beyond The Brain.* S.U.N.Y. Press 1985

Harris, Thomas A., M.D., *I'm OK—You're OK.* Avon 1973

Heard, Gerald, *The Third Morality.* Cassell & Co. (London) 1937

Heidegger, Martin, *Basic Writings.* Harper & Row 1977

Hick, John: (See Coward & Penelhum, Eds., *Mystics and Scholars*)

Higgins, John J., S.J., *Thomas Merton on Prayer.* Image 1975

Hilton, Walter, *The Stairway of Perfection.* Image 1979

Horney, Karen, *Self Analysis*. Norton 1942
   Neurosis and Human Growth. Norton 1950
Horney, Karen, *New Ways in Psychoanalysis*. Norton 1966
Huxley, Aldous, *The Perennial Philosophy*. Harper Colophon 1970
   The Doors of Perception, Borgo Press, 1990
Illich, Ivan, *Deschooling Society*. Harrow Books 1972
James, William, *The Principles of Psychology*. Dover
   The Varieties Of Religious Experience. Mentor Book 1958
Janet, Paul, *The Life and Works of Fénelon*. Pitman & Sons 1914
Jaspers, Karl, *Anselm and Nicholas of Cusa*. Harcourt Brace 1966
Jung, Carl G., *Analytical Psychology*. Pantheon 1968
   Two Essays on Analytical Psychology. Pantheon Books 1966
   Modern Man in Search of a Soul. Harcourt Brace 1933
   Man and His Symbols. Dell 1968
   The Portable Jung. Penguin 1978
John of the Cross, St., The Collected Works of,. I.C.S. Publications 1979
Jones, Rufus M., *Spiritual Reformers in the 16th and 17th Centuries*. Beacon 1959
Kandel, Eric, et al. *Essentials of Neural Science and Behavior*. McGraw-Hill 1995
Katz, Joseph, *Plotinus Search for the Good*. King's Crown 1950
Kelly, George A., *A Theory of Personality*. W. W. Norton 1963
á Kempis, Thomas, *The Imitation of Christ*. Penguin Books 1973
Klivington, Kenneth A. *The Science of Mind*. MIT Press 1989
Knowles, Dom David, (See Woods, *Understanding Mysticism*)
Krishnamurti, J., *Commentaries on Living*. Quest Book 1979
Laing, R. D., *The Divided Self*. Penguin 1990
   The Politics of Experience. Pantheon 1967
Latner, Joel, *The Gestalt Therapy Book*. Bantam 1974
Law, William, *A Serious Call to a Devout and Holy Life*. Dent & Sons 1967
   The Spirit of Love and The Spirit of Prayer. James Clarke & Co. 1969
   The Way to Divine Knowledge. G. Moreton 1893
   An Appeal to All Who Doubt or Disbelieve the Truths of the Gospel.
Le Shan, Lawrence, *How to Meditate*. Bantam Book 1984
Leen, Edward, Rev., *Why the Cross*. Sheed & Ward 1938
   Progress Through Mental Prayer. Sheed & Ward 1935
   In the Likeness of Christ. Sheed & Ward
Leonard, George B., *Education and Ecstasy*. Delta Books 1968
Lewis, Thomas, et al., *A General Theory of Love*. Random House 2000
Lilly, John C., M.D., *Simulations of God*. Bantam 1976
Loyola, Ignatius, St., *The Autobiography of St. Ignatius Loyola*. Harper & Row 1975
   The Spiritual Exercises of St. Ignatius. Newman Press 1963
Lozowick, Lee, *The Only Grace is Loving God*. Hohm Press 1982
Maloney, George A., S.J., *The Mystic of Fire and Light, St. Symeon The New Theologian*. Dimension Books 1975
Maltz, Maxwell, *Psycho-Cybernetics*. Prentice Hall 1960
Mandelkorn, Philip, Ed., *To Know Your Self*. Anchor Books 1978

Magoun, H. W., *The Waking Brain.* Charles C. Thomas 1969
Maharshi, Ramana, The Spiritual Teaching of,. Shambhala 1972
Maslow, Abraham, *Motivation and Personality.* Harper & Row 1970
   The Farther Reaches of Human Nature. Esalen 1977 .
   Toward a Psychology of Being. D. Van Nostrand Co. 1968
   Religions, Values, and Peak Experiences. Penguin 1970
   The Plateau Experience. Journal of Transpersonal Psychology 4(1972)
May, Rollo, *Love and Will.* W.W. Norton 1969
   Man's Search for Himself. W. W. Norton 1953
   The Courage to Create. Bantam 1980
   Freedom and Destiny. W. W. Norton 1981
   The Discovery of Being. W. W. Norton 1983
McNamara, William, O.C.D., *Christian Mysticism.* Franciscan Herald Press 1981
Merluzzi, Glass & Genest, Ed., *Cognitive Assessment.* Guilford 1981
Merton, Thomas, *The Seven Storey Mountain.* Image 1970
   Seasons of Celebration. Farrar, Straus & Giroux 1964
   Introduction to The Monastic Theology of Aelred of Rievaulx. 1969
   Unpublished Material from the original mss. of The Seven Storey Mountain
   (Also see Higgins, John J., S.J.)
Missildine, W. Hugh, M.D., *Your Inner Child of the Past.* Simon & Schuster 1963
Murry, John Middleton, *Keats.* Noonday Press 1962
Naranjo & Ornstein, *On the Psychology of Meditation.* Penguin Books 1977
Nightingale, Earl, *The Strangest Secret* - (Recording). Nightingale-Conant 1966
Otto, R., *Mysticism East and West.* Meridian 1957
   The Idea of the Holy. Oxford University Press 1978
Pascal, Blaise, *Pensees.* Penguin 1973
Peck, M. Scott, M.D., *The Road Less Traveled.* Simon and Schuster1978
Perls, Fritz, *The Gestalt Approach and Eyewitness to Therapy.* Bantam 1978
Peterson, Jordan B., *Maps of Meaning - The Architecture of Belief.* Routledge 1999
Phillips, D. B., et al., *The Choice is Always Ours.* Re Quest 1977
Plotinus, *The Essential Plotinus.* Hackett Publishing 1975
Polanyi, Michael, *Personal Knowledge.* University of Chicago Press 1962
Prabhupada, A. C. B., *Bhagavad-Gita As It Is.* The Bhaktivedanta Book Trust
Rajneesh, Bhagwan Shree, *The Mustard Seed.* Harper & Row 1975
Richard of St. Victor, *Richard of St. Victor.* Paulist Press 1979
Robinson, Daniel N., *The Philosophy of Psychology.* Columbia Univ. Press 1985
Rokeach, Milton, *The Nature of Human Values.* Free Press 1973
   The Open and Closed Mind. Basic Books 1960
   B*eliefs, Attitudes, and Values.* Jossey-Bass 1968
Ruitenbeek, H. M., Ed. *Varieties of Personality Theory.* Dutton 1964
Ruysbroeck, Jan of, *The Adornment of the Spiritual Marriage.* John M. Watkins
   (London) 1951
Satinover, Jeffrey, *The Quantum Brain.* John Wiley & Sons 2001
Schacter & Scarry, Ed. *Memory, Brain, and Belief.* Harvard University Press 2001
Schwartz, Joseph, *Cassandra's Daughter - A History of Psychoanalysis.*
   Viking Penguin 1999

Shah, Idries, *The Sufis.* Anchor Books 1971
Smith, Huston, *The Religions of Man.* Perennial Library 1965
    Forgotten Truth. Harper & Row 1976
    Cleansing the Doors of Perception. Jeremy P. Tarcher/Putnam 2000
Smith, Margaret, *The Way of the Mystics.* Oxford 1978
Sorokin, Pitirim A., *The Ways and Power of Love.* Gateway 1967
Suzuki, D. T., *Zen Buddhism.* Anchor Books 1956
Szasz, Thomas, *The Myth of Mental Illness.* Harper & Row 1984
Tauler, Johannes, *Johannes Tauler Sermons.* Paulist Press 1985
Teresa of Avila, St., *The Way of Perfection.* Image Books 1964
    Interior Castle. Image Books 1961
Therese of Lisieux, St., *The Autobiography of St. Therese of Lisieux.* Image 1957
Thomas, Paul G., *Psycho-Feedback.* Prentice-Hall 1979
Tillich, Paul, *The New Being.* Charles Scribner's Sons 1955
Tolle, Eckhart, *The Power of Now - A guide to spiritual enlightenment.* New
    World Library, 1999
Tyrrell, Bernard J., S.J., *Christotherapy.* Seabury 1981
    Christotherapy II. Paulist 1982
Underhill, Evelyn, Mysticism. Dutton 1961
    Practical Mysticism. Dutton 1943
Vitz, Paul C., *Psychology as Religion.* Eerdmans 1977
Vivekenanda, *The Yogas and Other Works.* Ramakrishna-Vivekananda Center
    1953
von Hildebrand, Dietrich, *Transformation in Christ.* Image 1962
von Hugel, Freidrich, *The Mystical Element of Religion.* J. M. Dent & Sons 1961
Walsh & Vaughan, *Beyond Ego.* Tarcher 1980
Wapnick, Kenneth, *Mysticism and Schizophrenia - Understanding Mysticism.*
    Image Books: Garden City, 1980.
Watts, Alan, *The Supreme Identity.* Vintage 1972
    Cloud-Hidden, Whereabouts Unknown. Vintage 1974
    The Way of Zen. Vintage 1974
    The Wisdom of Insecurity. Vintage 1968
    The Book on the Taboo Against Knowing Who You Are. Vintage 1972
Wilber, Ken, *The Spectrum of Consciousness.* Quest 1980
    No Boundary. Shambhala 1981
    The Atman Project. Quest 1982
    Up From Eden. Anchor Press 1981
Wilson, Edward O., *On Human Nature.* Harvard University Press 1978
Woods, Richard, O., Ed., *Understanding Mysticism.* Image Books 1980
Wooldridge, Dean E., *The Machinery of the Brain.* McGraw-Hill 1963
Yogi, Maharishi Mahesh, *On the Bhagavad-Gita.* Penguin 1971
    Transcendental Meditation. Signet Book 1963
Zaleski, Carol, *Otherworld Journeys.* Oxford University Press 1987

Index of Subjects

Index of Names

Index of Subjects

Index of Names